THE TRIPLE BIND

THE TRIPLE BIND

Saving Our Teenage Girls from Today's Pressures

Stephen Hinshaw, Ph.D.
with Rachel Kranz

Ballantine Books New York

Published in the United States by Ballantine Books,
an imprint of The Random House Publishing Group,
a division of Random House, Inc., New York.

BALLANTINE and colophon are registered trademarks
of Random House, Inc.

Library of Congress Cataloging-in-Publication Data

Hinshaw, Stephen.
The triple bind : saving our teenage girls from today's
pressures / Stephen Hinshaw with Rachel Kranz.—1st ed.
p. cm.
Includes bibliographical references and index.
ISBN 978-0-345-50399-2 (hardcover : alk. paper)
1. Teenage girls—United States—Psychology.
2. Stress in adolescence—United States.
I. Kranz, Rachel. II. Title.

HQ798.H55 2008
155.5'33—dc22
2008042781

Printed in the United States of America on acid-free paper

www.ballantinebooks.com

2 4 6 8 9 7 5 6 1

First Edition

To all families who are struggling
with how best to nurture, support, and guide
their daughters (and sons)

CONTENTS

INTRODUCTION

Girls in Crisis

If you were in any U.S. mall or movieplex toward the end of 2007, you probably saw dozens of teen, tween, and elementary-school girls crowding into *Enchanted*, the holiday-season film from Walt Disney Pictures. And if you had followed them into the theater, you would have seen a movie that seems to embody the dreams and daydreams of today's American girl.

A tongue-in-cheek romance, *Enchanted* begins with an animated section that slyly recalls the classic Disney "princess movies." A beautiful maiden sings cheerfully to the little woodland creatures, who respond by helping her with her tasks. She dreams of the handsome, valiant prince, who of course loves her at first sight. Then the prince's wicked stepmother foils the marriage by ejecting the would-be princess out of her cartoon into a strange and faraway land—the non-animated real world of Times Square.

Meanwhile, elsewhere in New York City, a handsome workaholic lawyer plans to marry an equally workaholic career woman. The lawyer's six-year-old daughter isn't happy about the marriage, however. She wants a *real* mother, not the busy, career-oriented stepmother who tries to engage her in "grown-up girl bonding." She *isn't* a grown-up, she points out, only a little girl. As such, she longs for fairy tales, not the book of real-life scientists, political leaders, and other heroines that her father tries to pass on. "Marie Curie discovered radium—and died of radiation poisoning," her father tells her—a gloomy image indeed of the working woman.

When the lawyer meets the princess, of course, they fall in love. The little girl is delighted: here is a fairy tale come to life. But there are also signs that our real world does the fairy tale one better. The princess is intrigued by the achievements of the women in the little girl's book of heroines. She starts to prefer our earthly custom of dating to the fairy tale's rush to marriage. In lieu of a fairy godmother, she relies on a credit card to outfit her for a fancy ball, enhancing her apparently effortless beauty with a trip to the hairdresser and manicurist. And when her beloved lawyer refuses to take her seriously, she feels the stirrings of a brand-new emotion—anger.

Will the princess remain a fairy-tale creature or become a modern American woman who shops, dates, makes demands on men, and obsesses about her career? In fact, she does it all. When the prince's evil stepmother becomes a dragon who follows the princess to earth, our suddenly athletic heroine picks up a sword, defeats the dragon, and rescues the man she loves. She kisses her beloved lawyer passionately, then marries him and opens a fashion boutique in which all the clothes are magically constructed by animals, giving her seemingly endless time to play with her new daughter. She even gets her new husband to play with them, effortlessly combining romance, marriage, career, and motherhood, all while looking beautiful and being nice to everybody.

At first glance, *Enchanted* might seem like a harmless or even positive fantasy. Who doesn't want to be loved and live happily ever after? Who doesn't want to be a strong, brave, athletic slayer of dragons? And who doesn't want to be beautiful? Does it really matter that in real life, no one person could possibly reconcile all these conflicting roles; that succeeding at even one of them takes an enormous amount of effort; that the pressures to look beautiful, not to mention sexy, take a toll of their own?

Well, when you consider the real-life situations of the girls who flocked to see *Enchanted*, maybe it does matter.

GIRLS AT RISK

At least 25 percent of today's teenage girls are in immediate danger from self-mutilation, eating disorders, violence, depression, or suicide.

This statistic seems unbelievable, but it's true. One-fourth or more of all U.S. girls between the ages of ten and nineteen face one or more of these threats. Hundreds of thousands, perhaps even millions, struggle with conditions that are only slightly less dangerous.[1]

There's no doubt about it: today's teenage girls are in crisis—and by all indications, the crisis is like a runaway train, picking up speed as it goes. For example, depression is now striking girls at ever earlier ages. When I was in grad school, we were taught that the average age for a person's first depressive episode was somewhere in the early thirties. That figure has since fallen to the twenties, and as far as we can tell, the age of onset continues to drop. As a result, 15 to 20 percent of U.S. girls ages ten to nineteen meet criteria for major depression, while an additional 10 percent or more will endure one or more bouts of mild or moderate depression by adulthood.[2]

The worst possible outcome of depression, of course, is suicide—and among adolescent girls, suicide rates are spiking. Between 2003 and 2004, the suicide rate among girls ages ten to fourteen rose by a whopping 76 percent. True, only a small fraction of U.S. girls actually commit suicide. But by some estimates, 10 percent have made the attempt, and a distressingly high number will seriously consider it at least once between their last day of grade school and their first day of college.[3]

Meanwhile, many girls who do not consider taking their own lives nonetheless perform such self-destructive behaviors as cutting, burning, and otherwise injuring themselves. Although "cutters" are notoriously secretive, any clinician will tell you that self-mutilation is becoming more common—again, at an ever faster rate. According to both published reports and my own conversations with clinicians, girls are now wounding themselves more often and more severely than at any time in the past.[4]

If a girl doesn't turn her anger inward, she might very well turn it outward. Although rates of boys' violence have been falling since the mid-1990s, girls' rates are rising. During the 1990s, aggravated assault rose sharply among girls younger than eighteen, while dropping among boys the same age. Overall, approximately one-quarter of all U.S. girls have reported committing a serious violent offense, while about 5 percent show repeated patterns of aggressive or antisocial behavior while they are teenagers. Countless more engage in "relational aggression": cyberbullying, gossip, rumor-mongering, and just plain meanness. By early adulthood, at least half of partner violence is now initiated by women.[5]

True, some experts argue that some of these figures may be deceptive—that at least part of the statistical jump has been caused by official counting of girls' offenses in a different manner than before, with a greater tendency to brand as "assaults" behaviors that would receive a different label if a boy committed them.[6] Still, there is little doubt that girls' violence is on the upswing, even if we can't yet measure its increase with complete certainty.

The increase in eating disorders is another indication of the crisis. Some 3 to 4 percent of all U.S. girls have been diagnosed with eating disorders. Rates of anorexia and bulimia seem to be holding steady, but the number of young women who binge has been growing. This trend, too, shows no signs of stopping. An estimated 10 percent of teenage girls struggle with obsessive dieting, a distorted body image, or hatred of their own bodies, while more than half of all teenage girls worry about their weight or engage in some form of dieting. The numbers of girls who have unhealthy body images is staggering—and they often develop this corrosive view of themselves well before they become teenagers.[7]

There are many reasons for this unprecedented crisis among teenage girls, which, as we've just seen, includes clinical conditions for one-quarter or more of our adolescent daughters.[8] Our culture's overly sexualized images of girls and women play a role. So does the spread of consumerism, the loss of community, and the growing influence of cyberculture and the media. And let's not forget the way both parents and children are facing ever-harsher competition, whether for jobs or for college admissions, so everyone in the family is working way too hard. For parents no less than for their teenage children, the pressure to perform is relentless.

All of these factors play their part. But they wouldn't have nearly as much destructive power if they didn't feed the contradictions that the Disney movie embodies, a set of conflicting expectations that I call the Triple Bind:

1. *Be good at all the traditional "girl" stuff.* Like the girls who grew up when those earlier Disney princesses first appeared, young ladies today are expected to be good at relationships, empathy, and bonding. They're supposed to be nice, obedient, helpful, and nurturing. And while they're supposed to attract boyfriends and eventually husbands, they're also expected to be "good girls" who either don't have strong sexual feelings or else are well able to control them.
2. *Be good at most of the traditional "guy" stuff.* Unlike their earlier counterparts, today's girls are also expected to be good at many of the tasks that were traditionally reserved for men: fighting for spots at a top college, preparing themselves for the job market, and playing at sports. Besides being empathic and obedient, they must also be competitive, assertive, and ambitious, if not outright driven. And alongside the culture that glorifies marriage is a new dating culture that encourages girls to "hook up" the way many guys traditionally have, engaging in multiple brief sexual encounters that are completely disconnected from intimacy, longevity, or even conversation.
3. *Conform to a narrow, unrealistic set of standards that allows for no alternative.* Once, girls could look to family or cultural role models for ideas on how to subvert, avoid, or transcend society's rules for women. Today, though, virtually all public images of women are ultrafeminized and overly sexualized. Instead of Martina Navratilova, the pioneering female athlete, we have fashion-conscious Maria Sharapova and "hot" Danica Patrick, whose *Playboy* article about her experience as the first woman Indy 500 driver is accompanied by a suggestive photo. Even fit, muscular Venus and Serena Williams dress provocatively on court, and Serena has

started her own fashion line. Instead of Eleanor Roosevelt, whose public statements were all concerned with social policy, we have Hillary Clinton, who openly obsesses about her weight. And while earlier generations of rock and pop stars—Janis Joplin, Chrissie Hynde, Cyndi Lauper, Annie Lennox—tried to craft an alternative image of femaleness, today we have Britney, Christina, and Beyoncé, all of whom present themselves as chic, thin, and ultrasexualized. For today's girls, the message is clear: even women who break new ground must fit the ever-narrower standards for looking pretty, hot, and model-thin.

The lack of alternatives extends beyond appearance to girls' ambitions. Whereas previous generations of girls might look to the counterculture, bohemianism, feminism, politics, or some larger notion of religious or community service as domains in which to craft their own unique identities, today's young women live in a world that is increasingly defined by the pursuit of money, power, and status. And the roles that might once have helped them get beyond society's narrow definitions of femininity have been recycled back into increasingly unattainable media images: hip artists who are nevertheless svelte and sexy; dedicated surgeons with devoted boyfriends and perfect figures; glamorous businesswomen who manage corporations, raise money for charity, and effortlessly tend to a husband and children. Girls have to succeed—brilliantly—in all these areas, within a culture that makes it virtually impossible for them to envision alternative lives, unique identities, or other models for success.

These impossible, contradictory expectations are fueling the crisis-level statistics for depression, self-mutilation, eating disorders, violence, and suicide. They've also prompted confusion, despair, and distress among girls of all types, including those who aren't suffering from clinical disorders. Across the board, girls are floundering, desperate for ways to come to terms with these three contradictory demands.

Does it sound as though I'm exaggerating? I only wish I were. Here are just some of the girls I've seen struggling with the Triple Bind.

Kelly is a pretty, blond high school freshman in an affluent suburb.* Once popular and outgoing, Kelly now hides out in her room. When I ask her to roll up the long gray sleeves of her sweatshirt, she slowly does so. Her arms are covered with cuts, scars, and burns, the traces of her self-mutilation. "I just want to feel *something*," she tells me.

Even when Alesia was only ten, her anger was a force to be reckoned

---

*When girls preferred to remain anonymous, I changed their names and other identifying details and in some cases have combined elements from several girls' stories. For all these anonymous girls, I give only first names.

with. When frustrated, she would punch, buck, and slap, until it took three staff members to haul her out of the classroom. All through her teenage years, Alesia fought in ways that even the boys wouldn't try: gouging, going for the genitals. A miniature "raging bull," she came close to seriously hurting several of her classmates and staff members. As a teenager, Alesia became the only girl to be invited into a local gang, where her unique combination of empathy, charisma, and steely determination led the boys to make her their leader.

Nicola Cooke is seventeen years old, a hardworking senior at an upscale Catholic high school in northern California. A former basketball star, she had to quit her team because of debilitating panic attacks that started in her sophomore year. Although she never actually attempted suicide, she often thought about it as her anxiety and panic morphed into depression. A self-described "rescuer" and "worrier," Nicola felt overwhelmed by the conflicting pressures of doing well at school while remaining emotionally available to her family and friends. Between homework, college applications, sports, and preparing for the SATs, she felt as though she were cracking under the strain. Yet everyone around her seemed to find her schedule normal. She confesses:

> The worst words I ever hear are "I am disappointed in you." But how are people *not* going to be disappointed when they are setting these huge, high limits? When you make a mistake, [not only your family but also] your teachers will be disappointed, your friends will be disappointed in you. Everything kinda coincides with one another, you can never make just one mistake and have one person upset about it. . . . No one says what is expected of you, you're just expected to know—and you have a pressure to exceed even that.

Cecy agrees. A junior at a northeastern public high school, she feels torn by the conflicting expectations she sees coming at her from all directions. When I ask her what expectations a twelve-year-old girl might face as she plans to enter high school, Cecy's face softens with pity for this imaginary newcomer. "Like [she's supposed to get] good grades, and, um, [have] a social life," she begins, and then pauses, overwhelmed by even the thought of what might lie ahead.

"I don't know," she finally says with exasperation. "It should look like she has everything together and she has no problems whatsoever and she basically puts on a façade. I mean, that's kinda what we're all taught to do to—like that's how we're supposed to go though life, I guess."

Randi is a free-spirited junior at a private prep school in the South. She enjoys wearing tight, skimpy tops and short little skirts, and she takes evident pleasure in her appearance and her physical self. When she talks about the "hookup" culture at her high school, she sounds enthusiastic at first, reveling in the sense of power she gets from making out with a new boy each week.

"Once you're in a relationship, you can get hurt so easily," she says matter-of-factly. "I've seen it with so many of my friends—they become sort of like slaves to their boyfriends because they're so afraid of losing them. I want to focus on getting into my top schools—I don't have time to feel that bad."

But when I probe for more information, Randi starts to tell a different story. Certainly she enjoys the attention she gets from her "hookup" guys, and she likes the status that comes with being sought-after. On the other hand, the sex itself isn't so great. "Sometimes I think I like the idea of it more than the reality," she says frankly.

Marcy has chosen the opposite path. Instead of pursuing boys, she ignores them; instead of flaunting her sexuality, she suppresses it. A loose T-shirt hides her large breasts; torn, ill-fitting jeans are her constant uniform. Although few of her girlfriends are still virgins, Marcy has barely been kissed. At eighteen, she's just finishing her freshman year at a top northeastern college, and, she explains, she's focused on her pre-law schedule; she doesn't have time "for that relationship stuff." Besides, she says, the boys at her school have a well-known system of rating girls for "hotness." "I'd never make their top-ten list, so why try?"

These six girls couldn't be more different from one another—yet they all share a similar quality, a kind of resignation. Beneath Marcy's ambition, Cecy's warmheartedness, and Randi's flirtatiousness lies a kind of quiet desperation, a weary acceptance that life is hard, relationships are disappointing, and success requires the right, effortless façade. These girls might dream of the handsome Disney prince; they might dream as well of slaying their dragons and finding their true calling. Meanwhile, however, they remain all too aware of how unlikely it is that either love or work will satisfy them. The sadness and anger that lurk beneath the surface seem only a few degrees removed from the more serious disorders that plague Kelly, Alesia, and Nicola.

I've worked for the past twenty-five years as a clinical psychologist, so my training and inclination are to identify disorders. In my field, there's a useful emphasis on distinguishing between an actual disorder—say, clinical depression—and what looks like a less serious version of the same problem, including the sorrow, hopelessness, or helplessness we might all feel from time to time. And I'll admit that when I began this book, I thought I'd be spending a whole lot more time separating the "real" casualties of the Triple Bind from the vast majority of teenage girls, most of whom will eventually make a successful transition into adulthood.

But the more time I've spent listening to teenagers and the more research I have done and read, the more I've come to see that in this case, a clinical focus on disorders may not be the most useful approach. Of course, there's an important distinction to be made between serious depression and a minor case of the blues, if only because we'd treat them so differently (if we'd treat the latter at all). But once we go beyond the specifics of treatment plans and prognoses, we might find it useful to take another tack, not separating out the serious from the nonserious so much as viewing the problems on a continuum.[9]

To understand the range of effects of the Triple Bind, imagine what might happen if we forced our teenage daughters to remain for several hours each day in a room that was full of cigarette smoke. Distasteful (and unethical) though this would be, the vast majority would probably emerge relatively intact. Yes, some would develop lung cancer (probably those with genetic vulnerabilities), and a few more would come down with emphysema, asthma, bronchitis, and other respiratory ailments as a direct or indirect result of the smoke. Another small but significant percentage might develop heart trouble. And a handful would be at increased risk for throat cancer and other serious conditions. Most, however, would not require medical care or hospital treatment.

But does that mean they would be truly okay? We would expect that most if not all of the girls would start to develop sore throats, red eyes, or nagging coughs in response to the smoke. Some might develop a mild form of nicotine addiction that would render them cranky and irritable during those times when they were nicotine-deprived. They might start to feel tired and run-down, or they might find themselves getting more colds. In other words, pretty much every girl in that room would pay for the strain of being there. Some might become seriously ill while others would escape with low-grade symptoms, but all would reveal, in a variety of ways, the toll taken by their toxic environment.

In the same way, I've come to see that even though most teenage girls are not at risk for serious psychological disorders, those with the most vulnerability are placed at even higher risk for major clinical conditions because of the Triple Bind—and all are affected by its messages. Girls like Marcy, who suppresses her sexuality, and Randi, who acts on it despite little physical fulfillment, may never mutilate their bodies or succumb to serious depression. But both of them are profoundly affected by the Triple Bind, just as Kelly and Nicola are. Alesia's rage likewise tells us something about what the cheerful Cecy may be feeling when she informs me that girls are expected to have "no problems whatsoever."

So in this book, I'm going to approach the Triple Bind as a continuum, something that helps us understand the full range of ways that our culture puts today's girls at risk. To enable you to grasp the true meaning of the Triple Bind, I'll bring you into the world of today's girls. In the first chapter I'll draw upon a provocative mix of statistics, pop culture, and my own work with girls to demonstrate how the Triple Bind threatens our daughters.

Next I'll turn to the world of science, dispelling some popular misconceptions. True, depression, like some other psychological conditions, is most likely to appear in people with a family history or a genetic predisposition to it. But we are not slaves to our genes or to our hormones. In Chapter 2, I'll sort through the confusing claims about the role of biology and genes in our girls' problems. I'll share with you the latest science, which has shown that our genes and our environment work together in unexpected and fascinating ways both to lay the groundwork for serious psychological disorders and to create more productive ways of coping with our problems.

Chapter 3 turns to girls' highly scheduled, overly pressured lives. Part of the power of the Triple Bind stems from our culture's new insistence that girls excel at *everything*: school, sports, relationships, and looks. The endless round of after-school activities and the compulsive effort to enter a top school all play a part in setting girls up for crisis.

In previous decades, young women could escape the double bind by entering a world of alternative identities—hippie, tomboy, punk, goth. As I'll show in Chapter 4, girls today have far fewer alternatives, and the ones that do exist are often deceptive: highly sexualized or ultrafeminized. As a result, girls are frequently trapped in "self-erasing identities," roles that *seem* to allow the authentic search for self—but don't.

Consider the popular TV show *Private Practice*. Successful ob-gyn Addison Montgomery is thin, rich, and gorgeous. But she's lost both a husband *and* a potential boyfriend to younger women and now she's agonizing over the discovery that she can't have a baby. Ten-year-old girls who looked at June Cleaver might have dreamed of breaking out of the mold and becoming a doctor. But the lovely and accomplished Addison has already freed herself—and she's miserable. How do our daughters make sense of her plight?

Within the Triple Bind, girls' greatest strengths can often become their most treacherous weaknesses. As I'll show in Chapter 5, girls are socialized to show empathy, self-awareness, and verbal ability, and from a very young age, they are better at these skills, on average, than boys. But these traditionally female qualities—which are often correctly viewed as strengths—may also put girls at an increased risk for depression, eating disorders, and other self-destructive behaviors. That's because, as any boy could tell you, focusing on feelings makes it harder to excel at sports, to compete in the classroom, or simply to "tough it out." Girls thrown into traditionally "boy" situations may find it far harder than boys to cope with the pressure.

And then there's sex. Girls having sex too early. Girls having sex too often. Girls convinced they're good for nothing but sex. Girls convinced they're not good enough for sex—too ugly, too fat, too awkward, too strong. In Chapter 6, I'll look at the disturbing messages our culture offers to girls of all ages, from the three-year-old "princess" to the twenty-year-old sorority girl. I'll explore the troubling ways that teenagers, preteens, and even little girls are overly sexualized, leading to a deeply disturbing trend for our daughters to view themselves as objects.

Chapter 7 takes on the role of the Internet and our electronic culture. The cover of a 2006 issue of *New York* magazine says it all: "I am not interested in privacy. Online, I reveal everything—my breakups, my bank balance, my breakfast cereal, my body. My parents call it shameless. I call it freedom."[10] I'll explore how the new cyberculture exacerbates the Triple Bind, as girls enter a world in which everything seems to be revealed without intimacy, effort, or any sense of consequence. We'll also look at cyberbullying and the ways girls express aggression online.

In Chapter 8, I'll consider physical aggression and the rising number of teenage girls who now commit violent acts. Although teenage boys' rates of violence have been falling slowly but steadily, key indicators show that girls' violence is increasing. As with so many aspects of the Triple Bind, there's a contradictory aspect to this problem. Girls who now grow up under Title IX are used to participating in the kinds of rough-and-tumble sports that have traditionally made boys feel strong and powerful. Yet many girls are now channeling the pressures they feel into slaps, punches, and even stabbing. We'll also look at the surprisingly vicious world of "relational aggression"—girls who wound with words and social manipulation, inflicting injuries that can be as grievous and long-lasting as those caused by physical violence.

In Chapter 9, I'll help you relate the stories of girls in crisis to the problems faced by more "normal" girls. The girls at greatest risk, I argue—those who develop clinical disorders or otherwise collapse under the strain—are our canaries in the coal mine, indicators of the pressures that all girls must contend with. In this era of unprecedented opportunities for girls, we can't ignore the strain that the Triple Bind is placing on each of our daughters. I'll also tell the story of one remarkable young woman whose victory over the Triple Bind offers hope for all our girls.

In this final chapter, I'll also explore some ways in which we can support our girls, offering them family and community bulwarks against the relentless cultural pressures created by the Triple Bind. Most important, I believe, is helping our girls to engage with a wider community as a way of transcending the consumerism, overfocus on achievement, and preoccupation with looks encouraged by the Triple Bind.

I'll admit it: I'm one of the last people you'd ever think of as making a life's work out of "girl problems." After all, I conducted programs exclusively for boys for many years, and I'm the father of sons, not daughters. But when you consider that girls often suffer in silence—their voices unheard, their problems often hidden behind a cheerful façade—then maybe it's not so strange.

After all, I, too, grew up with a secret that no one was supposed to talk about, a secret I didn't even know I had. Following the medical wisdom of the time, my parents kept silent throughout my childhood about the reason behind my father's long, mysterious absences. Finally, in my late teens, my dad told me the truth: he had spent a lifetime struggling with mental illness, misdiagnosed as schizophrenia. While supposedly "away resting," he'd actually been hospitalized, medicated, and given shock therapy. His illness wasn't properly identified until after I graduated from college, when I helped to get him a correct diagnosis of bipolar disorder. One of my goals ever since has been to fight the shame and stigma that still cling to mental illness.[11]

Not surprisingly, this childhood experience inspired a lifelong interest in helping troubled children, especially kids who no one realized needed help. So when attention-deficit/hyperactivity disorder was barely recognized as a widespread problem, I was already running summer programs to study boys with ADHD. Every year, a few girls applied as well, but it didn't seem fair to include them as such a tiny minority. Besides, experts insisted that ADHD wasn't even a "girl problem": virtually all the children who had it were boys.

Maybe my background has made me extra sensitive to hidden suffering, or maybe I'm just contrary. In any case, I applied for—and received—one of the largest grants ever awarded by the National Institute of Mental Health to study girls with ADHD.

"You'll never get enough to fill a program" was the general consensus—until we opened our phone lines. The voice mail filled up faster than we could return the calls, and that first summer we had more than five hundred inquiries.

Clearly, girls were suffering—too often, in silence. Troubled boys acted out. But too many troubled girls were more likely to turn their anger inward, concealing their self-mutilation, eating disorders, and depression behind a mask of cheerful obedience.[12]

The girls were out there, I realized. Anxious, angry, depressed, and sometimes violent, the troubled girls were clearly there, and every year, their numbers grew. Having grasped the dimensions of teenage girls' crisis—the crisis that produced the statistics I've quoted in this Introduction and that I'll explain further in Chapter 1—my focus expanded. I wanted to address the concerns of all girls, not just the ones with attention disorders.

True, girls with ADHD face special challenges and need special support. But if the figures I had been reading were correct and if the life stories I was hearing were to be believed, *all* girls needed more support than they were getting, and I felt a deep responsibility to say so.

As I learned the stories of a wider range of teenagers, I was struck by how pressured their lives were, how unsupported their explorations of sex and their bodies were, how overwhelmed they often felt by the consumerism and wall-to-wall media of our culture. I was appalled at how discouraged they were and saddened by how many of them seemed to have already given up on finding meaningful work and satisfying relationships. Even the hardest workers among them seemed worried about whether their efforts would ever pay off. Even the cheeriest and most optimistic seemed to have a premature sense of how much could go wrong, burdened by fear regarding their futures.

Because my work had always included kids from low-income families, I was used to classrooms where far too many had lost a friend or family member to violence, inadequate medical treatment, or just the rigors of poverty. But I did not expect to find the same "survivor mentality" among the middle- and upper-middle-class high school students whose stories also fill this book. I did not expect the words of Michelle, who told me, "Every week, we go to a different funeral of someone who commits suicide," or Jasmine, who explained that a third of her classmates were on some kind of medication, or Lori, who rattled off a long list of friends lost to eating disorders, cutting, or breakdowns.

I was also moved by the eagerness with which girls sought to share their stories.[13] Cecy was so grateful that someone was finally listening instead of telling her to "buckle down and get to work." Anya was relieved to share her confusion about putting on "sexy" clothes that she didn't feel ready to wear. ("My mom says I'm selling myself short by wearing sweatshirts all the time, and I know she's right, but . . .") Toni couldn't wait to vent her frustration with the girls in her class who dumbed themselves down while the guys were around—and then sniped at the weaker girls after the boys had left.

Perhaps the most moving words I heard were from Kirsten, a freshman with a women's studies major at a small liberal arts college. Recalling Betty Friedan's famous "problem with no name," the mysterious malaise that seized so many 1960s housewives who could not explain why they felt so trapped and frustrated, Kirsten said, "[Our situation] sort of feels like this problem with no name. Like people just say, 'Oh, girls are crazy. Oh, it's just adolescence, the girls are hormonal,' or 'You're just PMSing, aren't you?' . . . It's really nice for someone to say, 'Wow, you have a lot of pressures on you,' rather than 'Wow, you are hysterical.' "

Of course, part of a teenager's job is to complain about parents and teachers and grown-ups in general. But after reading the scientific and clinical literature and listening to these girls, I can assure you that there is a crisis, and it is real. We ignore it at our peril—and worse, at our daughters' peril. On the other hand, if we listen, if we understand, and if we take action, there's a real chance that we could liberate our daughters from the power of the Triple Bind—and perhaps free our culture from it as well.[14]

THE TRIPLE BIND

CHAPTER I

Impossible Expectations

Sixteen-year-old Lupe leans forward, so eager to share her thoughts that she almost knocks her schoolbooks on the floor. "The expectations are impossible!" she tells me.

Her classmate Eugenia, a high school junior, agrees. "No one says what is expected of you, you're just expected to know—and you have a pressure to exceed even that. I think you're expected to be well-rounded, be intelligent, be outgoing, but also do, like, community service and do extracurricular stuff, just have the whole package."

"But sometimes that's really hard!" Lupe insists.

Fifteen-year-old Jessica chimes in. "I think we're supposed to know what we're supposed to be doing with the rest of our lives. They expect you to know what you are doing at, like, sixteen or seventeen, and you're supposed to have a big life plan, but sometimes you just don't. I think also you get a lot of pressure from your parents to do well in school, and you get a lot of pressure from your friends because you want to go out and have fun, and you get pressure about guys, too. . . . You have to do *everything*!"

Her classmates nod vigorously as Jessica continues, her fervor building with every word. "And you're supposed to handle it beautifully. Be completely graceful, poised, have a boyfriend you've been seeing for the past year, know everything, make sure nothing's wrong, talk to your teachers, be best friends with them, everything has to be perfect. Love your siblings, love your parents, no fighting, and of course, you should be going out with your friends—but don't party, 'cause you don't want a bad rep. But you still want to have fun and be a kid—and you can't. It's so hard."

Eugenia shakes her head. "And the second you make a mistake, everything comes crashing down. You feel like the world just kind of stops. I've known some people who have kind of gone down the tubes, they just can't handle it anymore."

"Yeah," say the others.

Lupe sighs explosively and leans back in her chair. "It all goes back to the expectations," she repeats. "First of all, they are impossible, and second of all, we don't know what they are."

GIRLS IN DANGER

At first glance, this conversation with a group of prep school girls in the Seattle area might seem like run-of-the-mill teenage angst. Sure, they're worried about homework, parents, and getting into college—so what? Why should *we* worry about these routine teenage complaints?

The numbers tell us why—and their message is disturbing indeed:

- *Up to 20 percent of girls ages ten to nineteen are experiencing episodes of major depression.* Information from the general population about depressive disorders—which include withdrawal, tearfulness, lassitude, repeated negative thoughts, sleep disturbance, and self-destructive acts—shows that over the past fifty years or more, the average age of onset of female depression has fallen from the mid-thirties to the mid-twenties, with a significant portion of young women becoming depressed by their early to mid-teens.[1]
- *As of 2005, about one-tenth of all teenage girls had made an attempt to end their lives.* Whereas teenage girls once tended to make "nonserious" suicide attempts—attempts that were considered primarily a cry for help—an increased number are now genuinely trying to kill themselves. The teen suicide rate went up more than 300 percent between the 1950s and late 1980s. Although teen suicide rates fell somewhat during the 1990s and early years of the current decade, between 2003 and 2004, they spiked: the number of girls ages ten to fourteen who killed themselves rose by 76 percent, while suicides of girls ages fifteen to nineteen rose 32 percent.[2]
- *Self-mutilation among teenage girls—cutting, burning, biting, and other forms of serious self-injury—appears to be on the increase.* Because girls go out of their way to hide this practice, statistics are hard to come by. But almost every clinician will tell you that rates are increasing—dramatically.[3]

- *Close to 5 percent of U.S. teenage girls and young women suffer from some form of eating disorder—anorexia, bulimia, or binge eating—with some estimates placing that figure at more than twice that rate.* When girls and women are specifically asked about binge eating, more admit to this practice than we ever suspected. And even "normal" girls are preoccupied with weight, diet, and body issues at alarmingly high rates and at distressingly young ages—according to some studies, as young as first grade.[4]
- *Girls' rates of aggression and violence are on the rise, while boys' rates have shown either less of a rise or an actual decrease during the past fifteen years.* Boys are more physically violent than girls throughout their lives, so it is particularly distressing to review the latest government statistics that reveal alarming rates of self-reported girls' violence. Some experts contend that rates of official violence are distorted because of a tendency to include aggression at home (fights with siblings, for example) as "assaults" for girls, whereas the same acts would be given another label if boys committed them. But there is no doubt that girls have become more aggressive than previously, and that relational and social aggression (spreading rumors, getting even by forming coalitions against a target, and the like) continue to be a major issue for our daughters.[5]

These figures add up to a staggering sum: *at least one-fourth of all U.S. teenage girls are suffering from self-mutilation, eating disorders, significant depression, or serious consideration of suicide—or are perpetrating acts of physical violence.*[6] And the rest of the girls, the ones who escape without a clinical label, are hardly home free. Too many of them are struggling with hatred of their bodies, obsessive dieting, sexual confusion, and the persistent sense that they just aren't good enough: that no matter how much they work or how hard they try, they'll never be able to achieve all that is expected of them.

If we only had to worry about serious clinical conditions plaguing 25 percent of our teenage girls, this would be alarming enough. But in my clinical and personal experience, virtually *all* of today's teenage girls are struggling with challenges that threaten to overwhelm them. When I've spoken with these girls, both those at risk and those who seem to be doing fine, I've heard a persistent note of dismay. Listening to Lupe, Jessica, and Eugenia, I was struck not by how much they complained but by how desperate they were to please their families, their teachers, their friends. "Give us expectations that we *can* meet," they seemed to be saying, "and look how well we'll perform!" They didn't mind working hard; they minded feeling that they were doomed to fail.

The underlying current of despair reminded me of some of the most famous animals in the history of psychology—Seligman's dogs. Martin Seligman is a psychologist who set out to understand learning and motivation. So he put three groups of dogs into harnesses through which he could administer painful electric shocks. The first group of dogs was shocked while in the harness and later released. The second group of dogs was likewise shocked but had access to a lever that could make the shocks stop. The third group of dogs was also given access to a lever—but their lever had no effect. No matter how long and hard this third group pressed the lever, they were unable to affect what happened to them.

None of the dogs liked being shocked. But it was the dogs in the third group whose response was most disturbing. All three groups of dogs were later placed in a "shock box" from which they could escape by leaping over a low partition. The first two groups of dogs quickly left their unpleasant situation—but nearly all of the third group simply lay down and whined.[7] Seligman concluded that when the dogs realized their responses did not affect their situation, they fell prey to "learned helplessness," which he came to see as analogous to the human condition of depression.

Today we know that depression is a far more complicated condition, with significant biological and genetic components. (We'll talk more about that in Chapter 2.)[8] But any of us, regardless of our genetic heritage, can experience the helplessness, hopelessness, and joylessness that come from feeling unable to affect our own lives. That feeling isn't necessarily an indicator of clinical depression, so let's call it "distress." In that sense, the hardworking, eager-to-please prep school girls with whom I spoke were distressed. So, by their account, were virtually all of their classmates.

Indeed, a whole generation of teenage girls is struggling with an impossible set of expectations, one that I've termed the *Triple Bind.*

WHAT IS THE TRIPLE BIND?

The original notion of a double bind came from social scientists in the 1950s who studied children growing up with contradictory, impossible demands. For example, a child might be told, "Tell me everything that's going on with you," and then told (either with or without words), "Don't bother me with so much information." Trying ever more frantically to do the impossible, the double-bind child was thought to be at risk of mental illness.[9]

Of course, mental illness has more complex origins than this picture indicates, nearly always including biological and genetic underpinnings.[10] And the types of family messages most associated with serious disorders aren't necessarily those of the double bind. But even if double-bind-style messages don't produce clinical conditions, they certainly produce distress. When we're asked to do two contradictory things, and especially when we fear being punished for not doing them, we're in a bind: confused, frustrated, and likely to blame ourselves. Our feelings might turn into anger, despair, resignation, or an ever more desperate attempt to go in two directions at once.

Today's girl faces not only a double but actually a Triple Bind: a set of impossible, contradictory expectations. Like Seligman's dogs, our teenage girls are baffled, distressed, and overwhelmed as they try ever harder to meet these ever more punishing demands. They've responded with a lower age of onset of depression, increases in aggression and violence, and skyrocketing rates of self-mutilation, binge eating, and suicide. They've also responded by sacrificing key portions of their identities, developing feelings of self-hatred, and becoming overwhelmed with a general sense of pressured confusion. The Triple Bind is possibly the greatest current threat to our daughters' health and well-being, an enormous obstacle to their becoming healthy, happy, and successful adults.

Each portion of the Triple Bind is challenging enough. But it's the combination of all three aspects that makes it deadly:

1. Be good at all of the traditional girl stuff.
2. Be good at most of the traditional guy stuff.
3. Conform to a narrow, unrealistic set of standards that allows for no alternative.

Let's take a closer look.

1. *Be good at all of the traditional girl stuff.* Today's girl knows she's supposed to fulfill all the traditional "girl" expectations—look pretty, be nice, get a boyfriend—while excelling at the "girl skills" of empathy, cooperation, and relationship building. Any girl who wants to feel normal knows the drill: bond with your girlfriends, support your boyfriend, and make your family proud. The essence of these girl skills is maintaining relationships: doing what others expect of you while putting their needs first. It's the quality that leads a girl to spend all evening talking a friend through a crisis rather than using those hours to write her own A-level paper. It's also the quality that might lead her to suppress her own abilities or desires in order to boost a boyfriend's ego or reassure an anxious parent.
2. *Be good at most of the traditional guy stuff.* Female skills might once have been all a girl needed—but no longer. Today, a girl isn't just looking for marriage and family; she expects to succeed at what were once traditionally considered "boy" goals, such as getting straight As and being a superathlete. Girls, especially those from the middle- or upper-income

brackets, are often expected to win acceptance to a top college. A poor or working-class girl's family may also look to her for the kind of financial support or upward mobility, through school, sports, or entertainment, that was once expected only of her brother.

So in today's competitive environment, girl skills are not enough. A successful girl must also master the ultimate boy skills of assertion, maybe even aggression: the commitment to becoming a winner at anything you undertake, regardless of your own or others' feelings. It's the quality that leads the star football player to charge through the line, suppressing any fear he might feel, ignoring both the pain he experiences and the pain he causes. It's also the quality that might lead a boy to promise himself, "Someday, I'm going to discover a cure for cancer, no matter how hard I have to work, no matter how many hours I miss with my family, no matter how many people think I can't do it."

As you can see, there are pluses and minuses to both approaches, but what's really difficult, if not impossible, is to master both of them at the same time. How do "best friends 4ever" fight each other over a diminishing number of college slots? What if the empowered basketball star doesn't fit into the size-2 miniskirt or can't stand letting her boyfriend win at ping-pong? What about the girl who wants to get off the merry-go-round and explore an alternative identity that allows a little more breathing room?

3. *Conform to a narrow, unrealistic set of standards that allows for no alternative.* Enter the third component of the Triple Bind: the way that alternatives of all types—different ways of becoming a woman, relating to society, or constructing an authentic self—have been virtually erased by the culture. This is the truly insidious aspect of the Triple Bind, which seems to offer choices with one hand only to take them away with the other.

At first glance, you might think that a girl was free to become anything she chooses. Look a little closer, though, and you'll see that whatever *else* she may decide, she must also always be sexy, thin, and pretty; have either a great boyfriend or a husband and kids; and be wildly successful at her career.

Girls used to be able to escape the narrow demands of femininity through such alternative roles as beatnik, tomboy, intellectual, hippie, punk, or goth. They'd embrace the ideals of feminism to proclaim that women didn't always have to be pretty, nice, and thin; that they didn't always have to have boyfriends; and that not all women wanted to become mothers. Or girls might follow a counterculture that challenged the notion of ascending the corporate ladder or fulfilling men's notions of the ideal woman. They'd imitate pop stars who presented alternate looks and styles of femininity: Janis

Joplin, Patti Smith, Tina Turner, Cyndi Lauper. They'd take up basketball or hockey; they'd turn into bookworms or dream of being president. All of these alternatives to traditional female roles gave independent girls a little breathing room, the space to insist that they didn't necessarily have to fit into skimpy clothes or learn how to flirt at age eleven. Other types of alternatives—bohemianism, the counterculture, activism, art, humanitarian ideals—helped girls challenge the achievement-oriented culture that insisted on straight As, elite colleges, and seven-figure incomes as the only prizes worth having. A free-spirited girl might even find a way of being sexy that wasn't about how she looked, a sexual style that was uniquely her own.

Now virtually all of these possibilities have been co-opted, consumerized, and forced into an increasingly narrow, unrealistic set of roles. Standards have become narrower and less realistic for both looks ("girl stuff") and achievement ("boy stuff"), even as the cultural alternatives that might have helped girls resist these standards have been erased.

First, the definitions of "sexy" and "pretty" have narrowed enormously in recent years, with an ever-escalating demand that girls turn themselves into sexual objects. For a girl to fit the acceptable look now requires an almost superhuman commitment to dieting, waxing, applying makeup, and shopping; for some girls, plastic surgery has also come to seem like a minimum requirement. These trends begin at frighteningly young ages. Even many lesbian girls, whose choice once seemed to free them from the "male gaze" of conventional beauty, are now also expected to present themselves in sexually objectified terms, sporting the same lipstick and lingerie as their heterosexual sisters.

At the same time, girls face increasingly unrealistic standards for achievement. Only the top grades and test scores, combined with the most impressive extracurriculars, will fit a girl for a top college, a destination that is becoming virtually a requirement for more and more middle-class girls. Poor and working-class girls now dream of becoming superstar athletes, top models, or self-made entrepreneurs—and attending the Ivies as well. I'm all for dreaming, but girls are being given the message that anything less than the absolute best counts as failure.

So both the "girl" and "boy" requirements have become harder to meet, even as the alternatives that might have freed girls from either set of demands—feminism, bohemianism, political activism, community spirit—have all but disappeared from the cultural landscape. Our girls are truly trapped, and the crisis-level statistics I have shared with you are a key consequence.

This third aspect of the Triple Bind is particularly insidious because it's so deceptive. On the surface, all jobs, all activities, indeed all possibilities are open to every teenage girl. Look a little deeper, though, and you can see the constraining need for girls to objectify themselves in order to fit the feminine mold. Yes, you might be able to do something "alternative" and unique—you can become the first female Indy driver, like Danica Patrick, or the first female presidential contender, like Hillary Clinton—but you still have to pose in a sexy outfit for *Playboy* or obsess publicly about your weight. Instead of Chrissie Hynde, we have Britney Spears; instead of Annie Lennox, we have Lindsay Lohan; instead of Queen Latifah, we have Beyoncé Knowles. Political pundits toss their hair and sport short skirts; women are told to exhibit empowerment, originality, and pride even as they don swimsuits to become the next top model. Our daughters might admire a whole roster of female athletes, but they, too, are expected to look skinny and "hot." (A colleague of mine, a sports psychologist, tells me that this is a recurring worry among the top female athletes he treats each week.) The 24/7 barrage of media images contributes to the sense that the walls are closing in. Skinny, sexy, scantily dressed teens and preteens appear everywhere, an airtight world that seems to offer no way out, reinforcing the notion that the only possible way to become a woman is to turn oneself into an object. Even the pioneering Nancy Pelosi, who will go down in history as the first female Speaker of the House, seems polite and ultrafeminine compared to such forebears as the hefty, abrasive congresswoman Bella Abzug.

Despite the apparent wealth of choices, our girls are ultimately presented with a very narrow, unrealistic set of standards that allow for no alternative. A seemingly boundless and hermetic culture insists on every female looking thin, pretty, and sexually available, whether she's a political pundit, a professional athlete, or a ten-year-old girl, even as it also demands that every girl aspire to being a wife (lesbian or straight) and mother—and all while climbing to the top of her career ladder, becoming a millionaire, and triumphing over every possible competitor.[11] No wonder our girls are increasingly becoming depressed, expressing their anguish through binge eating, self-mutilation, acts of violence, and even suicide.

As I lay out the elements of the Triple Bind, they sound neat and discrete, easy-to-separate qualities that are clearly at odds with one another. But for the teenage girl caught in the middle of that bind, the contradictions seem to blend seamlessly together. If you want to understand how this works, just watch a few episodes of *America's Next Top Model*. The show is wildly popular with teenage girls; nearly every one of the girls I spoke with told me she loved the show, including feminists, lesbians, and girls who wouldn't be caught dead wearing makeup, let alone prancing down a runway or posing for a swimsuit ad.

The show's format is simple: it gathers a group of thirteen young women of various shapes, backgrounds, and sizes, and asks them to compete for a top modeling spot. Every week, one more contestant is eliminated as the women are put through the complicated demands of photo shoots, runway modeling, and extreme athleticism. They might have to don mermaids' tails and dangle in fishing nets suspended above a canal, or pose, shivering in skimpy clothing, upon ice sculptures. They also have to endure twenty-four-hour surveillance from the show's cameras and find some way to get along with the other women they're competing against. And they have to learn how to make it all seem effortless, keeping a smiling, pretty face constantly on display in case some photographer snaps an unflattering "casual" shot and sells it to the tabloids. As the show's press release puts it, "Participants are asked to demonstrate both inner and outer beauty as they learn to master complicated catwalks, intense physical fitness, fashion photo shoots, and perfect publicity skills."

Looks count: a model has to have a lovely face and body, and usually she needs to be thin, though the show almost always includes a voluptuous woman or someone with unusual looks. (In fact, on the Spring 2008 cycle, a "plus-size" model won the competition for the first time.) However, a model can't be *just* a pretty face; the judges speak contemptuously of "beauty queens" and "ordinary" pretty girls. A model, especially a top model, has to have something extra—an unusual face, a signature walk. She must both fit the mold and break the mold, and of course, no one can ever quite tell her when she must do which. One contestant is told to leave the show because she refuses to cut her hair in the style that the judges have decided is best for her. Another is informed that if she doesn't let the show's dentist fix the gap in her front teeth, she won't be eligible for the Cover Girl contract that is part of the prize package.

Both girls agonize over their decisions: they see their hair, their gap-toothed smile, as aspects of who they are, their own sort of signature. No, the judges insist, those parts of their body are the wrong ground on which to take a stand. Get rid of those elements—and then find another way to be unique. "Confidence," "personality," and "being yourself" are probably the words most often spoken on *America's Next Top Model*, but unquestioning obedience is also a requirement.

The show's creator and producer is Tyra Banks, herself a groundbreaking African American model who clearly cares deeply for her young charges. But like many caring parents of today's girls, Banks has to teach the next generation how to fit into a system that she readily acknowledges is often unfair. Accordingly, she urges the girls to "be themselves" even as she demands that they conform.

In one episode, Banks explains to one young woman that her "country" accent is getting in her way. You shouldn't cut yourself off from your roots, Banks says firmly, but you can't be bound by them, either. Learn to turn your accent on and off, or you'll never be able to sell makeup on TV. Then Banks demonstrates how to play with a non-mainstream accent, teasing the model in her own childhood "street" speech and then reverting immediately to a more cultured voice.

No one minds where you actually came from: on one episode, the runway coach talked about himself as someone who had grown up in the projects, and fashion icon Twiggy, who was one of the judges for several seasons, referred frequently to her own working-class background. (Significantly, Twiggy herself started the fashion for thin models; before she came on the scene, models were full-figured.) But your background has to be incorporated into the larger ideal of an infinitely malleable woman who is nevertheless always unique. We should be able to identify your signature walk even in silhouette, says Tyra, but you also need to speak without an accent.

Imagine, for a moment, being one of the millions of teenage girls who watch this show. What message is she supposed to derive from this? *Be yourself—but not too much yourself. Be proud of who you are—but cover it up the moment someone else says it's offensive. Be unique—but unique in the* right *way, not in the wrong way. And if you want to know how to follow these contradictory instructions, well, we can't tell you exactly how, but don't worry, we'll know it when we see it. So just keep trying and trying and trying. If you're lucky, you'll figure it out. If not, well, you're off the program!*

On another episode, Tyra confronts a voluptuous young woman whose body doesn't fit the model stereotype. "Being a big girl is almost harder than being a black girl," Tyra says, pointing out that, like any minority, the "big girl" will have to work harder and present herself more cheerfully than her mainstream counterparts. The judges see no problem with giving the girl contradictory advice: she is encouraged both to glory in her unusual body (unusual by models' standards) and to compensate for it.

Clearly, looks aren't all that matter: ambition counts, too. Girls don't see their families or their boyfriends for several weeks as they remain shut up in the "model house" or travel to some exotic location, all the while working around the clock on each week's task. Any girl who loses focus is reprimanded, by the judges and by her fellow models; everyone agrees that boyfriends must come second if you expect to win. The show's theme song drives the point home: "Wanna be on top?" it asks, again and again and again.

Accordingly, Danielle, the model with the gap-toothed smile and "country" accent, drags herself out of a hospital bed, fighting the aftereffects of dehydration, exhaustion, and food poisoning to pose for a photo shoot on top of an elephant. She seems haggard and frail as she climbs on the beast's back, but the moment the cameras start to click, she looks dreamy and beautiful. She overcomes her physical weakness like a man but offers herself up to the camera like a woman, all in the service of a unique identity that is nevertheless ultrafeminized and overly sexualized.

To her credit, Banks wants to send a positive message about body image and race: the show always includes several African American and Latina models, as well as one or two girls who don't fit the mold. One season, that girl is Kim, a self-avowed lesbian who openly agonizes over her gender presentation: does she want to come across as a boy or a girl? The judges praise her androgyny and are obviously reluctant to cut her from the show. Clearly, Kim's no traditional girl; she even has a mini-affair with one of the other contestants. (Significantly, the other models object not to the homosexual activity but to the way the affair seems to distract both girls from the contest.)

Still, like all the women on the show, Kim is *also* ultrafeminine and overly sexualized: made up, dressed up, obediently allowing herself to be styled and posed however the client wants. Sometimes the judges want her to keep her boyish air; at other times, she's expected to look girlishly cute and sexy. Her unconventional qualities—androgyny, sexual difference—don't free her from traditional femininity so much as give her a unique spin on it. Even a gender-bending lesbian doesn't get a free pass: she has to retain her own style *and* be a "girly girl," sometimes switching back and forth, sometimes doing both at once.

Learning to be America's Next Top Model is clearly a balancing act even more demanding than staying on the back of an elephant. In true girl style, the models seek to please, to obey, to look good. In true boy style, they seek to prove their physical prowess and to reach the top. ("Suck it up," say the judges when the models complain about working in the cold or dangling upside down in the heat. "I'm here to win, not to make friends," say the models when asked about their competitors.) And any alternative identity or personal style they might develop, no matter how unique or apparently transgressive, is always cycled back into the demand to be ultrafeminized and overly sexualized, to make money for whatever corporate client has sponsored the photo shoot, to do whatever it takes to reach the top. Being a proud black woman, Danielle nonetheless accepts a long, silky hairstyle; being a boyish lesbian doesn't keep Kim from wanting to sell makeup. They don't see any contradictions, and perhaps girls watch the show so eagerly because they, too, need to reconcile so many conflicting demands.[12]

"I like the show while I watch it, but it makes me feel bad afterwards," says fifteen-year-old Madeleine, a junior at a public high school in a small midwestern college town. When I ask her why, she explains, "Well, it's intriguing, but it's sort of sad. I feel bad about myself, because I don't look that way. And I feel bad for them, because they want to reach the top but you know most of them aren't going to. They're never going to get what they dream about—but they just don't realize it."

Yet Madeleine watches the show every week, riveted by the balancing act that is her own struggle writ large. Like the contestants she watches, she needs to be herself—and to please others; to radiate confidence—but not to be arrogant; to look sexy—but not slutty; to be ambitious—but not mean. And if she stumbles on her own private runway or falters at her personal judge's latest demand, she at least has the comfort of knowing that thinner, prettier, more famous girls are also struggling with the impossible contradictions posed by the Triple Bind.

THE BEST OF TIMES, THE WORST OF TIMES

To be honest, it took me quite a while to figure out the nature of the Triple Bind because in so many ways, this is the best time in history to be a girl. In the 2004–5 school year, 57 percent of the bachelor's degrees in our country went to women. Women's right to be in the workplace has been well established, and among two-income households, one-quarter of wives now earn more than their husbands.[13]

Politically, too, women have made great strides. As of this writing, our Congress had eighty-nine female members—the highest number in history, including a female Speaker of the House. Also as of this writing, for the first time in U.S. history, a woman was a serious contender for a major-party presidential nomination. Teenage girls who watch the news will see women at all levels of politics and political commentary, and at least a surface acceptance that they belong there.

In one of the most striking shifts of the past thirty years, girls are also involved in sports in ways that used to be reserved for boys, allowing our daughters to engage with their bodies in new and more empowered ways. Madeleine, for example, is a champion swimmer, and her sister, Renee, excels at cross-country running. Athletic girls can see active women engaging with basketball, tennis, golf, soccer, track. They can aspire to play professionally with the Women's National Basketball Association or thrill to the "Just do it" message of the Nike ads. Long gone are the days of my baby boomer youth, when girls were patronizingly organized into six-person basketball teams—half on offense, half on defense—so that no frail female would be forced to run the whole length of the court. Instead, superbly conditioned female athletes are dunking in college and even high school games, while at some schools, girls' sports are even more popular than boys'. And for the first time in history, at least some girls are going to college on the strength of athletic scholarships in basketball or soccer, and others are being recruited on the basis of their athletic ability.[14]

But to some extent, the numbers are deceptive. Yes, looked at in one way, the Triple Bind is a triple set of opportunities, allowing girls to excel in or at least to explore every field. But looked at from another angle, the Triple Bind is a cruel hoax, as though we'd invited our daughters to the world's most sumptuous banquet and then kept them from enjoying their meal.

True, female college students now outnumber males, and women have nearly caught up with men in terms of med school and law school enrollment.[15] But at the same time, women are earning only 77 cents for every dollar earned by men—despite the fact that 37 percent of women over the age of sixteen work in management, professional, and related occupations, compared to only 31 percent of men. Women still predominate in such low-paid, low-status jobs as preschool and kindergarten teachers (97.5 percent female), child care workers (95.5 percent), dental assistants (97.3 percent), dental hygienists (96.1 percent), and secretaries and administrative assistants (96.7 percent).[16]

Moreover, the earnings gap between men and women persists even in the highest-paid occupations. For example, among both men and women, physicians and surgeons make the most money. Yet in 2000, female physicians' median income of $88,000 was only 63 percent of the $140,000 that the men were averaging. In only five occupations—hazardous materials removal, telecommunication line installation and repair, meeting and convention planning, dining and cafeteria attendants, and construction helpers—were women earning as much as men.[17]

Likewise, although the new acceptance of women in sports is a huge step forward, inequality persists there as well. On both the college and the professional level there is a major gender gap in terms of scholarships, funding, and salaries. Girl athletes may have become acceptable, even admired—but they're still not getting equal support.[18]

Certainly, too, adult women are facing impossible expectations of their own, a situation of which teenage girls can't help but be aware. In a November 1, 2007, article in the *New York Times*, columnist Lisa Belkin sums up the mixed messages that plague adult women in the workplace: "Don't get angry. But do take charge. Be nice. But not too nice. Speak up. But don't seem like you talk too much."[19]

Belkin was reporting on a recent spate of studies on working women, all of which came to rather discouraging conclusions. For example, a group called Catalyst, which conducts research on women in the workplace, published a July 2007 report with the gloomy title "Damned if You Do, Doomed if You Don't" that surveyed 1,231 senior executives from the United States and Europe. According to the report, the "default" image of a leader was still male, which meant that women were generally judged as failing to achieve true leadership. If they drew on what we have called their "girl skills"—showing "concern for other people's perspectives" or focusing on "work relationships"—they were considered less competent, since those were the qualities that marked them as women, not men. When they behaved more like traditional men, using what we have called their "boy skills" to "act assertively, focus on work task, display ambition," they were more often perceived as competent—but then they were disliked. In a classic example of the double bind, women who acted like women were "too soft," while women who acted like men were "too tough."[20]

Teenage girls today look at their parents, many of whom share the attitudes chronicled in the study, and they hear the mixed messages they are getting, especially from their fathers: "I want you to win one of the few places at a top school so you can go on to achieve huge success in a brilliant career. But I will never think it's as natural for you to be in charge as for a man (and if you had that great job right now, you probably still wouldn't earn as much as a man)."

Joan Williams agrees. She's the author of *Unbending Gender* and head of the Center of WorkLife Law at the University of California Hastings College of the Law in San Francisco. Belkin quotes a November speech Williams made at Cornell: "Women have to choose between being liked but not respected, or respected but not liked."[21]

For a teenage girl, this is a dreadful choice indeed, especially if she feels that her parents and teachers and coaches now expect—demand—that she do well. Should she please them with her straight As, her extracurricular triumphs, her winning games? Or should she try to win the affection of her peers, including the boys who, girls tell me, still generally prefer to feel smarter and more successful than their girlfriends?

Certainly, things have improved since the 1950s and 1960s, when parents were primarily concerned with finding husbands for their daughters while teachers were likely to disregard girls' abilities, especially in math and science. But to expect a girl to "live up to her potential" and then dislike her for doing so puts her in a difficult, if not impossible, situation.

Girls would have even more reason to be ambivalent if they knew about the research showing that men view sexy women as less competent. It's well documented that people of both genders do better at work if they're perceived as attractive, leading to better evaluations and greater success on the job. But when women are seen as not just attractive but sexy, they tend to be viewed as less competent.

Psychologist Peter Glick and his colleagues explored this issue, as they reported in a 2005 article in *Psychology of Women Quarterly.* They showed people videotapes of women who talked about their jobs while wearing either sexy clothes (low-cut blouse, tight skirt, high heels) or conservative ones. The women's scripts were identical, but viewers were variously told that they were receptionists or managers. The secretary, in her traditional female occupation, wasn't judged harshly for her sexy attire, but, says Glick, "participants viewed the sexy manager as less competent and less intelligent than the conservatively dressed manager," and they also had more negative feelings about working with her.[22]

The double bind for adult women includes anger as well as sexuality. An August 2007 study by Victoria Brescoll, a postdoctoral scholar at Yale University, found that angry men at work are admired, whereas angry women are often considered incompetent and "out of control." Working with randomly recruited men and women, Brescoll showed videos of a job interview in which candidates delivered identical scripts with one slight variation: they described themselves as either angry or sad about losing an account because of a colleague's late arrival to a meeting.

When the candidate expressing anger was a man, participants assigned him an average salary of $38,000. But a woman delivering the exact same "angry" script was given only $23,500. Women who expressed sadness were viewed more favorably than men who expressed the same emotion—but both were assigned salaries somewhere in the region of $30,000.

Not only did people react badly to angry women, but they were even more disapproving as the woman climbed the corporate ladder. Brescoll conducted another experiment in which the angry candidates were presented as either trainees or senior executives. "Participants rated the angry female CEO as significantly less competent than all of the other targets, including even the angry female trainee," Brescoll wrote. Adding insult to injury, they saw angry females as not only less competent but also "out of control."[23]

As these studies demonstrate, adult women face a double bind: they're expected to succeed like men, but not allowed to use the very tools—anger, assertiveness—that help men get ahead. And these attitudes eventually trickle down to teenage girls. Young women who are being groomed for top colleges or encouraged to compete for athletic scholarships may genuinely believe that they have the same opportunities as men. But on some level, they hear the same discouraging message that adult women receive, even if they haven't read the research. When I asked Jessica and her friends if they were treated differently than boys, they shook their heads in frustration.

"There's so many things we have to be, we have so many jobs that we have to do, and we have to do them perfectly," Jessica said. "I feel like there are a lot fewer roles for guys. They have to be a jock or popular, but that's it. And they don't have to be all that intelligent, either! They just have a very limited amount of roles. But we have to be the perfect student, and the perfect daughter, and the perfect sister—you know, work hard, and all this stuff—and it all piles up, and then you just can't do it all." She adds ruefully, "It holds us back."

Her friend Lupe agrees. Referring to the "glass ceiling" for women that she's heard about in her social studies class, she describes it poignantly: "You can see where you want to go but you just can't get there."

WHAT'S NEW ABOUT THE TRIPLE BIND?

As a baby boomer, I grew up at a time when it was unusual for girls to engage in sports or even to look forward to work after marriage. So to me, the changes represented by the Triple Bind are even more striking, a dramatic contrast to the values and styles I grew up with.

All this started to change dramatically following the women's movement. Indeed, if you came of age in the 1980s and 1990s, you may be wondering what I'm making such a fuss about. After all, girls—especially middle-class girls—have been playing soccer, striving for the Ivies, and planning their careers for more than two decades now. Is the Triple Bind really a new phenomenon?

Sadly, I believe it is. Although every era has put girls under a variety of pressures, there's something qualitatively different about the strains of the Triple Bind, and the crisis-level statistics for girls' mental health reflect that difference. Suicide rates are rising, depression is occurring at ever-earlier ages, binge eating and self-mutilation are increasingly common, and the percentage of girls involved in violence is growing.

Certainly, the cultural changes of the Triple Bind are an outgrowth of trends that began during the last part of the twentieth century. But the Triple Bind's unique features are putting our girls at a whole new level of risk, which continues to escalate at increasing speed.

So what's behind these alarming numbers? What has triggered this disturbing change?

I think that even though opportunities expanded for girls in the 1980s and 1990s, the expectations for girls were not so contradictory in those decades. True, girls were expected far more than previously to get good grades, apply to good schools, plan careers, and excel at sports. But in many cases, girls experienced these as additional demands in the "girl" mode, new ways to be obedient. Pleasing boyfriends took one set of skills, pleasing friends required another, and perhaps a third set of skills was needed for pleasing parents, teachers, and coaches. Yet a girl could still construct a consistent identity around "people pleasing" or being a "nice girl," even if she now had access to more activities and bigger dreams than her counterparts of early decades.

Another crucial aspect of the Triple Bind is its lack of alternatives. In former years, if a girl *didn't* want to conform to these traditional female demands, she could look to politics, sports, the arts, and even some aspects of pop culture for an escape from the mainstream ideals. She had pop icons such as Cyndi Lauper, Annie Lennox, Queen Latifah, or Tracy Chapman, who resisted the mold of the thin, pretty, ultrafeminine girl and offered other visions of femininity. She could look to movie characters, such as the quirky, offbeat girls and women in John Hughes movies (think of Ally Sheedy's moody artist in *The Breakfast Club*, Mary Stuart Masterson's punky drummer in *Some Kind of Wonderful*, and Annie Potts's ex-hippie record store owner in *Pretty in Pink*). She could even imagine becoming an athlete or dream of going into politics, believing that these career choices might free her from traditional feminine requirements for "hotness" or "cuteness." And she had access to a range of social movements—hippie, punk, goth, and a variety of religious and political groups—that might help her challenge the mainstream focus on money and success.

Then, around the turn of the millennium, a major cultural shift took place.

First, the economy tightened up, not just for people at the bottom but also for people in the middle. Now, getting into a good school has become a major challenge, while the prospects of employment for middle-class professionals are not nearly as rosy as before. (For more on the economic shifts of this period, see below.) The parents of middle-class girls look at what appears to be a bleak future for their children and fear that it's no longer enough for their daughters (and sons) to get good grades—they must now strive for a tiny number of places at a handful of top schools.[24] As columnist Judith Warner noted in the February 21, 2008, *New York Times,* the middle class now fears downward mobility. She quotes Columbia University historian Steven Mintz:

> We believe we're living in a new world where the avenues of success are harder to get into and there's no guarantee that things will work out. There's tremendous worry that our kids won't be able to recreate our class status. This creates an adversarial relationship between our kids and other kids.[25]

And, he might have added, it also puts tremendous pressure on children to succeed at ever-earlier ages.

For poor and working-class girls, the pressure is even more intense: jobs are fewer, and degree requirements are going up, even as state and community colleges have been raising their tuition and cutting back on aid. Even though the elite schools may offer low-income girls considerable financial assistance, admissions are far more competitive than ever before. To succeed in this new environment, a girl has to care not only about pleasing but also about winning, beating out her classmates or neighbors for access to an ever-shrinking pool of resources.

Likewise, girls in the 1980s and 1990s might have seen sports as a newly available "extra," a pleasurable way to use their bodies and hang out with their friends. As soon as sports for girls were taken seriously, though, girls had to engage the same competitive drives that characterized their male counterparts. Like the young women on *America's Next Top Model*, they had to care more about winning than about making friends.

To some extent, of course, female athletes—especially the successful ones—had always felt this way, even when they were high school students, and it must have been a liberating moment when they got more cultural permission to do so. But as girls' sports became more acceptable, they also became more of an obligation. Nearly every middle-class girl I spoke with talked about sports not primarily as a beloved activity—even if it also was—but as a college requirement. For too many poor and working-class girls, sports might be their only access *to* college. With these new opportunities, then, came new pressures to strive, compete, and succeed, pressures that are diametrically opposed to the ongoing expectation that a girl will do the "relationship work" of staying connected, putting others' needs first, and making people feel good.

For many girls, extracurriculars now take on the same obligatory quality as sports, becoming less a route for expressing their identities than one more burdensome pre-college requirement. Middle-class girls might strive for the Ivies while poor and working-class girls seek state schools, but either way, grades and test scores are rarely enough: thanks in part to the increased competition generated by fears of downward mobility, a long list of "extras" is now expected.[26] Suddenly the class play or the school paper or the volunteer work that had once offered girls an alternative space—a place to learn more about themselves, their abilities, and their world—has been channeled back into the twin demands of pleasing ("Show the admissions committee what it wants to see . . .") and competing (". . . or else you'll never beat out your classmates").[27]

The girls coming of age in the 1980s and 1990s also had far more chances to escape from the omnipresence of the media. Although twentieth-century kids watched TV, listened to music, and went to the movies, they didn't live in the 24/7 electronic culture that exploded into our lives as the century ended.[28] Again, the media have been a mixed blessing: they offer many girls a chance to explore alternatives, connect with others who share their interests, and keep alive their sense that life holds far more possibilities than are evident in their family, neighborhood, or school. To girls who feel trapped by their environments, the Internet can be a godsend, offering new worlds to dream about and maybe even some resources to make those dreams come true.[29]

But the media can also create the overwhelming sense that "everybody" is wearing this or thinking that, the sense that no matter what else a girl aspires to, she must always also be pretty, thin, and hot; she must always want a boyfriend or a husband and family; she must always try for the most public, prestigious, and financially rewarding version of success (and then consider herself a failure if she doesn't succeed). A girl who watches television may see a wide variety of female characters—far wider than in previous decades—but she also sees a far narrower range of acceptable female body types. A girl who surfs through Facebook or browses through blogs may meet girls with alternative interests and hobbies, but she may also see page after page of supposedly "ordinary" girls who look far thinner, hotter, and better-dressed than she does, and who present their look as effortless and natural. The relentless media barrage also makes it essential that our teens must relentlessly multitask, with negative consequences for their learning and even their health.[30]

So to a girl's long list of duties—studying, sports, extracurriculars, family responsibilities—add the very real work that goes into looking good: shopping and wardrobe maintenance, shaving or waxing, manicures and pedicures, keeping one's hair styled, and applying makeup so skillfully that it looks "natural." Every season, a new requirement is added: eyebrow waxing, perhaps, or shaving one's pubic hair, some new item of self-care that, as the years go by, becomes less an option and more a requirement. As we'll see in Chapter 6, an increasing number of teenage girls are even undergoing plastic surgery. Any girl will tell you how much work it all takes, but if she acknowledges the work, either to complain about it or to revel in it, she'll be accused of being vain or unfeminine or of "trying too hard." Or she'll be told that she should do what makes *her* feel good, as though she were somehow immune to the judgment of her peers and the cultural standard she encounters at every turn, as though she had the power to make herself feel good in the face of all the contradictory expectations that surround her.

For twenty-first-century girls, the Triple Bind has upped the ante. Now girls must strive like boys to succeed at school and sports, but they're still not exempt from the traditional "girl" demands: pleasing people, looking good, and presenting their achievements as effortless and natural. And if they seek a way out—an alternative view of being female that might fit better with their own hopes and dreams and desires—they are confronted with a seemingly endless parade of options that are nonetheless relentlessly similar: all pretty, hot, and thin; all seemingly happy with perfect boyfriends or husbands and children (or sometimes same-sex partners and children); all eagerly striving for power, money, and corporate success. No wonder so many girls went to see *Enchanted*, whose fairy-tale heroine perfectly fulfilled these conflicting expectations—all while succeeding brilliantly at romance, motherhood, and career. No wonder they love *America's Next Top Model*, where real-life girls seem to be learning not only runway walks and makeup tips but the secret of meeting these impossible demands.

No wonder, too, that as the political and cultural alternatives of previous decades seem to have faded from the public view, girls hunger for any sign that a person might maintain alternative values or that there is another way to be a woman. Ellen Page, star of the 2007 movie *Juno*, commented in a February 22, 2008, radio interview that she'd met teenage girls who'd seen the movie five times, thrilled with the movie's smart, quirky teenage heroine whose identity seemed to transcend the consumerized clichés and ultrafeminine imagery so prevalent elsewhere in the media. Responded radio host Kurt Andersen, "It does suggest that there is a yearning for something different."[31]

Until alternatives such as *Juno* are presented, teenage girls may even not realize how desperate they are for another view, another set of values, an escape hatch that might give them access to a kinder, more welcoming world. If all they know is their own time, their own school, they might have trouble even imagining other possibilities. They're all too aware, though, of how constraining their own era has become. "It's like mistakes aren't allowed anymore," Jessica sighs. "You aren't allowed to be like a normal person, you have to be like a robot."

Twenty-first-century girls might well see their newly expanded world not as a sumptuous banquet of new opportunities but as a demanding workplace with a long list of diverse—and contradictory—requirements. Many of them seem ready to shoulder any burden to please their families or teachers. Yet they are also supposed to maintain, as Jessica put it, the right façade, fulfilling their long list of duties with apparent ease and welcoming their many obligations as somehow "good for them."

For a time, they might comply. Then, especially if they have biological vulnerabilities or early experiences of abuse, they are likely to binge, cut themselves, self-medicate with pills or liquor, act out violently, or struggle with distress, depression, and suicidal thoughts. Or they opt out of whole areas of experience, like the desexualized Marcy or like Nicola, who gave up her beloved basketball because she couldn't handle the pressure. Or they simply soldier along, wondering, like Jessica, why it's so hard "to have fun and be a kid."

Certainly, if you walked down the corridors of a typical high school or visited the town soccer field on a Saturday morning, you'd see plenty of teenage girls wearing jeans and T-shirts, apparently comfortable in a wide range of sizes, shapes, and styles. But even the girls who seem to be doing fine are paying a price for their efforts: secret bingeing and purging, perhaps, or self-mutilation hidden under long sleeves and leggings, or simply the girl's own sense that she is somehow disappointing her family, her teachers, herself.

"Every time I get a report card," Eugenia says wistfully, "I know when my mom comes home she's gonna be like, 'Oh, you should have tried harder. All those times you were watching TV for half an hour or talking on the phone for twenty minutes, you could have gotten an A.' "[32]

Michi can't even say what's causing her sorrow; she only knows that something's missing. "We have to be really on top of everything," she says quietly. "But we can't get there. We have that stopping point. We can't get there. Something is pushing us back down. We can't move up if we are getting pushed back down. It's just kinda hard because then you are not meeting your expectations—so it just keeps pushing back and forth, so you're not getting there."

When I ask Michi *what* is pushing her down, she searches for the words and then gives up. "It's just something," she says. I can't help thinking of Kirsten, the women's studies major, who told me, "This is our problem with no name." And I can't help remembering from my own experience—both as a clinician and as a child—that the problems you can't find the words for are often the ones that hurt the most.

THE ECONOMY AND THE TRIPLE BIND

If the crisis I'm describing were confined only to teenage girls, that would be bad enough. Unfortunately, as I've come to understand it better, I've seen that the Triple Bind is also a by-product of larger changes in our economy, changes that are having far-reaching and disturbing effects upon us all.

Consider the 2005 national best seller *The World Is Flat,* by *New York Times* reporter Thomas L. Friedman. Friedman argues that we're in the process of moving toward a global economy, one in which work is almost infinitely transferable to anyplace on the planet. Industrial jobs, of course, were moved out of the United States in the 1980s and 1990s, with disastrous consequences for poor and working-class Americans. Friedman chronicles the process of middle-class and professional jobs being moved out as well.

Friedman is thoroughly positive about this transition, which he sees as opening up a wide variety of new opportunities. Reading between the lines, however, you get a much more disturbing story, one in which no American, no matter how well qualified or well trained, is safe from the prospect of losing not only a job but the very possibility of having a job.[33]

I was particularly struck by the story, early in the book, of Friedman's encounter with Jaithirth Rao, a Mumbai executive who has helped to move tax preparation from the United States to India. Rao assures Friedman that all the routine work of accountancy—tax returns, for example—can be done overseas, leaving U.S. accountants to focus on satisfying important clients by performing the more complex business of tax shelters, estate planning, income management, and so on.

Friedman appreciates the economic efficiency. But, he wonders, how will this affect the U.S. citizens who are now working as accountants? He asks Rao:

> What if I am just an average accountant? I went to a state university. I had a B+ average. Eventually I got my CPA. I work in a big accounting firm, doing a lot of standard work. I rarely meet with clients. They keep me in the back. But it is a decent living and the firm is basically happy with me. What is going to happen to me in this system?[34]

"It is a good question," Rao admits, without ever actually answering it. He does stress, however, that in the future, the U.S. accountants who can expect to be employed will be those who are skilled enough to do complicated work and who have good enough "people skills" to handle clients well.

As I read through the rest of Friedman's book, seeing how many middle-class jobs were being lost to globalization, I began to understand a bit better the pervasive anxiety of parents who freaked out when their daughters took twenty minutes to talk on the phone instead of doing their homework. On some level, we're all aware of the changes Friedman chronicles, and we know that at least for now, they've made us less certain about our futures. Despite Friedman's reassurances, it's hard not to feel that the economic future he describes is one in which only a few top people can succeed, and to fear the downward mobility that Steven Mintz described. It's also clear that in Friedman's new "flat" world, people will need both "girl skills" and "boy skills" to rise to the top: competitive enough to snag the top jobs, accommodating enough to please wealthy clients.

Barbara Ehrenreich offers another spin on the economic insecurities that may be driving the Triple Bind. In her 2005 *New York Times* best seller *Bait and Switch*, she describes her experience of trying to get work in corporate America. The picture she paints is a gloomy one indeed. White-collar workers at all levels frequently find themselves fired or laid off and often spend months or even years without work. Personality seems to count more than achievements, which has the paradoxical effect of making people work harder than ever to achieve even as they also succumb to a paralyzing despair. Ehrenreich explains:

> Middle-class Americans, like myself and my fellow seekers, have been raised with the old-time Protestant expectation that hard work will be rewarded with material

> comfort and security. This has never been true of the working class, most of which toils away at wages incommensurate with the effort required. And now, the sociologists agree, it is increasingly untrue of the educated middle class that stocks our corporate bureaucracies. As sociologist Robert Jackall concluded, "Success and failure seem to have little to do with one's accomplishments."[35]

The parents of the girls I met may not have read Mintz or Friedman or Ehrenreich. Certainly the girls had not read them. Yet when I thought about the profound anxieties that both authors chronicled, I began to see that at least one aspect of the Triple Bind is an effort to guarantee security in an insecure world. Both Friedman and Ehrenreich make clear that what I've been calling "girl skills"—making people feel comfortable, figuring out what they need, and then giving it to them—are central to success in the new economy, whether in Ehrenreich's corporate bureaucracy or Friedman's globalized "flat world." At the same time, given the relentless competition, anyone without the "boy skills" of striving and winning at all costs may have a very tough row to hoe. And from both books—as from *America's Next Top Model*—you get the sense of how important it is to have both a unique personality and yet one that seems completely obedient to the prevailing ethos, to make a unique contribution even while submitting wholly to the people in charge.

Indeed, in our insecure, "flat" world, even those who make a unique contribution may not survive. As I was working on this chapter, I came upon a December 11, 2007, story in the *Wall Street Journal* about the precarious nature of the pharmaceutical industry. Big Pharma has long been touted as one of the industries of the future, in which U.S. cutting-edge research is supposed to assure economic success. But the story also revealed that Robert Sliskovic, the inventor of Lipitor, had recently been laid off. Despite having developed a medication that has saved countless lives and made hundreds of millions of dollars for his employer, in the end, this talented scientist was simply another corporate employee. Retaining no patent rights in the drug he developed, Sliskovic was a casualty of his company's decision to shut down a whole research division that was deemed obsolete.[36]

In a world where even so successful a man can't keep a job, how can parents prepare their daughters for the future? Who can blame parents for wanting their daughters to succeed at everything—girl skills, boy skills, and everything in between—if they think that will guarantee them a financially secure life? Who can blame girls for feeling that if they *don't* get into a top college, their lives have been ended at age eighteen?

I'm a psychologist, not a sociologist or an economist, and so the rest of this book will be devoted to the cultural and psychological aspects of the Triple Bind. But as you read about girls staying up all night to study or girls rushing from activity to activity in a desperate attempt to enter a top school, remember Friedman's hypothetical B+ accountant, Ehrenreich's anxious executives, and Robert Sliskovic. Their stories also form part of the Triple Bind.

UNDERSTANDING THE TRIPLE BIND

It's hard to imagine a time of greater opportunity for girls. This is in many ways a time to revel in girls' and women's unprecedented accomplishments and to savor their many new opportunities. Yet we cannot escape the horrifying statistics presented in this chapter. Sadly, the flip side of all the new achievements by women and girls is a new degree of psychological devastation for far too many of our daughters.

When teenage girls speak for themselves, one can sense vividly their utter frustration at not being able to name or fully describe their pervasive sense that they cannot hope to meet the contradictory, impossible challenges of acting simultaneously as nurturers and as competitors in an oversexualized, consumerist environment that offers few genuine alternatives. For unprecedented numbers of our daughters, the extraordinary opportunities of the current era have come to seem, to invoke Ehrenreich's title, like so many games of bait and switch, promising self-expression but delivering self-erasure. Amidst all the activities foisted upon teenage girls, where is the time for them to find out what they like to do? Amidst all the pressure to enter a top college, how can they decide what's important to them? Amidst all the premature maturity, oversexualization, and self-objectification, how can they make friends with their bodies and discover their own desires? Amidst the consumerism and relentless drive to buy, how can they develop a sense of community, or a sense of priority regarding a larger purpose in life?

We must do better by our daughters—and I believe we can. The first step, though, is to understand what we're up against. So let me share with you my research, my experience, and my conversations with the young women who are struggling with the Triple Bind.

CHAPTER 2

Blue Jeans and "Blue" Genes

Depression and the Triple Bind

Jeannie had always been a quiet child and even somewhat shy, but she was the kind of girl who drew smiles and praise from nearly everyone for her sweet and helpful nature. She wasn't always comfortable with boys, but by the time she turned fourteen, she had started going out with Mike, a guy who went to her school.

Jeannie felt that she and Mike were perfect for each other—both loved animals, both liked sports—and she was also relieved to have found a steady guy, which she felt excused her from the "hooking up" dating culture that her other friends were part of. She liked Mike a lot, and sometimes she even thought they were in love.

Everything went well until Jeannie started taking a demanding biology class, an important step in her plan to become a veterinarian. She knew how competitive the best schools were, and she worried about whether she'd have the chance to pursue her dreams. She studied hard each night for the class and was thrilled when she got an A on her first assignment.

Mike, who hadn't yet settled on a career path, felt frustrated and left out. He took to calling Jeannie every evening in the middle of her study time, even though first she and then her parents asked him not to. He seemed to have one problem after another for which he needed comfort—a tough coach, a difficult family situation, a falling-out with a friend. Jeannie tried to be helpful, but she never had the sense that her suggestions or condolences made much difference. She felt she was failing Mike, and she was also increasingly worried about her grades: time on the phone was time she didn't have for studying. Soon she was losing an hour or two of sleep each night, trying to help both Mike and herself.

Sometimes Jeannie would try to end the phone call so she could get back to her studies. Then Mike would pout, calling her selfish and even saying she was mean. Finally, the inevitable happened: Mike broke up with Jeannie, saying that she was too immature, self-centered, and insensitive to have a boyfriend.

Jeannie was devastated. She was tormented by the sense that she had let Mike down and by the fear that what he had said was true. Maybe she *was* selfish and immature. Maybe she was a truly bad person. Maybe she would never find another boyfriend. Her friends were outwardly supportive, but Jeannie began to suspect that they secretly agreed with Mike. She started worrying over little things—the day she was half an hour late meeting Lissa at the mall, or the time she forgot to call Kira back about an important math assignment. In Jeannie's mind, these minor transgressions magnified into major crimes. When her biology teacher scolded her for getting a B- on a pop quiz, Jeannie felt that she had failed at everything and that she had let everyone down: Mike, her friends, her teachers, even her family, who expected her to get good grades. She was sure now that she'd never get into vet school. She'd lost Mike—she'd lost everything—and all for nothing.

Jeannie became preoccupied with the idea that she was ugly. She started avoiding social times even with her family and hiding out in her room at every opportunity. From being a quiet but mostly happy young woman she became withdrawn, tearful, almost catatonic, with a pervasive sense that she wasn't worth anything anymore.

Jeannie's mother was all too familiar with the signs of depression. Although she herself had never been depressed, her older sister had a history of suicide attempts and her mother had come close to being hospitalized. She knew that this family history meant that Jeannie, too, had a potential tendency to suffer from depression. "I don't want to be one of those mothers who hover over every little thing," Jeannie's mother told their pediatrician. "After all, her grades are still good and she's not acting out. But I'm beginning to worry that she really is pretty depressed."

The doctor was inclined to brush off these fears and suggested that Jeannie's mother just give her daughter "time to grow out of her bad mood." Then one day Jeannie's mother went into her daughter's room looking for a permission slip and found some sample suicide notes, as though Jeannie had been practicing how she might say goodbye. Jeannie's mother was fairly certain that she'd been meant to find the notes. But she was now more convinced than ever that her daughter was struggling with serious depression.

Melinda was also a quiet but happy fourteen-year-old who had never given her parents any trouble. She, too, had recently started going out with her first boyfriend, Rick, a guy from her AP history class. When Rick got a C and decided to switch down to the regular class, he asked Melinda to come with him. College-bound, ambitious, and idealistic—she planned to become a civil rights lawyer—Melinda refused.

Rick seemed first hurt, then angry, that Melinda had chosen to remain in her AP class. When she continued to stick to her guns, Rick (as Mike had done with Jeannie) called her selfish and immature, and eventually broke up with her in a particularly hurtful way. And, like Jeannie, Melinda was devastated. Distraught over her broken relationship, she found it harder to concentrate when she studied. Soon she, too, was faltering in school, particularly in the AP class that she and Rick had fought about. Concerned, her teacher went so far as to meet with her parents to find out why Melinda had stopped participating in class, gotten a C+ on the midterm, and seemed to be falling behind on an important semester-long project.

Significantly, Melinda also had an aunt and a grandmother who'd suffered from severe depressions. This family history should have made her vulnerable to depression, just as Jeannie was. Yet, although Melinda had a few bad weeks, she never responded to her setbacks as Jeannie did. Melinda never hid out in her room, didn't become preoccupied by her appearance, never encountered a sense of being worthless, and was not suicidal, though she did seem sad. What made the difference?

As it happened, Melinda came from a strong African American family with working-class roots, membership in a local church, and a deep involvement in their community. As a result, Melinda had friends not only at her high school but also at Sunday school and among the children she knew through her father's fraternal organization and her mother's union. Melinda wasn't especially close to these other friends and she never started dating any of the guys in those groups. But because she moved in so many different social circles, she had a larger sense of the world than Jeannie did. Melinda could see for herself that life didn't begin and end at her high school—there were other options.

Melinda also felt a powerful sense of mission: by going to college and then to law school, she believed she'd be helping the people she'd grown up with and making a real difference in the world. Her sense of social responsibility was further strengthened by the weekly activities of her church's youth group, which included raising money for a local scholarship fund, reading to people at a nursing home, and preparing the Christmas pageant at their church.

Thus, even when Melinda was at her lowest, she was surrounded by people who helped remind her that she had a place in the world, useful work to do, and the hope of a better future. True, Melinda was wracked with pain for several weeks. But she never developed major depression.

ONE GIRL IN FIVE

Depression is one of the most serious crises facing our teenage girls today. Girls surge ahead of boys in experiencing serious depression during the early teen years, and by age sixteen, girls face twice the risk of depression as boys, a ratio that persists for the rest of their lives. One in five girls will have experienced an episode of major depression by the time she reaches age nineteen, with many more encountering minor or mild depression. To me, though, the most devastating statistic is that nearly 10 percent of adolescent girls report that they've made a suicide attempt, with an alarming increase in the rate of actual suicides for girls ages ten to nineteen during the years 2003–4 (as of this writing, the last period for which good figures were available).[1]

Experts disagree over whether we're in the midst of an epidemic of child and adolescent depression. But one thing is clear: the age at which serious depression first hits is becoming younger and younger. Although depression is a complex condition, with genetic, biological, and emotional components, I believe that one of the primary reasons for the ever-earlier display of depression and for the dramatic increase in adolescent girls' rates of suicide is the Triple Bind.[2] I also believe that the extent to which adolescents feel connected to larger issues, involved in some kind of community, and supported by a world beyond their families can make a huge difference in keeping them from developing disorders or in helping them to recover if a disorder develops. (For more on how a social perspective can help prevent and combat depression and other clinical problems, see Chapter 9.)

But when I express these opinions to some of my colleagues, or point out that Jeannie and Melinda, with virtually identical family histories of depression, nonetheless weathered their challenges very differently, they look at me with skepticism. Although the orthodox view in 1950s psychology was that all mental health problems were caused by bad parenting, we've now taken up a new orthodoxy: that the root of all evil is in our brain chemistry, and ultimately in our genes. Depression, after all, *is* a biochemical condition, and one that's likely to be passed down through the generations. A clinician might well be tempted to believe that Melinda and Jeannie, presenting with the same two-generation history of female depression, were equally at risk for depressive episodes of their own.[3]

And yet that's not how the stories went. Given similar family histories and similar stresses, one girl became depressed while the other remained simply sad. Why?

"NATURE VERSUS NURTURE" OR "NATURE *PLUS* NURTURE"?

In this chapter, I'm going to help you sort through the confusing scientific claims about the role of genetics and brain chemistry in depression. Although the debate has often been framed in terms of "nature versus nurture," it's far more accurate to see it as a combination of nature *plus* nurture. And given that more accurate perspective, the Triple Bind looks like an even greater danger, increasing the risk for any girl who has even a mild biological tendency to depression.[4]

First things first: let's define depression. *Depression* is the condition of feeling helpless, hopeless, and often worthless. A depressed person is often unable to find pleasure in life. She's likely to sleep too little or too much; to either gain or lose excessive weight; and to spend a lot of time crying or on the verge of tears. Her motivation is low, and her thought patterns are gloomy, pessimistic, and too often cast in all-or-nothing terms. She is frequently irritable, even more than she might be sad, and her sense of self-worth has plummeted.

Of course, we all feel blue occasionally, and when things are going badly—particularly when we've lost a loved one to death or divorce—we may experience pain for weeks or even months. But depression often goes a step beyond pain to the conviction that we don't deserve to live and the world would be better off without us. And serious depressions are highly likely to recur, with repeated episodes throughout the person's life, which are often devastating for relationships, schoolwork, employment, and even physical health.[5]

Depression comes in many degrees. Clinicians tend to talk about "minor" versus "major" depression, or, in another terminology, "mild," "moderate," or "severe" depression, depending on the symptoms. These aren't hard-and-fast categories, however, but rather ways of trying to get a handle on an elusive condition that can appear in a wide variety of guises.[6]

Women are far more vulnerable to depression than men, beginning with the onset of adolescence. Depression is still rare in children, and boys may be slightly more likely to show it than girls, though before adolescence the rates are just about fifty-fifty. Once kids hit puberty, though, girls quickly overtake boys, so that by the age of fifteen or, at latest, sixteen, females are twice as likely as males to experience major depression.[7] As our measurements have improved over the past fifty years or more, we've found that at least one woman in five (and maybe more) is likely to experience at least one depressive episode sometime during her life.

So what causes depression? That's a complicated question that scientists are hotly debating, and our ideas have been changing rapidly as our knowledge advances. Currently, what I and most of my colleagues believe is that depression is at least partly the result of our genetic heritage. If you don't have the combination of genes that makes you vulnerable to depression, you may well become distressed: sad, angry, despairing, listless. You may even become depressed for a few weeks or even a few months, especially if you've suffered a major bereavement or loss. But without the "vulnerability" genes, you aren't likely to show the most severe signs of clinical depression: a sense of worthlessness, a belief that the world would be better off without you, and a tendency to consider suicide. Nor are you necessarily at risk for recurrent episodes throughout your life.[8]

So genetic heritage does play a key role in depression. However—and here's a key point—even people who have the "vulnerability" genes will not necessarily become depressed. These genes don't doom you to a life of depression; they only give you the *potential* to become depressed.

How can that be true? Why do some people with "vulnerability" genes fall prey to the worst ravages of depression while others, with what appears to be the same genetic heritage, escape?[9]

To answer that question, we can't look just at our genes *or* at our life circumstances: we have to consider the relationship between them. So if you leave this chapter remembering only two key points, here are the ones I want you to take away:

1. Our life circumstances can turn some genes "on" or "off"—activating or deactivating them—and this may well be true with the genes that make us vulnerable to depression.
2. The "depression" genes don't make us depressed: they make us more vulnerable to stress. So even with such genes, we won't necessarily become depressed, *depending on what kinds of stress we experience.*

Surprised? Along with many of my colleagues, I was too when we first came upon this new understanding of our genes. Most of us had been trained to believe that genes were the absolute masters of our fate, and many of us had a hard time grasping the newer concept: that we and our environments have the power to affect the way our genes operate.

Once I've shared this concept with you, though, you'll never think about genes in the same way again.[10] So let's take a closer look at our two key points:

1. *Our life circumstances can turn some genes "on" or "off"—activating or deactivating them—and this may well be true with the genes that make us vulnerable to depression.* At first glance, this may seem shocking. How can

our genes be turned on and off? Aren't we born with our genes? Aren't we stuck with them?

Well, yes. And no. We *are* born with our genes: all twenty thousand or so in each and every cell, and they do not change throughout our lifetimes. But these same genes are dynamic. Many can be activated or deactivated in response to our internal chemistries and our life circumstances.[11]

Here's one very simple example: getting a suntan. If you're a light-skinned person and you're never exposed to the sun, what happens? Naturally, you stay pale all the time. But bring a new factor into your environment—a hot, blazing sun—and what happens then? If you have the genetic ability for it, you'll tan.

Tanning occurs when your body produces enough melanin to turn your skin brown. If you have naturally dark skin, of course, your body is already producing lots of melanin. This is a genetic effect: your melanin-producing genes are constantly active, keeping your skin dark. But if you're fair, your melanin-producing genes are less active—"turned down," so to speak. You have a potentially greater capacity to produce melanin, but most of the time you wouldn't know it.

Then, when the sun comes out, your body reacts to its new circumstances. To protect your light skin from getting burned, your body "turns up the volume" on those dormant genes and instructs them to produce melanin. Your new life circumstances have actually altered the way your genes behave.

This is such a new idea for most people that I'm going to repeat it: *your life experiences can actually cause your body to turn some genes "on" or "off."* Under some circumstances (such as when the sun is shining and you are outside), your "suntan" genes are active. Under other circumstances (when the sun is weak or hidden), your "suntan" genes are far less active. Your life circumstances can't change your genetic heritage. But it can determine how you *experience* that heritage—and whether your genes become activated or not.

Of course, if you live in an extreme northern climate all your life, you might never find out about your "suntan" gene. You *have* the genetic capacity to produce extra melanin, but that capacity lies dormant, waiting for the right circumstances to activate it.

Although the specific genes and the underlying biology are different with depression than with suntans, the principle is the same. A person with a vulnerability to depression might never find out about this part of her genetic heritage if her life circumstances don't set it off. Her genes may make her *vulnerable* to depression, but they don't necessarily ensure that she will become depressed. Likewise, the genes that make us vulnerable to ulcers, diabetes, and other mental disorders can also be activated at different times—and in different organs of the body—again as the result of experiences and/or internal chemical influences.

That's why I'm so concerned about the Triple Bind. I believe this set of cultural circumstances is putting our most vulnerable girls at increased risk, and later in this chapter, I'll tell you how.

First, though, let's make sure the science is really clear and that we've cleared up all the misinformation that's often conveyed in the media. So here's the second key point about genes and depression:

2. *The "depression" genes don't make us depressed: they make us more vulnerable to stress. So even with such genes, we won't necessarily become depressed, depending on what kinds of stress we experience.* We don't really know as much about "depression" genes as we'd like to. We do know there isn't one single gene for depression, but rather a number that seem to be related to this debilitating condition. In fact, the genes that make us vulnerable to depression may also be involved in a number of other conditions, including migraine, sleep disorders, and several other kinds of mental disorders as well. In that sense, they aren't even "depression" genes but rather "vulnerability" genes.

Possibly, one or more of these "vulnerability" genes can be activated by certain life experiences. Also, these genes may interact with one another in different ways; it's combinations of genes that may matter most, rather than any particular gene by itself. In any case, there's another crucial point: *we now know that the kinds of life experiences we have can help determine whether these genes affect us or not.* Scientific research into this fascinating topic is continuing, and we hope to know a lot more in the next five or ten years.

Meanwhile, here's something we *do* know: *none* of the genes that seem to be related to depression actually *causes* depression. Instead, they set off biological reactions that make us more *vulnerable* to depression by affecting how we respond to stress. A person without these "vulnerabilty" genes may respond to difficult life events by simply feeling sad or angry. A person with one or more of these genes might respond to the same events by becoming clinically depressed.

But what if the vulnerable person never experiences major losses or other negative life events? Or what if she has developed excellent coping mechanisms, so even when she suffers a loss or a challenge, the stress doesn't hit her so hard? She may still have a genetic *tendency* to depression. She may also have more than the usual amounts of negative emotion, regardless of circumstance. But she's found a way to keep stress at bay. Her vulnerability exists—but it's never triggered.

Think again of how this works with suntans. Many of us are genetically vulnerable to them. We're light-skinned, and we *don't* tan easily; we burn. Expose us to the sun and, unlike our melanin-rich neighbors, we're going to suffer. That's genetic.

But that doesn't mean we're doomed to sunburn. Yes, we were born with a genetic vulnerability to the sun's burning rays. But we can protect ourselves from those rays by avoiding the sun, loading up on sunblock, or putting on a hat and wearing long sleeves. Our genes haven't changed, but our life circumstances have. Because we're responding to the sun in a different way, our vulnerability doesn't matter.[12]

Of course, with the erosion of the ozone layer, *all* of us are being exposed to ever brighter and more intense sunlight. Those of us who could withstand an hour of sunlight before we burned may now start to redden after only a few minutes.

Likewise—and crucially—the Triple Bind is a kind of toxic psychological environment that puts far more teenage girls at risk. A girl with only a slight vulnerability to depression might have survived past decades without ever experiencing a serious episode. Now, when faced with the power of the Triple Bind, she succumbs, and at an earlier age.

Later in this chapter, I'll explore what exactly is "depressing" about the Triple Bind. But first, let's take another look at the biology of depression. Again, there's so much misinformation floating around out there, I want you to understand exactly what the latest science tells us.

CHEMICAL CONDITIONING

For many conditions, including depression, eating disorders, addiction, impulse control, and aggression, a key substance is serotonin, a powerful brain chemical that helps regulate our feelings of well-being and optimism. Serotonin is technically known as a *neurotransmitter,* because it literally transmits information from neuron to neuron. (There are small gaps, called *synapses,* between neurons. In order for information to travel throughout our brain, neurotransmitters must fill these gaps as the neurons send signals to neighboring neurons.)

At least three other neurotransmitters are also involved in depression, as well as a variety of other mental disorders: dopamine, epinephrine (aka adrenaline), and norepinephrine (aka noradrenaline). The right levels of these three chemicals (and many others) in our brains and bodies keep us feeling energized and capable of coping with stress. If our levels are too high, we're likely to feel angry and agitated; if they're too low, we'll feel sluggish and listless.

How do our brain chemical levels get out of whack in the first place? For one thing, our genes shape the ways that neurotransmitters function. Our brain chemistry also alters in response to a number of factors, including diet, exercise, sleep, mood, thought patterns, and external stressors. Certainly, losing a friend, breaking up with a partner, facing an important test, or worrying about the future might make any teenager feel sorrow, anger, despair, or even a kind of self-protective numbness. A certain range of emotional responses is normal, and most of us, even during adolescence, can handle that range without becoming seriously depressed.

But a girl who is vulnerable to depression has probably inherited a tendency to brain-chemistry imbalance, particularly when negative life events multiply. So when stress or tragedy hits her, she feels it more deeply than other girls. Depending on how she processes her experience, she may find that her serotonin levels fluctuate more drastically, making her feel hopeless and worthless. Her dopamine levels may drop, leading her to feel sluggish. Or her dopamine levels may spike, making her feel angry and agitated, or causing her to act in compulsive, seemingly uncontrollable ways.

The most specific risk for depression appears to result from a gene variation related to serotonin. Boys and girls appear to have this "vulnerability" gene in equal frequencies. Yet despite this identical genetic risk, teenage girls and adult women suffer from depression at more than twice the rate of males. Why?

First, the onset of puberty floods a girl's body with female hormones, some of which may help to activate that girl's vulnerability genes in response to life stress. Second, as we've seen, girls are subject to far more intense and complex pressures than boys, especially as they reach the teenage years. The painful challenges of female adolescence may well trigger the genetic vulnerability of teenage girls even as genetically similar boys manage to emerge intact.[13]

Although genetic risk is by definition passed down through the generations, we can't always identify a family history of depression, a condition that's often masked in a variety of ways. People with drinking problems, for example, are often struggling with depression. For them, alcohol may become a form of self-medication. That painfully shy aunt or perpetually irritable uncle may also have been showing signs of depression. And previous generations of vulnerable family members may simply never have faced life circumstances that propelled their sensitivity into a clinical condition, living in less stressful small towns, for example, rather than encountering the challenges of big-city life.[14]

As you can see, a genetic vulnerability interacts with the environment in a wide variety of ways. Moreover, the vulnerability to depression tends to grow over the course of a person's life. We all tend to seek and create circumstances that accentuate our initial tendencies. A girl who is prone to feeling negative or pessimistic may well seek out the poor relationships and frustrating situations that accentuate her tendencies, fueling a spiral toward depression.[15] Alternatively, a girl who learns that the world is basically a safe and happy place may develop a habit of optimism that helps protect her against depression, even if she's inherited a genetic vulnerability to it. If she faces her first serious loss or stress later in life, she may well have developed coping mechanisms that can help protect her further.

In contrast, a teenager who experiences even a single depressive episode is encountering a crisis when she's at her most vulnerable. Accordingly, she has more than a 50 percent chance of going through another depressive episode at a later point in her life. After two such episodes, the odds of a third rise dramatically.

Quite possibly, there is a biological component to this increased vulnerability: once the brain chemistry imbalance is triggered by stress, the brain finds it that much easier to go out of balance again.[16] Possibly, too, there are emotional factors: having learned that she *can* become depressed, a teenage girl is more likely to view the world as a fearful and upsetting place, which may trigger further incidents of depression. Belief systems—especially those that make a girl feel that the causes of negative events are global ("It's the same everywhere") and stable ("Nothing is ever going to change")—also fuel depression.[17] (This is why the "no alternatives" aspect of the Triple Bind is so dangerous.) Finally, tendencies to ruminate over one's feelings or to take on other people's problems, both typical of "girl" habits, put already vulnerable girls at even greater risk of depression. (We'll talk more about that pattern in Chapter 5.)[18]

Whatever the reason, teenage girls who become depressed are far more likely to struggle with depression for the rest of their lives, and the depression they encounter is far more likely to be serious. That's why the falling age of onset of a first depression is of such grave concern to all of us who deal with mental health. A teenage girl may muster all her resources to resist depression, as Jeannie and Melinda both did, but if the pressures are too great and her resources too limited, she may, as Jeannie did, succumb. And once a teenage girl does fall prey to depression—a risk greatly magnified by the Triple Bind—the specter of future episodes may haunt her for the rest of her life.

HOW MUCH OF DEPRESSION IS INHERITED?

Now at this point you may be thinking, "Okay, I understand that depression is *both* inherited *and* a response to life circumstance. But isn't there a way to tell just how much of any person's depression comes from genes and how much comes from the environment?" You may have read about the different rates of heritability for other disorders, such as breast cancer or Alzheimer's disease, and wondered whether we can assign a similar number to depression.

Well, yes . . . but only if we do so accurately. This concept of "heritability" helps us look at the role of genes in all sorts of traits and conditions, including height, optimism versus pessimism, many physical disorders (including breast cancer), and mental illness. But this term is often misunderstood, so let me clear it up for you.

For any given person, a trait or behavioral tendency is always 100 percent inherited *and* 100 percent environmental. To display the trait, a person needs to have both the genetic ability to do so and the environmental opportunity to express her genes.

Let's return to our example of the person who gets a suntan. Without the genetic ability to tan—without skin light enough to turn dark, and without the genetic ability to tan instead of burn—she *can't* tan. But if she's never exposed to the sun, she can't tan, either. So in her individual case, she is completely dependent upon her genetic heritage *and* upon her life circumstances: both are necessary for the tan to occur. That's why, for any particular individual, it makes no sense to say that a trait or condition is more genetic than environmental, or vice versa. It's always completely both.

Likewise, with a biological feature such as height, we are each conceived with a certain genetic potential. But to reach that potential, we need to be well nourished, both in the womb and during early childhood. If our life circumstances allow for good nutrition, we may grow into more of our potential. If we're unlucky enough to be malnourished, we may grow into less. Either way, the outcome was 100 percent genetic (we needed that potential) and 100 percent life circumstance (we were able to express all, most, or only some of it based on what we and our mothers ate).

So where does the concept of heritability come in? Well, that's a figure that scientists use to determine how features such as height, traits such as shyness or negativity, and disorders such as mental illness vary across a population. Heritability measures the genetic reasons that *I* am likely to experience a condition while *you* are not.

Height, for example, is 90 percent heritable. Suppose you get a large group of people in a room. A few people will be very tall, a few will be very short, and most will be somewhere in the middle. About 90 percent of those differences can be explained by genetics, while only 10 percent of the difference is due to such life circumstances as nutrition, illness, or other factors. Again, the height of any given individual in that room depends fully on genetics *and* life circumstances—the unique combination of these forces creates the person's specific height. But throughout the room, if *I* am taller than *you*, that's almost entirely because of our different genes.[19]

Some conditions are 100 percent heritable, usually those caused by the presence of a single gene. Sickle-cell anemia falls into this category. Basically, if you've got it, it's because both of your parents had the genetic heritage for the condition (in this case, they each had to have a copy of the recessive form of the gene), and together they passed it on to you. If we look at a room full of people, once again, the *only* reason some people have sickle-cell anemia and some don't is because some people have both copies of the recessive gene for the condition and others don't. What they ate, whether they got enough sleep, and how their schoolmates treated them have basically nothing to do with it.[20]

Most conditions, though, are less heritable, especially if they are the product of many different genes. Depression, for example, is only 30 to 40 percent heritable. That means when we look at a roomful of people—a room that might include both Jeannie and Melinda—and consider whether and how much each is depressed, only about a third of the differences we observe are caused by genes. More than half the differences among the people in the room are due to life circumstances: diet, exercise, emotional events, attitudes, and a number of other factors (including the cultural environment of the Triple Bind).[21]

When we think about Jeannie and Melinda, this makes sense. The two girls have very similar family histories. But Melinda, who presumably has genes that make her vulnerable to depression, didn't become depressed, because she faced significantly different life circumstances than Jeannie and was lucky enough to have some coping mechanisms that Jeannie did not. As a result, Melinda was able to prevent her genetic potential from being triggered by the environment.[22]

Jeannie was not so lucky. With a similar genetic vulnerability, she had far fewer defenses against a stressful environment. Without Melinda's coping strategies, Jeannie succumbed.

The fact that depression is *only* 30 to 40 percent heritable tells us what a huge role life circumstances can play in triggering it or holding it off. That's why I'm so concerned about the Triple Bind—because I believe that it is triggering depression in vulnerable girls who might otherwise find ways to triumph over their genetic heritage.[23]

THE DUNEDIN STUDY: A BREAKTHROUGH IN UNDERSTANDING DEPRESSION

If I had any lingering doubts about the way genes and life circumstances interact to produce depression, they were set to rest by a crucial study that appeared in 2003, a piece of research that changed the way most scientists and clinicians view depression, as well as changing their view of how genes and environments interact.[24] This study actually started a generation ago, when every child born in Dunedin, New Zealand, in a twelve-month period during 1972–73 began to participate in a major investigation. In order to see how mental health problems might unfold over time, the children and their families—and later, their teachers; and later still, their employers and spouses—were asked to complete regular evaluations concerning a wide variety of psychological and physical qualities.

Some three decades later, more than 90 percent of this sample is being followed. This extraordinary study has provided great insights into numerous mental health issues, including ADHD, delinquency, partner violence, problems with physical health, and a host of other topics.[25]

One of the most interesting aspects of the study comes from the work of psychologist Avshalom Caspi and his colleagues, who assessed the DNA of every person in the sample. Caspi's team was interested in the findings of geneticists who had discovered that we have a particular gene in each of our cells whose job is to tell the brain how much serotonin transporter to produce. This transporter molecule helps to regulate our serotonin levels—right at the synapse—affecting mood, the potential for depression, and many other conditions. (Serotonin and its transporter molecule are the specific targets of SSRIs, the most common type of antidepressant.) Caspi and his colleagues thought that people with an "inefficient" version of this gene would be at greater risk for depression.

But Caspi's team was also aware that the sheer number of negative life events in late adolescence and early adulthood might increase a person's chances of becoming depressed. Accordingly, the team also collected reports of all such events.

The findings were powerful. By itself, the "inefficient transporter" gene itself did not predict depression or suicidal attempts or thoughts. Nor did a person's negative life events tell the whole story: the number of those events in a person's life was only a mild predictor of depression, at least by the time people in the sample had reached their mid-twenties. (When the sample gets older, we'll know more.)

When the two factors were combined, however, that's where the action was. If someone had *both* the "inefficient transporter" gene *and* a history of negative life events, his or her risk for depression and suicidality rose dramatically.[26]

So indeed, we can't change our genes. Once you're born with that "inefficient transporter" gene, that's it. You're stuck with that genetic heritage for life.

But we can change our environment—and our children's environment. We can try to control the life events to which we are all exposed. We can make sure to teach our children coping mechanisms. And we can make every effort to create a culture that supports their healthy transition into adulthood.

That's where the Triple Bind comes in. As the statistics I've cited in these first two chapters make clear, our teenage girls are in crisis. The Triple Bind hasn't created our girls' genes. But it *has* thrown our daughters into a culture that is often stressful, painful, even overwhelming. And, like the people in the Dunedin study, the most vulnerable of our girls are responding with depression—along with the anxiety, self-mutilation, eating disorders, and violent acts that also characterize today's crisis.

DEPRESSION AT YOUNGER AGES

As we've seen, depressed teenage girls are vulnerable to a whole host of problems, including disrupted relationships, a sense of worthlessness, school failure, future episodes of depression, and even the risk of suicide. Accordingly, my fellow health professionals and I are extremely concerned about a disturbing trend that's continued over the past three decades: the steadily falling average age at which depression first occurs. When I was in grad school in the 1970s, we learned that most women who are vulnerable to depression will have their first depressive episode during their thirties. Now, the average age of onset has fallen to the mid-twenties, with a sharp spike during the midteens as well. As I've indicated earlier, up to 20 percent of adolescent girls—even more by some estimates—are experiencing episodes of major depression during their teenage years.[27]

This gradual decline in depression's age of onset is upsetting enough. What's even more disturbing, however, is the serious spike in self-destructive behaviors that began in the twenty-first century. The Triple Bind may not be responsible for the past three decades' falling age of onset of first depression. But it may very well be behind girls' sudden jump in rates of binge eating, self-mutilation, and suicidal thoughts and actions.

You've seen these statistics in the Introduction and Chapter 1, but let me briefly repeat them here:

- Rates of actual suicides during adolescence—not just thoughts or attempts of suicide, but actual teenage deaths—tripled between the 1950s and late 1980s. (Even though suicides probably were underreported in the "silent fifties," every credible expert believes there has been a genuine, significant increase.) After a downward trend in the 1990s, suicide rates have suddenly spiked, and especially for girls. Between 2003 and 2004, the last year for which figures are available, rates have jumped 76 percent among girls ten to fourteen and by nearly one-third in older teenage girls.
- According to the most recent national survey, binge-eating rates are far higher than most professionals expected, which means they too have risen in the last few years. And as we've seen, an alarmingly high percentage of teen girls struggle with distorted body image as they diet and experiment with diet pills: all signs of a terribly unhealthy preoccupation with appearance, size, and weight.
- Self-harm and self-mutilation appear to be skyrocketing. For girls, these practices are especially likely to lead to major health-related and interpersonal problems later in life, increasing the lifetime risk of suicide.[28]

As I review these figures, I can't help being grateful for science's new insights about genes and the environment, because otherwise I'd be totally at a loss. Sure, there's a genetic vulnerability for all of these disorders—that's been well documented. But genes alone can't explain the sudden spikes in these problems: our genes have simply not had the time to mutate so quickly.[29]

What *has* changed, though, is the level and type of stress to which our daughters are exposed. Subject to more stress, their preexisting genetic vulnerabilities are being triggered. That, in my view, is the work of the Triple Bind.

WHAT'S DEPRESSING ABOUT THE TRIPLE BIND?

As we've seen, genes may help explain—at least to some extent—why Jeannie collapses under a blow that a classmate or sibling might shrug off. But genes don't explain why Jeannie and many other girls receive such blows. They don't tell us why these girls live in a culture in which they feel torn between pursuing their own dreams and taking care of others, in which having a boyfriend is often central to a girl's identity, in which girls worry inordinately at ever younger ages about fulfilling so many different roles—friend, girlfriend, student, budding professional—while maintaining an impossibly thin and attractive look. To understand that crucial aspect of Jeannie's experience, we have to look at the Triple Bind.

Think for a minute about Jeannie's situation. She defined herself overwhelmingly in traditional "girl" ways: through her relationships with her boyfriend and her friends. Being successful at these relationships was crucial to her identity. Even more important to her than the actual companionship, perhaps, was the sense that she was successfully meeting others' needs, helping, caring.

Yet at the same time, another set of expectations—ones that have traditionally been assigned to boys—was also important to Jeannie. Understanding that she would undoubtedly work before and probably after marriage, Jeannie wanted to prepare for a successful and satisfying career. Living in an increasingly competitive world, in which college admissions and graduate programs become ever more demanding, Jeannie knew that she'd have to go the extra mile to have a shot at her career dreams.

To us adults, Jeannie's problems may seem trivial. Shouldn't a teenage girl be able to study *and* have a boyfriend? How could either activity be so demanding that a normal girl couldn't handle both?

But in the heavily scheduled, pressurized world of the Triple Bind, teenage girls often are struggling with near-adult levels of responsibility. They do worry about caring for their friends, reassuring their families, and pleasing their teachers. As Lupe, Jessica, and Eugenia testified in Chapter 1, that type of caretaking can seem almost as demanding as a full-time job. So can the pressures of schoolwork and college admissions. (For more on these demands, see Chapter 3.) And the feeling that there's no margin for error, that you have to do everything perfectly, effortlessly (in Jessica's words, "be completely graceful, poised") makes the burden even greater. In that sense, Jeannie was right: she *was* failing at all the many roles assigned to her, but only because no human being could be expected to handle them all at the level Jeannie expected of herself, and to do so without anyone noticing the superhuman effort that was required.[30]

In my view, teenagers living under the severe stress of the Triple Bind are massively challenged. Despite the material comforts in our culture, every day they must negotiate situations that are far more demanding than those faced by previous generations, all while lacking any viable alternative identities that aren't also ultrafeminized and overly sexualized—and that aren't also hyperfocused on the most lofty levels of conventional success. Under the extraordinary stress of the Triple Bind, any inherited tendency to a psychological problem is far more likely to be expressed.

Moreover, our culture helps us decide what counts as stress. To Jeannie, losing her boyfriend was a devastating blow to her sense of herself as a loving, caring person. Not having a boyfriend also meant she had no excuse for avoiding the "hookup" parties that her friends liked to attend, where they'd get drunk and make out with random boys. Jeannie wasn't comfortable with that behavior, but she didn't want to seem to be a prude or as if she were judging her friends. The prospect of either "hooking up" or looking for another boyfriend seemed daunting to this fourteen-year-old, who was already drowning in a sea of homework assignments, soccer practices, and other extracurricular activities. Jeannie knew, too, that these supposed "extras" were actually necessities, the crucial elements that might determine whether she'd be accepted at the college of her choice.

Melinda, on the other hand, lived in a wider world. Her studies and career goals were important to her, but she also had some perspective on them. Surrounded by people who had faced a variety of obstacles, she had learned that there's more than one way to solve a problem. If you can't get into one school, another will take you; if you lose one boyfriend, you may be able to find another, or do without for a while. Jeannie was surrounded by adults who worried inordinately over every B- and missed homework assignment—not just her own parents, but her friends' parents, her teachers, and her coaches. Melinda, by contrast, lived in a world in which many of the adults had some perspective. Sure, school was important, but so were church, the union, the family, the community. Not doing well in school didn't feel to Melinda like the end of her world. She wasn't happy about her C+, but she wasn't devastated, either.

Make no mistake: the loss of her boyfriend and her struggles with her schoolwork were extremely hard on Melinda. She cried a lot, spent hours writing in her journal or going for long, solitary walks, and seemed generally shaken by the whole experience. But the perspective offered by her family, church, and community helped keep a possible tendency to depression in check.

So again we return to our basic question: if the girls had inherited a similar tendency to depression, why did they respond to their life stresses so differently? In my view, each girl's response was profoundly affected by the way she experienced her social world. Isolated at her upper-middle-class high school, Jeannie had few defenses against the Triple Bind. Living in a world of varied communities with a greater range of support, Melinda was better protected.

I think this distinction is of enormous importance. When we see how disorders are rising among teenage girls—the increase in binge eating, violence, self-destructive behavior, and suicide attempts—it's tempting to blame it on their hormones. Or on their genes.

But even though genes may be partly responsible for why some girls succumb and others do not, they cannot explain changes in the overall rates of such problems over a relatively short amount of time. Something in the environment is "pushing the genetic envelope" of the whole population of girls.

Whatever genetic tendency a girl is born with, and whatever hormonal surges are triggered by puberty, the Triple Bind makes it worse. The Triple Bind is why girls who might have accepted or even celebrated their size-10 bodies a few generations ago now feel disgustingly fat if they're not a size 2 or 4. It's why girls who might not have been all that interested in boys at ages fourteen and fifteen, even after puberty, now insist on having steady boyfriends by ages eleven and twelve, even before puberty. It's why girls who once had a bit of breathing room to figure out their futures now feel under the gun before they've finished sixth grade, already anxious about getting perfect SATs and a roster of impressive extracurriculars. And it's why girls who once might have identified with alternative female figures—a rock star, an athlete, a female author—now have trouble finding any role models other than those who are beautiful, hot, thin, and thoroughly focused on conventional notions of success.

No wonder binge eating disorders are on the rise and distorted body image and the desire to diet are almost universal. No wonder depression's age of onset continues to fall. The Triple Bind demands that girls who still live as children—financially dependent on their parents, with no genuine sexual or domestic autonomy—nevertheless make adult-level decisions about their bodies, their careers, their identities.[31] Any girl with a weak spot, whether that weak spot comes from her upbringing, her hormones, or her genes, is far more likely to succumb now than in a less pressured environment.

Jeannie and girls like her face yet another challenge: the hermetic, all-encompassing nature of today's consumerist, oversexualized youth culture. This culture encourages girls to view themselves as objects from an early age (and encourages boys to view them that way as well). The 24/7 electronic experience not only promotes self-objectification but also means that peers and dating take up far more mental and emotional space than family, community, or religious affiliation. Although in some ways, media and the Internet have greatly expanded our teens' horizons, in other ways they've vastly increased the tendency for girls to view themselves as objects, always imagining how they appear to the thousands of invisible eyes potentially observing their Web pages and blogs and posts. With its plethora of sexy, thin, and highly accomplished women, the media also contribute to the sense that a genuine alternative is almost literally unthinkable: this cyberculture and these media images come to seem like the sum total of human possibility.[32] (For a more in-depth discussion of popular culture, see Chapter 4. For more on how cyberculture affects our children, see Chapter 7.)

No serious scientist would deny that brain chemistry and genes are of crucial importance. But unless we put their role into context, and unless we factor in cultural issues such as the Triple Bind, we'll never really understand what's going on with our girls. Sure, genes shape all aspects of ourselves, including our behavioral and emotional responses, but it's the environments, settings, and pressures out there that have everything to do with how and when certain genes get activated. Understanding how nature and nurture work together helps to reveal how today's culture is helping to incite depression at ever earlier ages and placing ever higher numbers of girls at risk—just when the opportunities for girls seem to have reached an all-time high.

CHAPTER 3

Life in the Pressure Cooker

Impossible Expectations and the Culture of Busy-ness

Toni was a charming, upbeat girl who seemed to have boundless energy. A junior at a prestigious Berkeley-area public high school, she was blessed with a loving boyfriend, a warm circle of friends, an A- average, and a wide range of interests, including theater, music, and horseback riding. She also played soccer for her school team and was taking fencing lessons.

By any standards, Toni's academic, athletic, and social lives were rich and full. Imagine the surprise of Toni's mother, then, when she heard mysterious sounds coming from her daughter's room at 3:00 A.M. There was Toni, sobbing in front of her computer, surrounded by the script for her latest play, her history notebook, and her AP physics text. "I just can't do it," Toni wailed. "I thought I could—but I can't."

Although Toni hadn't been in any of my summer programs, Toni's mother was a personal friend, so she asked me to speak with her daughter. It soon emerged that the problem was twofold. First, Toni simply had far too much to do. She just wasn't able to excel at every single one of the wide range of activities she'd chosen—and she didn't feel good about doing anything that she *didn't* excel at.

But even more stressful was Toni's sense that she was supposed to make it all look easy. "I shouldn't have to try so hard," she kept saying, and I realized she was speaking not in protest but in self-blame. Toni honestly thought that successful girls were those who could accomplish their tasks effortlessly, a sort of high school version of "Never let them see you sweat." Her belief that she was supposed to accomplish superhuman feats without even trying made her situation far more stressful than it already was.

To me, that belief in effortlessness is an integral—and extremely destructive—part of the Triple Bind. For generations, girls have been taught that unlike boys, they don't have to try; indeed, that they *shouldn't* really try. That's because boys *do*, but girls just *are*. A girl who works hard on her looks and her sex appeal is a bitch, a slut, or simply shallow. A girl who takes her studies seriously is a bookworm, a brain, or a nerd. (Studious boys may be given similar labels, but at least they don't have the other aspects of the Triple Bind to contend with.) A girl who openly pursues popularity or social power is a Queen Bee; a girl who actively pursues the boy of her choice is just pathetic.

I wish I could attribute these beliefs to teenage naiveté. Unfortunately, girls get these messages directly from the larger culture. Just think of how we demonize the woman who strives to win political office or who openly declares her desire for professional success. When the 2005–6 TV show *Commander in Chief* featured the first woman U.S. president, for example, she hadn't even run for the job. Instead, she ascends from the vice presidency when the former president dies, and she comes very close to stepping aside in favor of the (male) Speaker of the House. Apparently, the only sympathetic woman in power is the one who got there by accident.

Negative portrayals of ambitious women were problematic enough for girls when women were supposed to focus only on marriage and ignore professional success. But today's girls are caught within the Triple Bind: expected to compete like a man while remaining as indifferent to personal achievement as a (good) woman. And because so many girls' role models are ultrafeminized and overly sexualized—pretty, chic, sexy, and ultrathin—the ante is upped even further. You *can't* meet those standards without working extremely hard: at the gym, in the mall, in front of the mirror. But like the grades, relationships, and all the other accomplishments we expect of our girls, the looks are supposed to come easily, the natural expression of a girl's "inner beauty" rather than the hard-won result of hours of painstaking labor. Consider the March 2006 *Self* magazine article about *Grey's Anatomy* star Ellen Pompeo, whose slender figure is one of the most notable aspects of her appearance. Explained the article:

> As for her physical health, you may have noticed her thinness. Well, don't assume it's a result of any disorder. Contrarily, the 5'7", 100-pound brunette requires 3,000 calories a day just to keep the pounds *on*. The only problem she has is her metabolism, which is simply too fast. During her 14-hour days on the Grey's set, Pompeo eats every two hours just to maintain her energy. A nutritionist keeps her in line during the week, but on weekends, Ellen says, she "eats whatever she wants."[1]

TV star Ellen Pompeo may succeed in making her looks—and her life—seem effortless. Girls like Toni have a harder time, finding that it's virtually impossible to make your life seem effortless when you are on a never-ending treadmill of classes, extracurriculars, after-school lessons, and sports.

Overscheduling used to be seen as a primarily upper-middle-class problem, suggesting the cliché of the privileged child being chauffeured from prep school to piano lessons to the stables to the fencing salon, mastering an endless round of after-school activities and then returning home to several hours of homework. That cliché, alas, has its roots in truth—and it's trickling down to middle-class and working-class girls as well.

First, as we'll see in this chapter, homework is increasing for students at many economic levels and, most disturbingly, for younger students. Second, sports, after-school activities, and other extracurriculars are no longer extras but requirements, as even "second-choice" and state schools are becoming more competitive. Finally, except for the wealthiest Americans, nearly all families have seen a drop in their incomes over the past years, which means that parents tend to be working longer hours, if not multiple jobs.[2] Thus, teens from lower-middle-class and lower-income families are also feeling the brunt, in the form of part-time jobs, greater household responsibilities, and, not incidentally, vastly increased family stress.

So girls at all economic levels are now struggling with life inside the pressure cooker, and it's not a pretty picture. Today's girls, with schedules packed every hour of the day—and too much of the night—are often overwhelmed with anxiety, frustration, and a sense of failure. They're skimping on sleep, with potentially disastrous consequences for their mental and physical health. And they're missing out on crucial opportunities to develop a sense of their own personal goals and to create the identities that will carry them into their adult lives, with results that may be destructive at best, devastating at worst.

I agree with Toni: she *shouldn't* have to try so hard. In this chapter, we'll find out how making that effort, especially while making it seem effortless, is affecting her and the hundreds of thousands of girls like her. And we'll see how the problems caused by the new culture of busy-ness are worsened still further by the Triple Bind.

ARE TEENAGERS OVERSCHEDULED?

The notion of the "hurried child"—the child asked to do too much and grow up too fast—has been around at least since 1981, when psychologist David Elkind published a book of the same name.[3] Since then, other books have appeared on the shelf beside it, including Alvin Rosenfeld and Nicole Wise's

The Over-Scheduled Child: Avoiding the Hyper-Parenting Trap, which first appeared under the title *Hyper-Parenting* in 2000, and William Crain's *Reclaiming Childhood: Letting Children Be Children in Our Achievement-Oriented Society*, which first appeared in 2003.[4] These books made it a watchword that children—or at least middle-class children—were losing their childhoods by being overly scheduled into a demanding round of lessons, activities, and after-school programs. Aimed at a generation of worried parents, these works predicted dire fates for the young people whose childhood and adolescence were presumably being destroyed.

Much of the general public may have bought the message, but researchers are skeptical. A team led by Joseph Mahoney, then a professor in the Yale psychology department, published a 2006 paper in *Social Policy Report* taking issue with the idea that overscheduling was bad for kids. In fact, the team discovered, through a nationally representative sample of five- to eighteen-year-olds, that only 6 percent of teenagers spend more than twenty hours a week in organized activities, and even this subgroup reported more well-being, less drug use, and more time at the family dinner table than kids who engaged in no activities. Indeed, about 40 percent of those sampled fell into the latter group: clearly *they* were not overscheduled!

Generally, Mahoney found, participation in extracurriculars was associated with children's feeling better about themselves, having better relationships with their families, experiencing lower rates of psychological problems and drug use, performing better academically, and (over the long run) completing school. Importantly, active young people most often reported that they *wanted* to participate in their activities; they hadn't been pressured to do so. (For most of the teenagers studied, the main structured activity was sports.) In short, the overscheduling hypothesis just didn't seem to be true.[5]

My colleague Suniya Luthar of Columbia University came to similar conclusions when she and her research team conducted a 2006 study of eighth-grade students at schools in suburban Connecticut. In this and related investigations with similar samples, Luthar compared upper-middle-class teens to those from low-income inner-city neighborhoods and came to a shocking conclusion: by the time they reached middle school, teens from wealthier backgrounds often had *higher* rates of mental health problems—mainly anxiety and depression, as well as more substance abuse.[6]

Significantly, though, the time spent on extracurricular activities was not itself the cause. In fact, as Mahoney also found, participation in sports, the arts, and civic projects was linked to *lower* levels of anxiety, depression, delinquency, substance abuse, and academic failure. True, girls who spent more time on academic extracurriculars (mainly receiving tutoring) seemed to have higher rates of delinquency, anxiety, depression, and substance abuse, with a tendency for girls who had the highest rates of involvement in such academic extracurricular activities to display the highest rates of substance abuse. But this finding may have indicated only that girls who were already troubled were also having more difficulties in class, which in turn had led to their being enrolled in tutoring programs. (For some reason, boys' spending more time on academic "extras" did not correlate with higher rates of problems.)

What *was* associated with anxiety, depression, and other concerns—for both boys and girls—was family dynamics. The children most likely to have problems had parents who were excessively critical, left their children alone after school, and failed to eat dinner with them. "Overscheduling" wasn't the core issue, family relationships were. In fact, the girls in Luthar's study who had the highest rates of difficulties were those struggling with what seemed to be a particularly lethal combination: more time spent in academic extracurriculars, excessive parental criticism, and parents who were overly focused on achievement.[7]

THE NEW CULTURE OF BUSY-NESS

So if all those activities aren't causing anxiety, depression, or substance abuse, then what's the problem? Why are my colleagues and I concerned about what I've come to see as the new culture of busy-ness: the expectation that teenage girls (and boys) should schedule every minute of their day?

The problem, I believe, is that teenagers' inner lives are being impoverished. If our girls were busy pursuing their own hopes and dreams, I'd be delighted. But a great deal of their frantic work is in the service of pleasing others: teachers, coaches, colleges, and especially, parents. Certainly, the families of the kids in Luthar's study, overly focused on achievement and often hypercritical of their children, may have created for their daughters (and sons) the pressure to do more and more and more. And this relentless round of mandatory activity—the long lists of extracurriculars, the excessive homework, the relentless academic pressure, even the economically necessary part-time jobs—is preventing our daughters from discovering their own unique strengths, interests, and passions. As Mahoney found, young people are often quite enthusiastic about their organized activities. The problems come when the pressured quest to accomplish ever more tasks is driven not by the teens themselves but by others.

For three-quarters of all teenagers, these problems will never rise to the level of a clinical condition. Yes, the girls who are most vulnerable to depression, anxiety, and other clinical conditions and the girls with overly critical or achievement-oriented parents have created the crisis-level statistics we've been looking at. Most girls though, may seem just fine—until you hear them talk about their lives. As I listen to girl after girl describe how compelled she feels to stay busy, and how much of that busy-ness is intended to please others, I can't help feeling that they're suffering from a type of distress that evokes the learned helplessness of Seligman's dogs, a kind of sorrow at their own incapacity. Like the overworked adults who surround them, they're trying desperately to juggle a number of conflicting demands—getting good grades, pleasing their coaches, reassuring their families—and they soldier on cheerfully, perhaps, but with an underlying sense of despair. They can't possibly accomplish everything they're attempting, and they know it. Hearing their matter-of-fact, resigned voices and seeing their wistful eyes, I can't help thinking of the poet Stevie Smith's famous image for an earlier version of female despair: "I was much further out than you thought / And not waving but drowning."[8]

Sixteen-year-old Michi, for example, is sweet and shy. A talented soccer player, she's hoping to win an athletic scholarship that will take some of the pressure off her parents, who own a small business and have struggled to send her to private school. She's unlikely ever to show up in the statistics I've been quoting, but I'm worried about her all the same. She seems almost grim in her determination to succeed at all the impossible expectations with which she's been saddled. And when I ask her what most concerns her, she replies in what to me are heartbreakingly adult terms:

> I think the biggest thing is, like, *time.* How you're gonna do everything—like if you have those expectations, how are you going to fit that in time, if you only have twenty-four hours in the day, and you have to sleep eight of those or nine or however many? It's basically like, time, and how you're supposed to manage it, or whatever.

Think about that for a minute. Michi isn't concerned about who she wants to be or what matters most to her. She isn't concerned about the state of the world, or hanging out with her best friend, or whether she agrees with the precepts of her church, or how to attract the attention of that cute boy she likes. Her biggest concern is how to fit everything into a twenty-four-hour day, minus the time she has to sleep. If she'd said those words with a big grin or bubbling with excitement, I might have heard them as adolescent excitement: "How can I possibly fit into a single day all the interesting things I might want to do?" Instead, she was lamenting her inability to "do everything," to meet all the expectations that she had of herself and that she knew her parents, teachers, and coaches had for her.

Seventeen-year-old Jasmine seems strong, confident, and self-assured. The first-generation daughter of immigrants, she's proud of her parents even if she often feels frustrated by the gaps in their understanding of the "American way." Again, I'm not worried about her developing a clinical condition. But I am concerned about her finding the time and space to discover her true path in life and create her own unique identity. How can she, when she's working 24/7 to meet the expectations of other people? Like Michi, when I ask her what she feels is expected of her, she too rattles off a dauntingly long list of activities—and doubts:

> [It's not only] time . . . [but also] energy. 'Cause like for my senior year I started swimming and my coach wanted double practices. So it was like an hour and a half in the morning before school and like two hours after school, almost every day. And then I had just run for student government so I was on student government, and I have a job on the weekends. So I was only swimming for only like three weeks and I couldn't do it anymore—I just had to drop something. Like, you can't meet all your expectations and sometimes you have to make sacrifices for the good of yourself, instead of what other people would say about you.

I ask Jasmine how she made the decision to drop swimming. Once again I have the eerie sense that I am hearing not a teenager but an overworked adult:

> I felt like just because swimming in itself made me so tired all the time, I couldn't focus at school. I'd go home, and I'd take a nap between [school and] practice, and then after practice, I'd go home and eat dinner, and I'd take a shower, and then I'd try to do my homework, and I'd almost fall asleep on my books every night. And then I'd be like, "Okay, well, I'll try to catch up during school." And then if I'd try to catch up during first period, then I'd miss the whole lesson of whatever class I'd have and that would just put me behind more. And then if I tried to catch up on the weekend, then I couldn't, 'cause I was at work and that's not allowed. So I was just completely swamped. It just felt like I was starting to lose a grip on my life.

And how did people react to her choice? Jasmine's voice is ironic, almost humorous, as she describes the responses she got. She doesn't sound anxious, but she does sound pressured:

> The girls on the swim team were pretty mad at me. . . . I got a call from the coach. . . . [T]he coaches put pressure [on me] because they didn't want me to give up. Because like also when I was swimming, I just felt like I was getting slower and slower times, like I didn't have the energy to swim as fast as I could, so . . .

Fifteen-year-old Jessica, the prep school girl from Seattle, had an even longer list of the accomplishments she felt were expected of her:

> Well, it starts with your parents, 'cause they want you to do well, 'cause they want you to get into college, but then of course . . . it's hard to get into now. Now

> they're even saying a bachelor's isn't even enough, you need a master's to get somewhere in society. You need the grades, you need a 4.0 all through middle school and high school, you need something above a 4.0 if you even want a chance of getting into a good school.* And then coaches put a lot of pressure on you because they think you should be thinking only about the sport and they are like, "Who cares about school, that doesn't really matter!" and when you go back and think about it, at least to me, school was a lot more important, and so I had a lot of trouble with my coach because he put a lot of pressure on me to play and I just didn't want to anymore, it wasn't worth it. . . . Colleges say you need work experience but you also need community service, and then you also need like five activities, you need like a bunch of activities, a bunch of jobs, you need AP classes, and you need to do really well on SATs and SAT IIs and if you don't, if you miss something, then you won't get in.

She makes a face and looks at me. "I can't do all this," she says, not so much complaining as acting out for me how pressured she feels. "Everything combined is horrible." Not waving but drowning, indeed.

STRESSED-OUT STUDENTS

Why are teenage girls feeling so pressured? Part of the problem is that above and beyond the time they spend in school, they're asked to do many hours a week of homework. Experts disagree over whether older teens' homework levels have gone up, though it seems that students in advanced math and science classes are indeed doing more than previous generations, perhaps even more than students in other nations.[9] Undoubtedly, though, younger teenagers—and even preteens—are doing far more work than previously. Data from the National Center for Education Statistics reveal that between 1980 and 2002, the percentage of sophomores spending more than ten hours a week on homework rose from 7 percent to 37 percent.[10] And a 2005 study found that the United States is now "among the most homework-intensive countries in the world for 7th and 8th grade math classes."[11]

Even though the precise amount of homework our teens are doing each night is difficult to estimate with complete accuracy, based on my own experience as the father of teenage sons and on my knowledge of other parents'

---

*Although the highest possible traditional grade point average (GPA) used to be 4.0—representing straight As—in many districts a student who gets top marks in an entire roster of advanced placement (AP) classes can now achieve a GPA as high as 4.7 or even 5.0. Consequently, even a student who gets straight As in regular classes may not have a GPA competitive enough for the top schools. The *median* GPA for entering freshmen at my own UC Berkeley, for example, has been greater than 4.1 for a number of years.

experiences, I would place the figure as high and growing. My own sense is that many children, particularly from the middle- and upper-middle-income brackets, are working on homework more or less continuously, from the time they get home from their after-school activities until the time they finally go to bed. Sure, they take time out for dinner and they may get to spend some time watching TV, answering e-mail, or talking on the phone with their friends. But the awareness of several challenging assignments—due tomorrow, by the end of the week, by the end of the term—shadows their evenings and weekends like a demanding second job. Whether they're actually working on their homework or not, they're aware (and their parents are aware) that the homework is there, waiting to be done. That sense of being perpetually obligated, never able to say "I'm done for the day" or "I have a free weekend," contributes to the low-grade despair I saw in so many dutiful girls.

I'm also struck, from personal observation, at how much more challenging homework has become. Chatting with a friend's teenage son from North Carolina, I asked him what he was working on in his biology class. "Oh," he said casually, "we're doing gene sequencing." If there had *been* gene sequencing in my day, we would have reserved its study not even for college but for graduate school. Yet here was a high school sophomore expected to master this material—and this was over a decade ago! I can only imagine what teenagers are being asked to do now: Nobel Prize–winning research, perhaps?

Of course, if students *want* to explore challenging subjects, I'm all for it. But these superadvanced topics are not being seen as "extras" or as special treats for the most eager students. Instead, more and more, they're coming to be seen as the norm, as are advanced placement courses, and lots of them, at least for those kids who are shooting for the top schools. If those are the standards, more and more children will come to feel that they are failing.

A huge additional source of pressure, as any teen will tell you, is the way getting into college has suddenly become a full-time job. Anya, now a freshman at a small liberal arts college, is still frustrated about the way the focus on college admissions interfered with her high school education:

> I was so stressed. College application time, oh, my God! . . . You've got your teachers preparing you to take these AP tests, and the AP tests are so you don't have to take certain classes in college, so it is almost like you are trying to get through with college [during your] junior and senior year of high school, you know? It's crazy. You have teachers having students write college[-admission] essays to grade in class, so they can help them with their college[-admission] essays, which on one level is a good thing, but on another level it is just awful, because you want—I sort of wanted my school to be a place where I didn't have to be thinking about all this stuff. I was grateful for the help, but I also really enjoyed English class when we were doing Shakespeare and cool British literature. And instead, we were doing college[-admission] essays!

The idea that a teenager was prevented from reading Shakespeare because she had to work on her college-admission essays is a heartbreaking thought for any educator. But Anya's whole school, she tells me, was focused on the process of college admissions, including a principal who promised to throw parties for the students who got high test scores. Whenever government officials wrote to the school to congratulate them on their scores, Anya reports, the principal "interrupts class to read on the intercom the entire length of the letter."

The competition for college continues, and it's getting worse. In recent years, it's become increasingly common for upper-income and even many middle-income teens to take test prep classes, get coached on college admissions, and seek professional help with their application essays. Check out the website for the Penn Group, founded in 1999 and staffed exclusively by "Ivy League graduates and admissions experts." Their website explains, "For students who need advice about applications, essays, or their junior or senior year class schedules, we provide a range of exceptionally valuable counseling services."

One of the Penn Group's proudest achievements is its college admissions calculator, which predicts a student's chances of being admitted to a particular college. Based on the school, the calculator weights such factors as "GPA, SAT score, high school classes, teacher recommendations, admission essay, extracurricular activities, affiliation with the college or university, minority status, and application effort." SAT scores and GPAs are weighted the highest, the Web site explains, but extracurriculars count, too. I invite you to look at the attractive website, which can be found at www.college-admissions-essay.com/formula.html. It almost seems like a parody of the effort that now goes into the college application process. Unfortunately, it's all too real.[12]

Given that 2008 saw the most selective spring in modern memory at America's elite schools, according to an April 1, 2008, article in the *New York Times*, perhaps such organizations are needed.[13] Or perhaps what's really needed is a change in parents' and students' belief that admission into an elite school is the prerequisite for a happy, financially secure life. (For more on economic pressures and the Triple Bind, see Chapter 1.) Meanwhile, though, the culture of busy-ness requires students to exert themselves to the max for those grades and scores, while demonstrating their proficiency and commitment to a long roster of extracurriculars. No longer a way for a teenager to express her true self or explore her interests, the "extras" have become a requirement.

For many kids at all income levels, time not spent on homework and college admissions is often taken up with part-time jobs. Recent data show that high school sophomores spend fifteen hours a week working for pay, while a

1995 study found that U.S. seniors spent an average of three hours a day working for money, about three times more than students in other countries.[14]

Again, if working is a family necessity, of course teenagers should pitch in. And I would never deny the value of hard work, which I believe does indeed build character, promote self-sufficiency, and help to prepare young people for adult life. But how many of those working hours are driven by the relentless consumerism of today's society, in which teens feel the pressure to buy themselves the latest clothes, music, and electronics? How many are the result of the astronomical rise in college tuition and the severe cutbacks in state and federal subsidies and scholarships? And how much do they contribute to the culture of busy-ness, in which teens are working so hard at everything that they don't have time to find out who they are or what they care about?

SLEEPLESS IN SEATTLE: THE TRIPLE BIND AND THE TRIPLE SHIFT

Listen to teenage girls sometimes, and you get the impression that they're working a double shift, first at school, then at home. If they have a job, make that a triple shift. Here's sixteen-year-old Lupe—the Seattle-area prep school girl whom we met Chapter 1—on the pressures of her day:

> When you come home from school, you've been at school for, like, eight hours, or more [in some cases] . . . you've been there since 6:00 A.M. or since, like, seven. You're, like, exhausted and you have a draining day, and you have all this homework you're not looking forward to. And my parents come in and are like, "What are you doing on the phone?" "My friend just called me like five minutes ago." "What were you doing before? You were on the phone before." "No, I was doing my homework for an hour, you came and saw me in between, you just happened to catch me when I was on the phone." My mom's gotten mad at me for that all the time and she'll take my phone, and I am like, "Mom, I have to talk to my friends, I don't want to do my homework right now." There are points where you just shut down and you don't want to do it. They don't care, they just want it done as early as possible.
>
> My parents go to bed at nine. They're like, "Why do you go to bed at twelve?" 'Cause I can't get my homework done! I'll start my homework at five, but then I have to eat dinner with my parents for an hour, 'cause my parents want to talk to me. They want to know everything that is going on, and then they get mad at me if I leave the dinner table early. I have to go do my homework, what do you want me to do? They want to talk to me but then they want me to go to bed at nine. I can't go to bed at nine! There is no way I can make it through my day, doing all my

school, come home at three, and do all my homework, and what? End at seven, eat, and then go to bed? How are you supposed to have a social life?

As Lupe describes her day, her friends Jessica and Eugenia are nodding in agreement. Lupe adds, "The thing that is always sacrificed, the thing that is first off your list, is sleep," and the other girls practically cheer in agreement.

"You feel like, you go to school and you should be able to go home and at least take a break before you start your homework," Eugenia says. "Home is supposed to be away from school and away from the pressure. There will be times when you are doing work and all you want is a break. Please give me a break! The sleep thing is the first thing we feel we can [give up]. Nobody is going to get disappointed if we lose sleep."

I am skeptical. "Really?" I ask them. "Your parents really don't mind if you don't get enough sleep?"

Jessica tries to explain. "Yeah, your parents feel bad and they are, like, 'You should get some sleep.' [But] you sacrifice sleep 'cause you don't want to sacrifice any other things, because the grades are important. . . . You want to have good grades. [But you also want to] at least talk to your friends and refresh. But then it gets later and later. And we think that the one thing we can sacrifice that no one will get mad at us about is sleep." She thinks about it for a moment. "But you need sleep," she admits.

"Yes," Eugenia chimes in. "Every day I go home, I'm tired from school. I want to go home and take a nap. If I go home and get into my bed, my mom will come into my room and start yelling, 'This is why your report card looks the way it does! This is why you aren't doing better!' "

I admit, I might have put the girls' descriptions down to typical teenage complaining if I hadn't observed too many other kids and their classmates working hours into the night and every weekend. Any lingering doubts I had were put to rest when I reviewed the National Sleep Foundation's 2006 Sleep in America poll, a nationally representative sample of sixth to twelfth graders. According to this highly respected study, only 20 percent of middle and high school students were getting the nine hours of sleep per night that is recommended for this age group, while 45 percent were getting fewer than eight hours per night on school nights. In fact, the average sixth grader gets only 8.4 hours of sleep on school nights, while the average twelfth grader sleeps only 6.9 hours on school nights.[15] Like Lupe, Jessica, and Eugenia, more than half the students in the survey complained of being tired or sleepy during the day. Like Eugenia, about a third of all teens say they nap regularly—but their naps are two hours or so in length, indicating sleep deprivation (as opposed to a thirty-to-forty-five-minute "refresher" nap). Some 75 percent of all teens rely on a daily Coke or coffee, a figure that is disturbing in itself. Even so, more than one-quarter of all high school students fall asleep during the day and nearly one-fifth are sometimes late or absent from school because of lack of sleep or tiredness.

These figures seem even more alarming when we take into account the latest research on how adolescents are affected by insufficient sleep. We used to think that kids (and adults) could make up for lost sleep on weekends. But my colleague at UC Berkeley, Matthew Walker, is one of a new generation of scientists showing that every day of sleep deprivation has serious consequences for young people.

Matt's research deals with the role of sleep in helping us consolidate and remember the things we learn during the day. Recently, he's also become interested in how sleep affects emotion. Several studies have now confirmed that people tend to recall a far greater number of negative events than positive ones when they are sleep-deprived, something that most of us can confirm by remembering how frantic, frazzled, and downright miserable we can become when we have missed a significant amount of sleep.

Matt's findings offer a biological explanation: he and his team found that sleep-deprived late adolescents and young adults show a great deal of activation in the amygdala, a part of the brain that helps to process negative, fear-related information. Normally, we rely on our frontal lobes to modify the amygdala's messages, but when young people are sleep-deprived, this happens far less. As a result, sleep-deprived teenagers are being flooded with negative emotions that their brains are less able to "edit." The consequences are likely to be grievous for sleep-deprived teenage girls in general and for those who are vulnerable to depression in particular.[16]

Matt also believes that sleep deprivation is particularly dangerous in these days when young people are being asked to learn more. "We have an incendiary situation today," he told *New York* magazine, "where the intensity of learning that kids are going through is so much greater, yet the amount of sleep they get to process is so much less. If these linear trends continue, the rubber band will soon snap."[17] Other researchers have linked sleep deprivation to lower IQ scores, poor school performance, headaches, diabetes, and obesity.[18]

The latest research shows that even adults suffer when deprived of sleep. But for children and teenagers, whose brains are still developing, every hour of lost sleep can have serious consequences. For teenage girls trying to juggle the conflicting demands of the Triple Bind, loss of sleep is just one more burden to carry, one more assault on a mind and body that may already be vulnerable to depression, anxiety, or just feeling bad.

Now at this point you may be thinking, "Let's get a little perspective here!" After all, for most of human history, children and adolescents worked alongside adults on a wide variety of tasks, taking their place as productive members of a household or community as soon as they were physically able. Although sometimes this took the form of punitive child labor in factories, farms, and workshops, work also gave many children a sense of purpose and belonging, helping them to feel important to their families and useful to their communities.

In theory, I agree. Hard work per se is not necessarily bad for children. But being made to feel like a failure—being given more to do than they can reasonably handle, or being expected to achieve at levels beyond their abilities, or being asked to show adult-level skills in work-flow and time management—*is* bad for children, just as the punishing work schedule that many families endure is bad for adults as well. Americans work longer hours and have less vacation than any other industrialized country, and since the 1980s, we've been working even harder and longer.[19] In my clinical opinion, it isn't good for us, and it isn't good for our kids. And based on the crisis figures I've cited in every chapter—the gradual drop in the age of first onset of depression; the alarming spikes in violent behavior, binge eating, self-mutilation, and suicide attempts—life in the pressure cooker is particularly bad for our girls.

LIFE IN THE PRESSURE COOKER: THE GIRL FACTOR

Why might a pressured life be harder on girls than on boys? First, as we've seen, girls are struggling with two different types of demands: the need to please, maintain relationships, and put others' feelings first, and the need to strive, compete, and win. The contradictory nature of these demands can put a teenage girl in an impossible position, feeling "damned if she does and damned if she doesn't." And while girls are trying to run in two directions at once, all they can see in their culture are images of women who seem to be able to pull off this remarkable feat, all while looking pretty, hot, and thin; all while achieving extraordinary levels of professional success; and all while seeming not to even try. Sometimes I think that the Triple Bind's lack of true alternatives is the cruelest aspect of all.

Second, because girls *have* generally been socialized to please, they take their failures more to heart. When they get a poor grade or a poor time in a swim meet, they don't just worry about their abilities, they worry about how they've affected their families, teachers, and coaches. When the pressure of their workday keeps them from helping out a friend or giving emotional support to a loved one, they feel like personal failures even if they're getting straight As. When their demanding schedules make them late to work or keep them from being super-alert and focused on the job, they feel bad for their bosses, coworkers, and customers as well as for themselves.[20] Certainly that degree of empathy and outward focus is not true of all girls. But it's true of enough of them to help create the crisis-level figures we've been seeing. (For more on empathy and girl problems, see Chapter 5.)

Finally, girls living in the pressure cooker have that much less time and energy to seek out alternatives, other ways of being female. And as we've seen in Chapter 2, if a girl lives in a homogenous world, in which most adults she knows are narrowly focused on their own careers and busy schedules, she may find it even harder to push past the cultural boundaries to create an identity that truly satisfies her. Instead, she may content herself with "just following orders," trying ever harder to please the harried and overworked adults who surround her, working ever more desperately to imitate the uniformly thin, sexy, and successful women she sees on TV, in the movies, and online. Trying to be good at girl stuff, good at boy stuff, and longing for an alternative, she may find life inside the pressure cooker intense indeed.

A LOSS OF MEANING

To me, the most disturbing aspect of life inside the pressure cooker isn't even the anxiety, depression, and lack of sleep; it's the way meaning and purpose are slowly being leached out of our children's lives. Endeavors that once might have helped them learn about the world, choose activities they enjoyed, and consolidate their identities have now been reduced to rote tasks, useful for getting into college, perhaps, or for pleasing the many adults who seem to care, but in themselves are meaningless.

"The most common question that people ask while we're reviewing for the test is 'Is this going to be on the test?' " Eugenia says ruefully. "The first day we start a new chapter—'Is this going to be on the test? Do I need to know this?' And then people just, like, star things, and memorize it. What's the point?"

"It's about the grades now," Jessica says. "A lot of people don't learn any of the material, really."

Lupe agrees. "If we had to take the test thirty minutes after we take it," she says, "we would probably get an F."

Often, girls tell me, the pressures to achieve are so great that students simply cheat. Anya tells me that "cheating was humongous" at her high school. Although both boys and girls cheated, she feels that girls faced greater penalties if they got caught.

> I think with the guys, it was almost like, "Oh, my God, it's expected, boys will be boys . . ." [I and my friends] felt like we were, on the surface . . . held to higher standards. But really, when we thought about it, we were really being discriminated against. We have to jump through more hoops than they do. We are going to get cut less slack, because we have to be both moral and intelligent. It's really a lot more easy to be intelligent when you don't have to be moral.

Anya attended a middle-income public school in a relatively small city. But cheating is clearly a concern at public and private high schools across the income spectrum, and at parochial schools as well. At a Catholic prep school for girls in Oregon, cheating was such an issue that it inspired the school to form a group called Stressed-Out Students, a committee of teachers, parents, and students who meet monthly to discuss ways of reducing student stress. But despite the group, cheating at the school continues. One member of the group tells me that a teacher the previous semester had received work that had been cut and pasted from other sources—not even edited or slightly disguised. The teacher was so distressed that she burst into tears in front of her class. Anya tells me a similar story, about a student who photocopied a test stolen from a teacher's office—and then got a better grade than the student who had originally submitted the test.

When I ask why cheating occurs, the same old themes recur: too much pressure, not enough time. One student explains, "People just don't have that many hours in the day because they are also doing, you know, basketball, cheerleading, whatever it is, they just don't have the time. So they feel like they need to go cheat and get the A and make their parents happy and make themselves happy."

"You feel like you have to meet all of these things," another student tells me. "And you just get to a point where 'I really cannot finish this, how am I gonna finish this?' You *can't* just not finish it! And so people get to the point where they are like, 'Well, how am I going to be able to do this in the least amount of time?' And that's when you get to cheating."

I ask the students whether they themselves have ever thought about cheating. One girl admits that she's been tempted, in what she calls a "defining moment":

> I was playing basketball, and doing a lot of other activities, and you just get overwhelmed completely, and you try to get everything done, and you just get to a point—*I* got to the point where it was just like, I didn't want to deal with the feeling of everything being so overwhelming. I didn't want to feel like that. I thought maybe if I tried to get out of it by cheating, it would make it better. But when I thought about it, I was like, "No, I'm not going to do that, I'm not going to disrespect myself. I am not going to risk this, because I'm not going to get anything from it. Like, in the greater scheme of things, in a cosmic view, it's this one small thing, my grades will be okay, and I will just try to find some other way to bring them up."

The student I spoke with was justly proud of her decision. But what struck me was her sense that what I have called the culture of busy-ness was actually encouraging her to cheat. For her and many of her classmates, the process of learning had devolved into a search for grades, while the experience of high school had degenerated into the chase for college. She respected herself too much to cheat, because she understood that she wouldn't "get anything from it"—she wouldn't actually learn what she had come to school to learn. But, as Anya also found, the predominant culture clearly valued the grades and the activities more than the actual learning.[21]

Some of the most interesting developmental research I know concerns the relationship between intrinsic motivation (doing something for its own sake) and extrinsic motivation (working in response to an external punishment or reward). We tend to think that teenagers need extrinsic motivation: grades, test scores, punishments, rewards. But the research, first conducted in the early 1970s and continuing today, comes to a startling conclusion: *the best way to ruin intrinsic motivation is to reward extrinsically the activities that a kid does naturally.*[22]

In other words, if your kid is reading for pleasure, terrific. But the moment that pleasure reading turns into a "reading journal" for which a teacher offers a reward, a grade, or some other extrinsic motivation, say goodbye to reading for pleasure. The child may go on to dutifully complete her homework assignments. But her love of reading will have taken a serious blow. (It's a tribute to how much some kids love learning that homework and grades don't spoil it for them completely.)

One of the primary jobs of adolescence, in my view, is to find something that you spontaneously love and are good at. Organizing four years of high school around grades and college admissions is a virtual guarantee that a teenager's natural commitment and enthusiasm are likely to be undermined.

Why does extrinsic reward destroy intrinsic motivation? There are probably several reasons. But the most salient, in my view, is the simplest: once you're rewarded for engaging in an activity and then come to expect that reward, you'll never know your *true* motivation. Are you *genuinely* committed to reading that book, learning that math, exploring that interest, working in that community group? Or are you basically just chasing the reward, ready to do anything for a good grade or some points on your college application?[23]

These questions plague all teenagers, but once again, they're harder for teenage girls, who tend to spend far more time than boys ruminating about whether or not they're "good people." (For more on girls' rumination and preoccupation with relationships, see Chapter 5.) Also, girls often founder on the need to do everything without effort—while simultaneously feeling guilty if something comes easily, especially if they see others struggle with it. Girls who can get good grades without studying hard, for example, often feel confused about whether they deserve their high grades, because they got them without the effort that their classmates seem to expend. On the other hand, girls who do work hard for their grades may feel confused, once again, by conflicting expectations: are they supposed to work hard, as boys do, or simply "express themselves," as girls theoretically should?

THE MYTH OF EFFORTLESSNESS

As we've seen, the Triple Bind asks girls to perform "effortlessly": that is, to present their appearance, their abilities, and their unique identities not as the product of enormous labor but as the "natural" expression of their inner beauty. Watch successful women speak about themselves and you'll be struck by how rarely they talk about themselves as ambitious, hardworking, or driven, as men often do. Instead, they'll smile modestly and say, "I was just lucky," or "I don't know—I guess I was in the right place at the right time."

My Stanford colleague Carol Dweck (formerly at Columbia University) has created a body of research that illuminates just how destructive it is to think of any type of achievement as effortless. Dweck and her team worked with fifth graders from two different U.S. regions—the Midwest and New York City—bolstering the contention that their results apply generally, at least to U.S. children. After working on academic tasks, some students were told, "You must be smart at this." Others were told, "You must have worked really hard."

Dweck and her associates found that students who were praised for their intelligence were far more likely to give up when given a second, more difficult test. They adopted a brittle style of becoming so concerned with how they and their intelligence appeared (both to themselves and others) that they failed to take advantage of feedback or try to improve.

Students praised for their effort, on the other hand, often chose voluntarily to take even harder tests and expressed pleasure in trying to come up with a solution. They seemed far more able to see "intelligence" as a practice, a way of approaching the world, and an activity that could be modified, rather than as a fixed entity that could never be altered.[24]

Dweck concluded that some students come to believe in intelligence as an "entity": either you had it or you didn't. Those students, she realized, had nowhere to go when things got hard. If intelligence were a fixed, inborn quality, then a girl praised for her "smarts" who couldn't complete a task easily simply assumed she was stupid, rather than concluding that she had to work harder.

On the other hand, if a girl saw her good results as the fruits of her efforts—what is sometimes called an "incremental" theory of intelligence—she felt empowered, even when she ran into roadblocks. The "effort girl" was far more likely to respond to challenges by increasing her efforts, a response that she welcomed as a chance to learn more about what she could do.[25]

How does this relate to the Triple Bind? Because intelligence has traditionally been viewed as a somewhat unfeminine trait, there's already a certain amount of cognitive dissonance in a smart girl's identity: she is two opposite things, "smart" (a boy quality) and "a girl." If, after failing to perform well on a test, she concludes that she isn't even "smart," then she suffers threefold: losing a part of her identity (intelligence); feeling that she was arrogant to even *think* she had been smart; and wondering why, though obviously a girl, she is nevertheless weird enough to *want* to be smart.

We'll talk more about sex, dating, and relationships in Chapter 6. But for now, please note that virtually every teen and preteen girl I spoke with told me that boys prefer less intelligent girls. No girl ever admitted to dumbing *herself* down for boys, but almost everyone I spoke with told me that many *other* girls did that. Despite all our advances, girls still fear—perhaps with some justification—that intelligence is likely to make them less sexy, less feminine, less desirable to boys. Lesbian and bisexual girls may be less concerned about the "boy" factor, but my sense is that they, too, worry about being "real" women and often feel a certain amount of anxiety about how intelligence fits in with that.

Yet even while they want to be "real" women, girls know that today, they must also succeed at "boy" skills: school, sports, and, ultimately, career. So they look around for an image for how to perform both "girl" skills and "boy" skills, and what do they see? A horde of thin, chic, sexy women, working as political pundits or playing surgeons on TV or driving racecars or engaging in any number of "boy" careers, but almost without exception fitting the narrowest possible definition of an ultrafeminine and overly sexualized presentation. None of these women admit to working hard at their look or at their career (if they do, they run the risk of being mocked for their vanity and/or their ambition). And, in Eugenia's words, if you make a mistake, "everything comes crashing down." When I asked her to explain what she meant, she sighed and her voice dropped almost to a whisper.

"Well, you have these expected guidelines that you're supposed to set your life to," she said, then paused. "If you make a mistake in the eyes of your parents, friends, school, you're supposed to view it as the end of the world." She started to say something else and then stopped. That was literally all she could say.

Nicola Cooke, the prep school senior struggling with panic and depression, had never read the work of Carol Dweck. But intuitively, she had grasped Dweck's point. "The worst thing about [school]," she said longingly, "is that grades aren't based on effort. . . . Now all that matters is how good you do on your test, how good you do on the final. . . . There is nothing that says effort."

Jessica, who presumably also hadn't read Carol Dweck, said almost the same thing: "Last year in French class," she told me, "my teacher graded us on whether we said something right. And you're like, 'But we're learning!' There's a point to learning, and if we do it wrong, how can you grade us on that?"

Even as they struggled with the new culture of busy-ness, Nicola and Jessica longed for room to learn. They wanted to be appreciated for their efforts; they wanted room to explore and fail. Contrary to the myth of the lazy teenager who won't open a book or go the extra mile without being forced, these young women were eager to find out more about what the world had to teach them. What they were tired of was being rated, measured, pressured, and judged, of being asked to accept that they either "had it" or they didn't. The wonder is that they were still willing, after so much evidence to the contrary, to believe in the value of effort and the worth of learning.

Dweck's research centered on intelligence, but she and others have shown that the basic principles apply to other areas, too. For example, people who think that their shyness is a fixed entity rather than a behavior that can be modified tend to avoid social interactions that might help them overcome their shyness.[26]

I wondered whether these ideas might also be applied to beauty. Might a girl believe in the "prettiness entity" as much as in the "intelligence entity"? If that is so—if a girl sees her looks as an inborn quality rather than as the product of her own efforts—then she is likely to suffer the same devastating insecurity that the smart girls expressed in Dweck's studies.

Certainly, the notion that a girl should work hard at her looks is problematic as well. But if a girl feels that her looks are inordinately valued, and further believes that she has no real ability to control her looks—no genuine choice about whether she is "beautiful" or "a dog"—then she is doubly at the mercy of the Triple Bind. If Dweck's ideas can be applied to beauty, we might imagine that any time a supposedly pretty girl *isn't* considered beautiful, her entire identity is thrown into question. She can't respond by deciding to work harder because she doesn't see her looks as the result of effort. She can only conclude that she's been wrong all along (and so have all the loved ones who have praised her). Perhaps she'll also begin to hate herself for her foolishness ("Who was I to think I was pretty?"), her arrogance ("I guess I must think I'm better than other people—but I'm not"), and her selfishness ("How can I want to be pretty when so many other girls aren't? Who am I to deserve such good fortune?"). And girls who, for whatever reason, believe they're not pretty are in even more of a bind: they believe they can't do anything to improve their chances in one of life's all-important contests, that they're permanently lacking in one of the most crucial "entities" for determining their identities and their futures.

There isn't any research I know of to support these speculations directly, but to me, they offer another intriguing perspective on the Triple Bind.[27] Meanwhile, as we've seen, virtually every girl today is at risk for distress if not for the clinical conditions that have produced today's crisis. Whatever her looks or abilities, every teenage girl deserves better than we've given our daughters so far.

CHAPTER 4

No Place to Run, No Place to Hide

The Popular Culture of "Self-Erasing Identities"

> "Hi," Serena said, beaming at Jenny and setting her tray down.
>
> God, she was beautiful. Her hair was the pale gold color some of the other Constance girls tried to achieve by spending four hours in the hair salon on the top floor of Bergdorf Goodman getting their highlights done. But Serena's was natural, you could tell.
>
> —Cecily von Ziegesar, *Gossip Girl*

> STARTING TODAY I WILL
>
> 1. Be nice to everyone, whether I like him/her or not
> 2. Stop lying all the time about my feelings
> 3. Stop forgetting my Algebra notebook
> 4. Keep my comments to myself . . .
>
> —Meg Cabot, *The Princess Diaries*

> The girl with Ben had the kind of effortless beauty that no amount of plastic surgery could replicate. You had to be born with it. The bitch.
>
> —Zoey Dean, *The A-List*

Welcome to the contradictory world of self-erasing identities, in which the very images that seem to offer a girl avenues for discovering her identity in fact demand that she erase herself so as to better blend in with the crowd. In this chapter, I'll explore the ways that popular culture reinforces the Triple Bind, instructing girls to be good at both "girl stuff" and "boy stuff" while conforming to the ever more stringent requirements of being effortlessly thin, gorgeous, and "hot." I'll also look at some examples of pop culture that might actually feed girls' hunger for genuine alternatives—alternatives that have become extremely difficult to find.

I don't promise a comprehensive survey of today's pop culture, which would be far beyond the scope of this book. But I am going to share some intriguing examples of what today's teenage girls are watching and reading.

For the most part, it's not a pretty picture. Despite what often seem to be the best intentions of the creators, far too many cultural products ultimately reinforce the impossible expectations of the Triple Bind, contributing to the pervasive sense that there's just no alternative. The prevalence of so many successful and empowered female characters who are also sexy, chic, and thin may reinforce an "ordinary" girl's belief that she's the only one who can't get it right, the lone oddball in the group. And the presentation of most pop culture characters' looks as effortless adds insult to injury, suggesting that the real-life teenager who *does* have to work at her appearance—let alone at her grades, her relationships, or her sense of self—has somehow gone terribly wrong.

On the other hand, you can also find some cultural products that take on the Triple Bind, either by showing what girls are up against or by offering a genuine alternative. Part of the problem, in fact, is the way these potentially healthy examples blend in so well with the vast ocean of pop culture. As we've seen before, this is truly the best of times *and* the worst of times, in which the media seem to encourage girls to fulfill every aspect of their identities in any way they choose. It's only when you look below the surface that you begin to see how many of the so-called opportunities are double-edged at best and traps at worst.

So let's look over our daughters' shoulders as they watch, read, and listen. And let's try to imagine what messages our teenage girls are getting from their favorite shows, books, and movies. They may not even be the messages that the creators intended—but the messages are powerful all the same.

BEAUTIFUL SURGEONS AND UGLY BETTY: TV TRIES TO EMPOWER WOMEN

The TV show *Grey's Anatomy* is geared toward adult women, but it's also a big favorite with teenage girls.[1] The story of a group of surgical interns in the fictional hospital of Seattle Grace, *Grey's Anatomy* is the first show to reflect the growing predominance of women in medical school. Three of the five interns who begin their residency in the show's first season are female, while their supervisor, Miranda Bailey (Chandra Wilson), is a powerful African American surgeon known as "the Nazi" for her fierce, unyielding discipline (though, naturally, she has a heart of gold).

Significantly, Dr. Bailey is the only recurring female character who *isn't* conventionally beautiful. Short and stocky, she is nonetheless a successful woman in conventional terms: we eventually find out she's been married for ten years, and later she becomes pregnant and delivers a child. In the 2007–8 season, though, the show began to question Dr. Bailey's female identity. In one episode, Bailey reveals an ongoing insecurity about her looks: she melts before a charming, manipulative patient she'd had a crush on in high school, revealing that there's still an awkward little girl inside. Then her marriage begins to fall apart, largely because of her husband's frustration with Bailey's overwhelming dedication to her work, even though he'd previously agreed to be a stay-at-home dad. From being a character who seemed the very essence of "having it all" and not caring about her looks, Dr. Bailey is reduced to an anxious, insecure woman whose rush to get to work one morning had very possibly endangered her son's life.

Almost all the other women on the show, including interns, residents, and even many of the patients, are gorgeous, and most of them are thin, though Callie (played by Sara Ramirez) is voluptuous and full-figured. Perhaps significantly, Callie is one of the few female characters on the show to be sexually rejected—and by George, the weakest, least desirable, and least "manly" of the show's men. (The other rejected women are Olivia, a plain nurse and decidedly minor character who lacks both the looks *and* the accomplishments of the female doctors, and Addison, a beautiful ob/gyn in her thirties who is rejected by two different men, in both cases for younger women.)

Despite their evident beauty, the show's female characters suffer an endless round of romantic problems, often in the form of men wanting commitments from them that they're not yet ready to make. Although the women are seldom shown outside the hospital, most of the episodes turn on personal conflicts rather than work-related ones.

Significantly, the show was discussed by a group of teenage girls featured in an April 1, 2007, front-page story of the *New York Times*, entitled "For Girls, It's Be Yourself and Be Perfect, Too."[2] The girls speak admiringly of Cristina (Sandra Oh), the most ambitious, competitive intern on the show. "She really stands up for herself and knows who she is, which I aspire to," says one of the high-achieving girls in the story. Then she adds that Cristina is "gorgeous . . . And when she's taking off her scrubs, she's always wearing cute lingerie."

So, on the one hand, the teenage girls watching *Grey's Anatomy* see a hospital full of powerful, skillful, hardworking women. They see authoritative surgeons and ambitious young residents, including women of color at all levels. Clearly, the show's African American creator, Shonda Rhimes, worked hard herself at creating a multiracial vision of empowered women. To a great extent, *Grey's Anatomy* is to be applauded for showing that ambitious women can also be attractive and sexually empowered.

On the other hand, the show also plays into some of the most troubling aspects of the Triple Bind, not least because the women's relentless beauty appears to be effortless. What message are girls getting about women who are ambitious but *not* as attractive as the supremely self-confident Cristina? ("I can do hot even in my scrubs," she mutters before a first date with an equally gorgeous male doctor. "*Hot* is not the problem.")

Any real-life surgical resident, male or female, will tell you that it's impossible to work those hours and remain glowing, thin, and beautiful: there's no time to exercise, you are incredibly sleep-deprived, and you're living on junk food out of the vending machine. The effortless beauty of the show's characters suggests that no matter what else you achieve—no matter what feats of surgery, what loves or friendships—beauty is somehow a prerequisite.

The show also maintains a clear hierarchy: in any romantic contest, the more conventionally beautiful woman almost always wins. Izzy, the thin, blond intern (played by budding movie star Katherine Heigl), is more conventionally beautiful than the large, olive-skinned, dark-haired Callie, and so, eventually, George leaves Callie for Izzy. Earlier in the series, George was hopelessly in love with Meredith (Ellen Pompeo), the show's heroine—a woman he clearly preferred to his plain girlfriend, Nurse Olivia (Sarah Utterback).

Sometimes looks aren't the issue, but then youth is. The handsome Dr. Shepherd (Patrick Dempsey), aka "McDreamy," eventually leaves his beautiful wife, Addison (Kate Walsh), for the younger Meredith. Later in the series, Addison begins a romance with a young doctor, only to lose him, too, to a younger woman. Then Addison gets her own series, *Private Practice*, in which a key theme involves her sadness about ending up without a man and her fear that she's now too old to have a baby. No matter how good she is at "boy stuff" (surgery), Addison must also be good at "girl stuff" (wife- and motherhood)—and of course, she has to remain effortlessly thin, hot, and beautiful. Although the Triple Bind apparently frees women to "have it all"—family, beauty, career—it also helps to silence the questions that previous generations of women (and men) have raised: *Do I agree with the roles traditionally assigned to women? Do I even want a family? How do I measure my career success: through professional achievement or by some other standard? What matters most to me? Who am I?* These key questions, central to crafting an authentic identity, are subsumed into fantasies of successful, happy, and beautiful women—or into sadder stories of women who try desperately to achieve those fantasies without ever questioning the values that produce them.

And so, as I said in the Introduction, the teenage girls who watch these shows must on some level find them terribly dispiriting: both *Grey's Anatomy* and *Private Practice* make it seem virtually unthinkable to be an ordinary-looking woman who creates her own unique identity. Instead, the programs are filled with extraordinarily lovely and talented women who are busily trying to fulfill the precepts of the Triple Bind. A teenage girl looking to these shows for ideas on how to forge her own unique self might well feel both inspired by the possibilities *and* discouraged by the impossibly narrow range of acceptable looks. The coexistence of both the new possibilities and the old-style emphasis on looks is in some ways even more demoralizing than had the show simply said, "Look, your professional life doesn't matter—only your appearance does."

These days, there is *one* unattractive female on TV, and she's so unusual that the whole show is named for her: *Ugly Betty*.[3] This show is also popular with teenage girls, who may identify with the title character (America Ferrara), a good-hearted would-be writer from a Latino working-class family in Queens trying to make it in the snooty Manhattan world of high-fashion journalism. Awkward, unpolished Betty is hired only because the magazine's publisher believes that she's too ugly to attract his son, the editor, who runs through assistants like Kleenex because he keeps sleeping with them. Over the course of the show, Betty and the editor become friends: she serves as his conscience and moral compass, and he serves as her protector and benefactor (when her father is having immigration problems, for example, he buys her family four first-class tickets to Mexico).

On the one hand, you can't help admiring Betty's spunk, integrity, and good heart. On the other hand, Betty is still a basically passive character whose goodness is expressed not by her striving for positive achievement but by saying no to other people's bad deeds. On *Ugly Betty* as much as *Grey's Anatomy*, ambition and talent are linked with beauty, hotness, and thinness. The "bad" women—glamorous editor Wilhelmina (Vanessa Williams) and sexy receptionist Amanda (Becki Newton)—are eager to rise to the top, no matter who gets hurt. But every time ugly, good Betty gets a chance to succeed, she gives it up to help somebody else. On the show's first episode she can't even bring herself to speak to her boss: her best friend has to present Betty's ideas for her, and when they catch on, Betty gives her boss all the credit. When Betty works hard, it's rarely to advance her own career but, almost invariably, to save her boss from yet another disaster.

One positive note in the show is that even while Betty is relentlessly mocked by the fashion world as ugly, she is nonetheless attractive to men. Although her first boyfriend is gawky and dull, her next is cute and charming, and he vastly prefers Betty to his traditionally attractive hometown girlfriend. Other men pursue Betty as well, while she, too, is portrayed as sexual and passionate.

The show's portrayal of beauty is in fact double-edged. On the one hand, looks are shown to be effortless: Salma Hayek, for example, one of the show's producers, had a recurring role as the smart, successful, and movie-star-gorgeous editor of a rival magazine, while the slender, sexy Amanda is never shown dieting (though she is often shown bingeing on candy or junk food whenever she hits an emotional low). On the other hand, we also see how hard the models and editors work at their appearance: starving themselves, obsessing over dress size, desperately trying new beauty treatments to make them look younger or sexier.

These portrayals play into the double-edged way looks are talked about in the culture at large. On the one hand, a girl who is preoccupied with her appearance is vain, maybe even slutty; on the other hand, a girl who neglects her appearance is "letting herself go" and "not loving herself enough." Teenage girls are expected *both* to work hard at their looks *and* to just "be yourself and do whatever makes you feel good." It's almost as though an employer were saying, "Oh, I don't know, just do whatever portion of the work that makes you feel good. But I won't pay you enough to live on if you don't do what *I* want you to do (even though I'll never quite tell you what that is), and I won't promote you unless you do *more* than I've asked you to do (and you're pretty much on your own in figuring that out, too, though I will be kind enough to drop some ambiguous hints). But, hey, it's your choice! What makes *you* feel good about yourself?"

Part of the reason, I think, that *America's Next Top Model* is so popular with teenage girls is that there you *do* see how much work goes into a look. Indeed, it takes a whole team to produce a top model, including stylist, runway coach, and art director. On that show, the girls are always told to "be natural" and "let your inner self come out." But they are also told to seek out the right hairstyle and wardrobe, work their angles, and pose in a way that compensates for their flaws. Contradictory messages, to be sure, but at least the show openly acknowledges that looking good is, literally, a full-time job.

The messages of *Ugly Betty*, on the other hand, are far less clear: Does Betty *choose* not to look like the fashionistas out of some high-minded integrity? Or is she simply sparing herself the indignity of failing at something that she is fundamentally incapable of doing? Is her goodness and supportiveness completely genuine? Or is it what she needs to compensate for the way that all the attention would otherwise go to women who are far more attractive than she is?

So what's a girl to do? Admire *Grey's Anatomy*'s Cristina and then wonder why she can't "do hot" as easily? Or accept *Ugly Betty*'s message that good girls take care of the men while bad girls strive for success? Of course, media images may have been equally dispiriting for previous generations, but at least girls could imagine some alternatives that the media excluded: a hippie chick, an ambitious woman, an intellectual, a tomboy. In the world of *Ugly Betty* and *Grey's Anatomy*, that imagination is precluded because when those figures are being shown, they, too, are beautiful, "hot," and thin. Every job that an ambitious Ugly Betty might aspire to fill (editor, writer, photographer) is already taken by someone who is sexy, model-thin, and chic, so that once again effortless good looks are linked with ambition and success. Betty can't distinguish herself by intelligence, talent, or drive—the pretty girls have cornered the market on those—so instead she relies on the old-fashioned feminine qualities of goodness, helpfulness, empathy, and innocence. It makes her the heroine of the show, but it doesn't leave her teenage viewers much room to create workable identities.

Significantly, the explicitly "alternative" character identity on *Ugly Betty* is Alexis, a male-to-female transsexual. Played by former supermodel Rebecca Romijn, Alexis looks like an Amazon—tall, stunning, bodacious, with big breasts and legs that go on forever. She's a living reminder of how far we've come from the supermodel era: today's models seem to be pale, timid, malnourished fourteen-year-olds from impoverished East European villages, unable to make the kinds of outrageous demands that women such as Naomi Campbell and Cindy Crawford used to be known for as they strutted down the runways.[4] In one way, then, Alexis seems like a throwback to the days before the Triple Bind.

In another way, though, the Triple Bind is her downfall. As a former man, she initially feels free to disregard everyone else's feelings: her only interest is in getting what she wants. But as she inhabits her female body, Alexis begins to soften. Instead of competing with her brother, she offers him support. Instead of resenting her father, she forgives him. She's still (male and) ambitious, but she's also become more (female and) caring—and, like so many girls and women, she doesn't know how to resolve the conflicting expectations she now has for herself. The show's writers clearly intend for her to be an object lesson, to show how difficult it is to find a "good" form of female ambition, as opposed to the evil Wilhelmina or the callous Amanda. But they also show that even a former man doesn't get a free pass: to be taken seriously, a woman *must* be beautiful.

One formerly common theme in pop culture showed the quirky, awkward girl as the one with the talent while the pretty girl coasted on her good looks. John Hughes' movies made a great deal of this distinction: Ally Sheedy's troubled artist versus Molly Ringwald's cheerleader in *The Breakfast Club*; Mary Stuart Masterson's punky drummer versus Lea Thompson's pretty "popular girl" in *Some Kind of Wonderful*. Those weren't ideal portraits, either, but at least they gave ordinary-looking girls something to pin their hopes on. If all the talented, ambitious professionals are also gorgeous, what roles are left for the other 98 percent of teenage girls?

Or consider the range of women who found their way into TV shows in the 1970s and 1980s. Mary Richards, played by Mary Tyler Moore on the series that was named for her, was sweet, pretty, and hardworking, but she wasn't successful at *everything*: although she dated frequently, she never had a steady boyfriend. Certainly Mary was attractive, but she also looked like a "regular" woman, someone the viewer might know or become. Her friend Rhoda was presented as less attractive than Mary, wisecracking about her weight or about the "loser guys" she dated, but she, too, looked like an ordinary woman, not the unthinkable extreme suggested by Ugly Betty. The contrast between her and Mary wasn't nearly as pronounced as that between the two categories of women (beautiful versus unattractive) on *Grey's Anatomy.*

Think, too, of the four teenage girls on the popular 1980s program *The Facts of Life.* Compared to today's thin, stunning teen actresses, the four characters seem heavy and almost funny-looking, though they were meant to be ordinarily attractive teenage girls for their time. Likewise, the four friends on the 1990s *Living Single* (whose cast included a grown-up actress from *The Facts of Life*) represented ordinary women in a range of shapes and sizes, including the queen-sized Queen Latifah. Compare that program to the more recent *Girlfriends*, whose characters, though diverse in personality, are uniformly glamorous, chic, and thin. One of the characters on *Girlfriends* is meant to be a kind of hippie, and much is made of her far-out ideas and her wacky diet. Yet she still looks like a model, demonstrating the rigid categories and implacable standards required by the Triple Bind.

It would be grievously unfair to say that *Grey's Anatomy* and *Ugly Betty* or even *Girlfriends* is responsible for the crisis-level statistics we've been seeing, especially when all three shows clearly want to provide positive, empowering views of women (and particularly women of color). But the fact that even programs with such progressive intentions participate in the narrowing of cultural alternatives shows us how powerful, and how destructive, the Triple Bind can be.

GOSSIP GIRLS AND UGLIES: THE NEW TRENDS IN TEEN LIT

Perhaps the most dramatic trend in teenage literature is the one begun by *Gossip Girl*, the 2002 novel by Cecily von Ziegesar. Based on von Ziegesar's own experiences as an Upper East Side prep school girl, the novel has been called a kind of *Sex and the City* for teenagers. It has spawned several sequels, a TV show that first aired in fall 2007, and a number of other similar books, including the It Girl series (by von Ziegesar) and the A-List series (by Zoey Dean).[5]

The style of these books is completely new in teenage literature, and not only because of the characters' casual attitudes toward sex, spending, and eating disorders. True, the focus on extremely wealthy, irresponsible teens and their endless repetition of brand names and labels is disturbing to anyone concerned about the ways that consumerism and materialism may be contributing to the crisis-level statistics among teenage girls. But the really upsetting aspect of these series, in my opinion, is the way they shift the focus from the traditional moral heroine of teen-girl books to an amoral group of girls who hate, envy, and scheme against the heroine. Rather than identifying with a character who has similar problems to theirs—friends, family, relationships, school, the future—teenage readers of this new type of book are invited to identify with all the girls who are mean to the main character. (For more on "mean girls" and relational aggression, see Chapter 8.)

In some books, such as the A-List series, the main character is presented as moral, although extremely wealthy and effortlessly pretty. Here is our heroine Anna, recently transplanted from New York to Beverly Hills, eating with some of her new classmates:

> "Jeez, Skye, won't you have a little roll with your butter?" Krishna asked, staring with distaste.
>
> "I've got the munchies." Skye took another bite of her roll. "Besides, it's not like you couldn't lose a few l-b's."
>
> "Hel-*lo*, who zipped up size-zero jeans at Barneys last week?"
>
> "Screw you," Skye said. But she put the roll down.
>
> That there was competition to be the thinnest was nothing new to Anna—so many of her friends in Manhattan had the same obsession. Anna knew how fortunate she was to be naturally slender. She'd taken ballet for years because she loved it; it was her main form of exercise.[6]

Anna is presented as thoughtful, moral, and—of course—effortlessly beautiful (and "naturally slender"). The reader is clearly supposed to like her and identify with her, as in passages such as the one I just quoted, which are presented from her point of view. Sometimes, though, the point of view shifts to the meaner, uglier, fatter girls who envy Anna for her looks, polish, and charm. The third epigraph to this chapter provides an example, coming from a scene in which one of Anna's rivals wonders about the new girl in town. Girls who read the book get to have it both ways: identifying with the good girl's effortless victories while also enjoying the thought of bringing her down.

Von Ziegesar, who invented the style, takes it one step further: all her female characters are equally materialistic, self-centered, and nasty. (The TV version of *Gossip Girl* has softened two of the characters, Serena and Jenny, to make them more sympathetic.) All, too, are equally at a loss when it comes to dealing with men: virtually every girl eventually loves someone who treats her badly, or whom she tries and ultimately fails to control. None of the main characters in either series has a passion for anything other than clothes, drugs, alcohol, or sex: no intellectual, artistic, or social interest, except insofar as expressing any such interest will get them into college. (There is some hint that Jenny, the heroine of *The It Girl*, likes art.) People make temporary alliances, but no one seems to genuinely like anyone. It's like reading an eighteenth-century French novel, only with teenagers.

Still, despite the general nastiness, some girls have more of "it" than others—and the "it" they have is the totally effortless ability to command a room's attention. Here, from von Ziegesar's *Gossip Girl*, are Serena's supposed best friends, observing Serena's first day back at school:

> "What the fuck is she wearing, anyway?" Kati Farkas hissed.
>
> "Maybe she thinks the maroon looks like Prada or something," Laura sniggered back.
>
> "I think she's trying to make some kind of statement," Isabel whispered. "Like, look at me, I'm Serena, I'm beautiful, I can wear whatever I want."
>
> *And she can,* Blair thought. That was one of the things that always infuriated her about Serena. She looked good in anything.[7]

Here is a similar passage from Anna's first day at school in Zoey Dean's *The A-List*:

> "Hi. You look great."
>
> Sweet of him to say so, but Anna hadn't given it a whole lot of thought when she'd dressed that morning—she never really did when she went to school. Back in New York outsized jeans—preferably from some vintage store—ancient sweats, and stretched-out sweaters with obvious holes were all considered not only appropriate, but hip. The idea was to look as if you didn't give a shit.[8]

Why are these books so popular with teenagers? I can imagine that some girls enjoy feeling superior to these apparently perfect characters, who despite their money, good looks, and lack of parental supervision seem pretty miserable pretty much all of the time. Some girls may like learning about all the products (in what is clearly von Ziegesar's formula, product names appear virtually every time a character enters a scene, while Dean uses brand names nearly as often). Perhaps some girls enjoy relief from the daily pressures of being "good," a brief "fantasy vacation" of behaving as badly as these characters do and of caring as little about other people's feelings. And some girls may appreciate the way the books skewer the shallow, college-oriented culture that marks too many schools:

> Mrs. McLean, or Mrs. M., as the girls called her, was their headmistress. It was her job to put forth the cream of the crop—send the girls off to the best colleges,

> the best marriages, the best lives—and she was very good at what she did. She had no patience for losers, and if she caught one of her girls acting like a loser—persistently calling in sick or doing poorly on the SATs—she would call in the shrinks, counselors, and tutors and make sure the girl got the personal attention she needed to get good grades, high scores, and a warm welcome to the college of her choice.[9]

I can appreciate why teenage girls would find these passages attractive. From my adult perspective, though, I find these books fairly disturbing. Once again, every significant character is thin, chic, and beautiful, while the overweight, the unstylish, and the less attractive are not so much mocked as simply dismissed. No man could ever want them. (Lesbianism isn't much discussed, at least in the series' first books.) No plan they create could ever succeed. No one could possibly take them seriously; how could they? Only the thin, chic, and beautiful matter.

Compared to this new teen lit, the best-selling books of Meg Cabot look positively old-fashioned. Like the teen-girl literature that's been around since the 1950s, Cabot's books center on a heroine with whom the reader is meant to identify as she works out the pressing issues of her age group: how to relate to friends, family, boys, and school. As in previous novels meant for teenage girls, Cabot's heroines struggle with moral issues: How many compromises should you make in order to become popular? How do you balance the claims of friends with your interest in an attractive guy? How do you decide what level of sexual activity is right for you? Unlike *Gossip Girl* and company, Cabot's books are clearly intended to model for readers the process of making good decisions in their own lives, holding out the promise of happy endings—a great boyfriend, renewed friendships, a dizzying degree of popularity—as a reward.

Yet a closer looks reveals that Cabot's books, too, are working the new territory of the Triple Bind. Consider Cabot's 2000 novel, *The Princess Diaries*, which also spawned a successful series as well as a movie.[10] The books are the story of New York high school student Mia Thermopolis, whom we first meet as a gawky, unattractive girl nursing a hopeless crush on a popular boy. Mia lives happily with her mother, a bohemian artist, and sees her father only occasionally. (In the movie version, the father has died.) Her folks were never married, but Mia has her dad's last name. Suddenly, she finds out why: he's the crown prince of an obscure European country called Genovia and she, the ordinary American girl, is a princess.

The fantasy of finding out you're really a princess apparently goes so deep that even the book's author shares it: according to her author bio, which appears even on her non-princess-themed books, "She is still waiting for her real parents, the king and queen, to restore her to her rightful throne."[11]

I find this rather chilling, to be honest, even if it is a contrived book jacket gimmick. Cabot is a grown-up, successful author whose photograph shows a happy-looking, attractive woman and whose bio informs us that she lives with her husband. Yet she still maintains the little-girl dream of becoming a princess? She's still waiting for her parents to transform her life?

These contradictions help to shape Cabot's heroines. They're also the contradictions that real-life teenage girls struggle with, which perhaps explains why her books are so popular. Mia, for example, is convinced she's unattractive. Her best friend is, too, but unlike Mia, Lilly is supremely confident:

> But Lilly doesn't care about things like that [being made fun of]. I mean, she's short and sort of round and kind of resembles a pug, but she totally doesn't care how she looks. I mean, she has her own TV show, and guys call in all the time and say how ugly they think she is, and ask her to lift her shirt up (*she* isn't flat-chested; she wears a C cup already), and she just laughs and laughs.
>
> Lilly isn't afraid of anything.[12]

Mia, however, is scared of Lilly and lets her best friend boss her around—until Mia becomes a princess. At first, Mia resists her transformation, which involves letting her royal grandmother give her a new hairstyle and some paste-on fingernails. But once Mia is made over, she turns out to be beautiful. Because Mia herself fights the makeover every step of the way, we can't accuse her of *wanting* to be beautiful or of putting any effort into it. Her beauty, like her princesshood, is not only effortless, it's something that's done to her. Yet Mia draws strength from her new look and the status that enables her to stand up to her best friend and, later, to an exploitative boy:

> I don't think I have ever told anyone to shut up before. It's just not something I do. I don't know what happened, really. Maybe it was the fingernails. I never had fingernails before. They sort of made me feel strong. . . .
>
> If it hadn't turned out that I'm a princess, maybe I might still be all that stuff. You know, unassertive, fearful of confrontation, an internalizer. I probably wouldn't have done what I did next [challenge the boy].[13]

With Mia's transformation comes a boyfriend (Lilly's brother), revenge on the mean popular girl who torments her, and even the chance to go out with—and reject—the most popular boy in school. All of these "girl" benefits just come to her without her making any kind of ambitious or self-promoting effort. What Mia *does* work at, as the second epigraph to this chapter indicates, is being nicer to people, even though that involves her in a perpetual contradiction: she wants to be honest about how she feels ("Stop lying all the time about my feelings"), but she doesn't want to hurt or offend anyone ("Be nice to everyone, whether I like him/her or not. . . . Keep my comments to myself").

Mia epitomizes the girl who wants to be attractive to boys without having to work at it, and in some ways that's a noble ideal. Yet Mia doesn't look like Lilly, with her round body and pug nose; Mia is a "natural" beauty too modest to recognize her own loveliness (lest we believe Mia's own first-person disclaimers about how ugly she is, we're told how often reporters praise her looks). Forced to become a beauty and a princess against her will, Mia expresses the contradictions of a Triple Bind that ask girls to work hard at girl stuff while pretending, to themselves and others, that they're just being "natural."

Significantly, the two teen-girl series I found that seem most in opposition to the Triple Bind culture were both written by men. Scott Westerfeld's Uglies series is set in a fantastic future where everyone gets a surgical makeover at age sixteen. "Ugly" until then, the remade teens are all uniformly pretty. "In a world of extreme beauty, anyone normal is ugly," says the tagline for *Uglies*, the first book in the series. Teenage girls might well feel that this describes not some fantastic future but their own lives.[14]

Westerfeld takes on the whole "pretty" culture by suggesting that the operation also includes a kind of lobotomy rendering the new "Pretties" docile and superficial. In the series' second book, *Pretties*, we see the shallow, hedonistic culture most Pretties engage in: an endless round of drinking, partying, and dressing up that looks suspiciously like the way teens behave in the Gossip Girl/It Girl/A-List series.[15] That teen readers have made Westerfeld's series a *New York Times* best seller suggests that at least some girls are hungry for a critique of their world (though I wouldn't be surprised if some of those same girls also owned all the *Gossip Girl* books).

Jerry Spinelli's *Stargirl* is set in a more realistic world, although the central character, Stargirl, has an otherworldly character, as her name suggests.[16] A true nonconformist, Stargirl dresses in outlandish costumes made by her mother—a ruffled pioneer girl's skirt, a 1920s flapper dress, a kimono. She doesn't wear makeup. She knows enormous amounts about obscure topics and nothing at all about standard school subjects. She joins the track team but runs the wrong way. She resists the pressures of the Triple Bind in every possible domain, secure in her own alternative identity.

Spinelli takes Stargirl through a number of emotional ups and downs. At first she is shunned. Then, miraculously, she is embraced: suddenly she becomes the most popular girl in school, with dozens of imitators. Then, in the fickle way of teenagers, she is shunned again when she refuses to join the other students in their mindless support of the school's winning basketball team. When the book's narrator falls in love with her, he convinces her to become "normal," even popular, and because she loves him, too, she goes along. Significantly, she is transformed via consumerism and an obsession with the very brand names that appear on every page of the Gossip Girl books:

> She was mad for shopping. It was as if she had just discovered clothes. She bought shirts and pants and shorts and costume jewelry and makeup. I began to notice that the items of clothing had one thing in common: they all had the designer's name plastered prominently on them. She seemed to buy not for color or style but for designer label size.
>
> She constantly quizzed me about what other kids would do, would buy, would say, would think. She invented a fictitious person whom she called Evelyn Everybody. "Would Evelyn like this?" "Would Evelyn do that?"[17]

Eventually, Stargirl gives up on her false self and embraces her true, unique identity. She explicitly rejects the designer label culture, stops wearing makeup, and returns to her outlandish costumes. She also resumes her quirky, inner-directed behavior, no longer concerned with Evelyn Everybody but following instead her own true star. She starts a ukulele club, for example, and manages to transform the big school dance of the year into a nearly utopian celebration, leading a long line of joyously dancing students in an ecstatic rendition of the bunny hop. Although she loses the boyfriend who wishes she were more like others, she holds on to a few true friends before her family suddenly leaves town. Her former boyfriend—an adult by the time he narrates the book—never gets over her, never stops regretting that he wasn't able to live up to the standard she set.

Teenage girls must have liked that ending, because they made *Stargirl* a best seller, inspiring not only a sequel (*Love, Stargirl*) but also a journal, with Stargirl's unique sayings printed on every page.[18] Again, the same girls who bought *Stargirl* might also buy their own designer labels, and they may turn to the Gossip Girl series to learn which ones to buy. But at least some girls, some of the time, want to read about those rare girls who manage to escape the pressures of the Triple Bind.

WITCHES, GODDESSES, AND DANCING QUEENS: *JUNO, HAIRSPRAY, QUEEN SIZED,* AND *WICKED*

As I was drafting this chapter, the newspapers and blogs were full of discussion about *Juno*, the 2007 movie about a bright, quirky teenage girl who gets pregnant, gives the baby up for adoption, and ends up with her boyfriend anyway. Some writers were appalled at what they saw as the film's "soft on teen pregnancy" attitude. Others cheered for its feisty heroine.[19]

One concern is that those teenage girls who would otherwise prefer abortion to adoption may find *Juno* discouraging. Given the virtual blackout on abortion as an acceptable choice for teenage girls, *Juno* may unwittingly play into the belief that a true heroine would have her child rather than abort the fetus. But I was also struck by the movie's effort to portray a genuinely alternative female identity. Though Juno's best friend is a stylish cheerleader, Juno herself is a far more unusual character. In the words of Ellen Page, the actress who plays her,

> I don't think we've ever had a character like Juno. . . . She is abrupt and unapologetic, extremely independent . . . and the film doesn't dwell on her uniqueness, you know? There's no, "Oh, look at this crazy outcast!" She's not interesting in relation to a stereotype—she wears flannel shirts and sweater vests, and it's just who she is.[20]

In other words, Juno is one of those rare female characters who seems to have created an identity outside of the Triple Bind. She's figuring out her own way of being a girl—significantly, both she and Page are big fans of seventies punk, when there were lots of musicians providing alternative female identities—and the film chronicles her efforts to discover and then pursue what really matters to her. As one perceptive critic pointed out, the movie ends with Juno singing, a sign that she has finally found her own voice.[21]

Page herself, according to a December 3, 2007, *New York* magazine profile, has to struggle to stay outside of the Triple Bind. She describes the photo shoots where she's asked to wear "lacy pink shirts," and harks back to an earlier version of a female alternative: "[Rock star] Annie Lennox used to be able to dress like a man and sell albums. . . . I don't think a big star could do that right now."[22]

The popularity of *Juno* and the Uglies and Stargirl series is a testament to how hungry teenage girls are for images that evade, attack, or transcend the Triple Bind. A similar testament can be read in the teen girls who love *Hairspray*, the story of a fat 1960s heroine (played by Nikki Blonsky) who loves to dance, does poorly in school, and unites with the African American community to integrate a local after-school dance show. *Hairspray* was originally a John Waters movie and later a Broadway musical. The latest movie, made from the musical, created stardom for Blonsky, who went on to play the lead in *Queen Sized*, a 2007 Lifetime TV movie about a fat girl who becomes her high school's prom queen.[23]

Both *Hairspray* and *Queen Sized* use their heroine's unconventional body size to symbolize girls taking up more space in general. Both heroines begin with individual ambitions—to win a dance contest, to be elected prom queen—but by the end of each movie, the girls have learned to think much, much bigger. In *Hairspray*, the main character sees her struggle for acceptance as part of a larger effort to transform society. She becomes far more concerned with racially integrating the whites-only local TV dance show than with winning acceptance from the popular kids at her school (though in happy Hollywood style, she actually manages to do both). In *Queen Sized*, the high school heroine comes to see her campaign for prom queen as an effort to revolutionize the hierarchical world of high school cliques. She learns to see her victory not as hers alone but as a collective triumph for all the kids who feel trapped by their labels: "pretty girl," "jock," and "cheerleader" as much as "fat girl," "geek," and "loser." From my point of view, both films point the way to a real Triple Bind solution: commitment to a larger community and to ideals beyond oneself. (For more on this potential solution, see Chapter 9.)

I love the optimism and utopian feel of *Juno*, *Hairspray*, and *Queen Sized*. But I'm also aware of a far less happy portrait of the Triple Bind: the Broadway musical *Wicked*, which has likewise become something of a cult favorite among teens and tweens.[24] In fact, *Wicked* (as well as *Hairspray*) is a recurring reference on *Ugly Betty*, as Betty explicitly identifies with *Wicked*'s "ugly" heroine.

Wicked, based on the novel by Gregory Maguire, is the prehistory of Oz, the story of how good witch Glinda and wicked witch Elphaba came to recognize the true nature of their fairy-tale country.[25] In *Wicked*, the Wizard is a demagogic charlatan who distracts citizens from his own shortcomings by uniting them in a campaign to suppress the country's talking animals. When humans decide that animals should not speak, the animals' abilities are undermined. Because nobody wants to hear them—indeed, because their speech disturbs and enrages the dominant society—they literally lose the ability to speak, a potent metaphor for the way teenage girls, "seen but not heard," lose their authentic voices.

Perhaps it's Elphaba's own outsider status that leads her to identify with the oppressed animals. Born with bright green skin, Elphaba would seem to be permanently disqualified from ever being popular, let alone loved. Feisty and talented—she has a huge store of natural magic that emerges whenever she gets angry—she is also empathic and compassionate (her anger is always on behalf of other, weaker creatures whom she tries to protect). Somehow, against all fairy-tale conventions, Elphaba wins the love of the handsome prince Fiyero even though beautiful, popular Glinda wants him, too. Yet the girls' friendship survives and thrives, as Glinda comes to admire Elphaba's integrity.

The story turns dark by the second act. When Elphaba is perceived as a threat to the Wizard's power, she goes into hiding, trying to rally the animals, but she is demonized as "wicked." Her beloved prince is beaten and tortured: she has to turn him into the Scarecrow so he can survive. In a version of "happily ever after" that is decidedly more bitter than sweet, Elphaba finally fakes her own death so that she and the Scarecrow can leave Oz.

Elphaba's very existence is a rebuke to the Triple Bind. She rejects the conventional female notions of beauty and popularity that Glinda embodies. But she also rejects the conventional male world of hierarchy and power. She isn't capable of looking beautiful or sexy in any conventional sense; after all, she's green, and plain besides.

Yet Elphaba develops her unique abilities, feels sexual passion, finds love, and even maintains a profound friendship with the prettiest, most popular girl of all. She fights for what she believes in and reaches out to a larger community. She inspires others with her compassion, her integrity, and her courage. And at the end of the play she must leave the story entirely, going to an unnamed country and an unknown destiny. True, she can survive the Triple Bind, but she cannot change the society that created it, a society that has so little room for her that she must escape into exile or face destruction. Teenage girls across America go to see *Wicked* not just once but several times. Shouldn't we hear what they're trying to tell us?

SELF-ERASING IDENTITIES AND THE TRIPLE BIND

In this all-too-brief survey of today's pop culture, one theme emerges over and over again: the apparent freedom for girls to become "anything" is all too often a trap, and a dangerous trap at that. Just as the supposedly happy land of Oz requires a huge portion of its citizenry to silence itself, so does this apparently liberated era for girls require them to erase a portion of their identities. Sure, any girl can become beautiful, but what about the girl who doesn't want to wear makeup or to focus on her appearance? Of course, any woman can undertake a challenging profession, whether surgeon or fashion editor, but only if she reassures the dominant culture by remaining sexy, pretty, and thin, and by accepting its definitions of success. Yes, there are some exceptions—Ugly Betty, for example, and the *Grey's Anatomy* character Miranda Bailey—but who would want to be like them when the pretty women are equally ambitious and often more successful? The real-life impossibility of being *that* beautiful and *that* successful (there simply aren't enough hours in the day) is conveniently overlooked. So is the possibility that anyone might define success differently: valuing artistic creativity or job satisfaction or humanitarian goals more highly than money, power, or status.

The popular culture of earlier eras was more overtly oppressive. Before the 1970s, you rarely saw a happy, successful working woman in the media, and even more rarely was such a woman married or a mother. Things started to change in the last decades of the twentieth century, but the default position for women was still marriage and motherhood, while the default position for career success was still male. Lesbians and women of color had virtually no pop culture visibility earlier in the century and mainly token representation later on.

So in many ways, the twenty-first-century trend of portraying a diverse, multiracial world of working women represents an enormous advance for women and girls, truly "the best of times." Yet, as we saw in Chapter 1, these very advances also signal "the worst of times," when girls are both allowed to be *anything* and required to be *everything*—loving and supportive like traditional women; ambitious and striving like traditional men; unable even to articulate a critique of the system that pushes them to reach for unrealistic standards of beauty and success. (One of the most recent lesbian characters on prime-time TV is a top executive at a makeup company.) Women are still prized for being natural, but today's standards for beauty make looking "natural" harder work than ever. Apparently allowed to have it all, girls struggle as never before, laboring under the burden of impossible, contradictory expectations.

The very roles that seem to promise new identities for girls also require them to erase huge portions of their experience, especially their resentment at having to be "onstage" all the time, endlessly judged for their appearance; or their anger at having to take care of others at their own expense; or their frustration at not being heard while having to pretend that those who ignore them have their best interests at heart. These frustrations are visible in *America's Next Top Model* as much as in any of the works I've discussed in this chapter. Also visible is the difficulty of understanding these feelings when all the choices are apparently yours. Those silenced animals in *Wicked* are sometimes beaten and caged. But sometimes they just lose heart. Unable to withstand the collective agreement that they should not speak, they simply give up their power. Apparently they, too, have something in common with Seligman's dogs.

Some girls collapse under the weight of these contradictions, especially those with other signs of vulnerability, such as genetic risk, early experiences of abuse, or a host of other risk factors. They're the ones whose statistics we've been reading, the ones who binge, mutilate themselves, behave violently, become depressed, or try to kill themselves. Most girls, though, will somehow find their way. It's up to us to listen to those girls even harder, so we can hear what parts of their identities might otherwise be erased.

CHAPTER 5

When Virtue Is Its Own Punishment

How Empathy and Verbal Skills May Put Our Girls at Higher Risk

When Nicola Cooke started high school three years ago, she was, in her own words, "a very lighthearted spirit, very outgoing." Tall and athletic, she played basketball, volunteered for community groups, and held down a part-time job. She was excited about her classes and about the chance to make new friends.

Then, as she described it in a talk she would later give at the girls' prep school she attended, "one event sent me into a spiral of anxiety, panic, and ultimately depression."

The event took place at a summer basketball game. As Nicola explains to me:

> I felt the pressure, 'cause my coach was like, "I need you to go in. There are only so many seconds to go, we're down two points, I need you to score, I need you to do this, I need you to get the ball to this person." . . . I felt like there was pressure for me a lot because I'm tall, and I was a good asset for the team, I think. I was feeling the pressure to always be there in a pinch.

Suddenly, Nicola found herself

> short of breath, dizzy, and feeling as if I were on the brink of death. I ran outside and everything tightened. My heart and lungs felt like someone was grasping it firmly with their fist, and my stomach felt as if I was on a roller coaster. Scared and confused, I tried to calm myself down, but the only thought going through my head was, "This is what death feels like."

In the talk she gave later, Nicola tried to make light of her feelings: "Being the dramatic girl that I am, I of course jumped to that conclusion." But the incident was the harbinger of a series of similar attacks that continued for several months—and not just on the court. First, Nicola started panicking whenever she went to the mall. Then she missed a week of school. "I didn't get out of bed. I stopped eating. . . . I spent the whole day crying."

Nicola's doctor suggested that the tightening in her chest might be asthma and gave Nicola an inhaler. But the steroids only made Nicola more jittery—and the panic attacks continued.

> I couldn't go to other people's houses, to church, to work, to concerts; I couldn't even go to the movies. I literally could not leave my house without nearly collapsing. I cried more than I had cried over the course of my life, and I began to shut down. After a year and a half of suffering, I wanted to give up. I spent two weeks in bed; scared of the world, of myself, and of the future. I didn't know how to describe my pain to anyone because I literally was completely numb. All I felt was fear.

Nicola endured a battery of tests—CAT scans, MRIs, blood tests—as her doctors responded to her own account of the problem: "I wasn't describing it as 'I feel stressed out, I feel sad.' I was being like, 'I am in pain. There is something wrong. I get headaches. I get stomach aches.' " Finally, though, Nicola came to accept the truth: she was suffering from an anxiety disorder, known as panic disorder, that had morphed into depression.[1] She began seeing a therapist, who taught her breathing techniques to help her relax.

For a while, things were better. Then it was time to take the SATs.

> I couldn't take the SATs. I passed out when I went to go take them the first time because I got so worked up over them. The stress of, like, sitting there, the stress, the pressure that if I don't do good on these tests, I'm not going to get into college, which means I'm not going to get a good degree and I am not going to have a good job and I am not going to have a good life. The idealism that they put into your head about tests like that just amazes me.[2]

When Nicola talks about her experience with the SATs, she begins by describing the pressure she felt on herself. But later, she was allowed to retake the test privately, and she did just fine. When I ask her about the discrepancy, she tells me that it wasn't so much the tests themselves as her sense of everybody else's anxiety. She feels most anxious, she tells me,

> [in] places where there are a lot of people, and I can feel like— You know when you can feel when people are stressed out, you can see it in their face. . . . Even before I was even in the classroom when I went to take [the SATs] for the first time, as soon as I entered the school, I could feel the stress, I could see the stress, I could feel it. That is what threw me off. . . . I kept trying to explain to people . . . when they would ask me, "Why can't you just go in and take the test?" I said, "It is not the test that I am worried about. Yeah, I know it means a lot, but I am a good test taker, I know I will do good on the test. It's just the stress, the tension, the

> quietness." . . . Seeing everyone's faces . . . I can sense stress. I can sense everything ten times better than everyone I know because I have such a sensitivity for it. So as soon as I pick up the slight [hint of stress], that is what makes me nervous.

I ask Nicola if she's always been so sensitive to the feelings of others. "I have always been the worry child in my family," she admits.

> Whenever someone in my family would be sick, or, like, in the hospital, I would literally get sick. I would be throwing up—nervous throwing up. I have always been . . . a nervous kind of person. I think it got out of control when the stress was always around me.

I ask Nicola to speculate about why she feels other people's stress so intensely. "I try to be the rescuer," she tells me. "Like, I try to notice what is wrong and try to fix it." She continues:

> I have always wanted to help people. And I think that it got to the point where I was taking other people's problems and putting them as my own and putting them *before* my own. . . . Not that someone blatantly said to me to put others before yourself. I think that was the idea that I developed . . . that my problems were secondhand to other people's problems. So instead of coping with mine first, I dealt with others, and I said, "Oh, I'll get to my issues eventually." Which ended up not happening. Which made it ten times worse.

MISPLACED EMPATHY

Nicola's story is a classic example of how empathy, compassion, and sensitivity to others' needs can derail teenage girls, especially those who, like Nicola, turn out to have a family history of anxiety and/or depression. To many researchers, it seems like a paradox: Girls come into the world and within their first few years surpass boys in many ways. They're more verbal, more attuned to others' emotions, and better at following adult rules. If all you knew of children was who they were at ages three and four, you'd have to predict that girls would have it made.

But a funny thing happens on the way to adulthood. The very qualities that empower girls as toddlers, preschoolers, and elementary school students begin to work to their disservice as they reach adolescence. Groundbreaking studies have shown that for many girls, the very verbal skills, empathy, and compliance at which they excel can lead to anxiety, depression, and a host of other disorders.[3]

Why does this occur? Once again, the Triple Bind is involved, demanding both that girls achieve in "boy" mode *and* that they take care of others in "girl" mode. And if they look outward, to cultural models who might seem to offer ways of resolving these contradictory expectations, all they see are a plethora of apparently successful women who not only seem to do the impossible but who look as though they're doing it effortlessly, all while presenting themselves as pretty, sexy, and thin.

Like Nicola, girls are typically encouraged to focus on others' feelings—especially the feelings of parents and authority figures. Boys are more often asked to focus on winning. Both genders pay a price. But because girls are being asked to succeed in male arenas, they pay an especially high price, given that they're not really socialized to have the kind of toughness and self-assertion that are needed to succeed in a man's world. The result is often anxiety, depression, and all the other self-destructive behaviors we've seen: eating disorders, self-mutilation, or simply self-hatred.[4]

For example, a boy who goes for victory on the basketball court knows that he's supposed to win—not to feel sorry for the opposing team or for the teammate who didn't make as many baskets as he did. He may be trying to make his coach proud, but he's not exactly worrying about his coach's feelings.

Nicola, trying for a similar achievement, was handicapped by her awareness of how much her coach was counting on her, how much her team was counting on her. When she talks about her first panic attack, she begins her account with what her coach needed, what the team needed: they depended on her, they were anxious about winning, they considered her height "a good asset." Her efforts to compete successfully on the SAT test were likewise blocked by her sense of other people's feelings, in this case, the anxiety of her fellow students. Even a trip to the mall could feel overwhelming as she picked up on the anxieties and frustrations of the other shoppers.

Thus, the (female) empathy that made Nicola loving and sensitive also made it hard for her to continue with (male) competition, while the culture of busy-ness we explored in Chapter 3 guaranteed that Nicola would continually be surrounded by people who seemed to be pressuring her: her coach, who worried about winning; her teachers, concerned about her grades; her parents, anxious about her college prospects; and her fellow students, stressed out over everything.

Nicola describes her parents as generally easygoing, and she feels grateful to both of them for getting her the help she needed. She's been attending school regularly for some time now and expects both to graduate with her class and to go on to college. But she's paid a heavy price for her sensitivity:

> I have lost a whole—the whole part of me that used to be. . . . I am never going to be able to be, like, spontaneous—like, I lost my spontaneity . . . I used to be like,

> "Let's go here, let's go there." . . . [Now] change scares me, it makes me nervous . . . I used to be the fun-loving kind of one and now I am like the kind of one that is like, "Let's be careful," "Why don't we just stay in tonight?" I still have my nervousness. . . . I still won't go to places that remind me of my anxiety by myself.
>
> . . . I love to sing. I was in the chorus at [my old school]. I was in my church choir. I had come to [my new high school] so I could also do musicals and stuff. . . . [Now] just the idea of crowds . . . just standing up there by myself—I don't sing anymore. I dropped chorus as a class. . . . I can't do it, I can't get myself to do it. Which is such a bummer, because it was, like, a big part of my life—I love to sing! . . . But then after . . . the anxiety attack, I just couldn't. I just couldn't do it anymore.

Nicola's struggles with empathy remind me of Susie, a fourteen-year-old group-home resident whom I'd met in one of our summer programs. At first glance, you couldn't imagine two girls who were more different. Unlike friendly, open Nicola, Susie appeared perpetually tough and self-possessed, with her swaggering step and her threatening demeanor. She stared out at the world through heavily made-up eyes as if daring you to cross her. Even some of the adults at the home were a bit unnerved.

Then one night, Susie had an after-hours guest, a nineteen-year-old boy who'd paid a lot of attention to her at an outing the week before. Susie let him in and stayed up chatting with him in the living room. They started making out, the boy got aroused, and suddenly Susie was having intercourse for the first time. According to the counselor who described it to me, Susie had basically been raped—but she hadn't resisted. Although the event had occurred in the midst of a crowded house with three adult counselors in residence, Susie had chosen to comply with the boy's wishes rather than assert her own. She sobbed through several counseling sessions, but then, a few weeks later, the boy paid another visit and the same thing happened. Longing desperately to please someone—anyone—Susie seemed to have lost all capacity to say no.

To those of us from less distressed situations, Susie seems like an extreme example. But I see her on a continuum with Nicola, the prep school girl. Feeling alone in the world, Susie had learned to take care of herself in street fights, while Nicola had a warm, supportive family she could count on. Yet both girls were nearly undone by their sensitivity to other people's feelings. What has so grievously disempowered these young women?

In my view, it's a combination of misplaced empathy and the Triple Bind. Needing to please like a girl, to succeed like a boy, and to make it all seem effortless (in Nicola's case) or to be perpetually hot and sexually available (in Susie's case) created panic and depression for Nicola and tragedy for Susie. Both girls struggled with problems they didn't know how to name and demands they couldn't talk about. Both girls blamed not their circumstances but themselves. Both girls deserve better.

So let's take a closer look at the plethora of research linking empathy to depression. This research provides valuable insight into the destructive power of the Triple Bind.

EMPATHY AND RISK FACTORS

As we've seen, depression is associated with genes that make some people more vulnerable to this condition. (For a fuller explanation of depression and genetics, see Chapter 2.)[5] For some medical conditions, genetic predisposition is pretty much the end of the story. If you're born with the genetic coding for sickle-cell anemia, for example, you'll get sickle-cell anemia, no matter what life circumstances you experience.

But behavioral and emotional conditions don't work that way, especially depression. Being born with certain genes isn't enough: life circumstances must trigger those genes in order to produce depression. (The genes are actually for *vulnerability* to depression, not for depression per se.) The technical name for those triggering life circumstances is *risk factors*: factors that put a genetically vulnerable person at risk.[6]

As we saw in Chapter 2, men and women are equally likely to have the "vulnerability" genes for depression. Although in women, the heritability of depression seems slightly higher—that is, genes appear to have slightly more influence relative to other factors than among men—basically, men and women have roughly equal genetic vulnerability to depression.

Yet the two genders do not go on to experience roughly similar incidences of depression throughout their lives. Instead, women are twice as likely to become depressed once adolescence hits. Therefore we must conclude that the higher rates of female depression are the product of either a greater number of risk factors that girls experience or their tendency to interpret negative life events in ways that make depression more likely to emerge—or both.[7] And one of the strongest risk factors turns out to be empathy, the tendency to understand others' feelings (cognitive empathy) and to experience such feelings as though they were your own (emotional empathy).

In a 2005 article, psychologists Kate Keenan and Alison E. Hipwell reviewed the research on girls and depression, concluding that girls' tendency toward emotional empathy and excessive compliance (doing what others want, even at the expense of your own needs) are key risk factors for female depression. For girls, it seems, taking on the pain of others and thereby denying their own needs may work for a while during childhood. But when adolescence emerges—the time to form an identity and become an individual—girls' excessive focus on others' needs and feelings can become truly problematic.[8]

Empathy and self-denial are especially likely to trigger worry and depression if a girl is distressed for other reasons: for example, if she has a depressed mother or other caregiver, or if there is excessive family conflict. A girl who identifies with a troubled mother may feel that she's not entitled to happiness, or that being happy would somehow constitute a betrayal of her mother. (You can find a moving portrait of this pattern in Mona Simpson's novel *Anywhere but Here* and in the film of the same name that was based on the book.)[9]

If an empathic girl identifies with her depressed mother, she may also conclude that being a "true woman" *means* being depressed. Even if a young woman understands consciously that she is a different person from her mother, empathy may undermine her ability to feel happy when her mother is sad.[10]

In this regard, boys tend to have an advantage. A boy with a depressed mother or a troubled family may be upset at his inability to make Mom happy or disturbed by the arguing and fighting. But he is probably better equipped to understand the distinction between his feelings and his mother's (or those of any of the adults who might care for him). A boy is also far more likely to become noncompliant: to refuse to go along with what adults want. In this case, that's a productive choice that will support the development of his new adult identity.

True, a boy with a depressed parent may be frustrated or discouraged by Mom's depression. He may even feel like a failure because he *can't* help her—feelings that bring their own grievous life consequences. Whatever other problems he struggles with, though, the average boy won't necessarily feel his mother's depression as his own, at least not as strongly as a girl will tend to. Even if he experiences cognitive empathy (understanding what his mother feels), he is far less likely than a girl to succumb to excessive emotional empathy—having to feel precisely what she feels, thereby bringing him down with her.

An empathic girl such as Nicola, by contrast, tends to feel *everybody*'s feelings as her own. This can be a valuable asset if the girl can also set boundaries. Then she could use empathy to understand others but at the crucial moment would be able to say, "Her sadness is ultimately *her* problem, not mine." This is the kind of empathy we ask of clinicians and therapists, who understand their patients' feelings—and who also feel with them, to a great extent—but who must nonetheless avoid becoming overwhelmed by their patients' problems.

Yet as any good therapist will tell you, empathic sorrow is not always so easy to resist. When you care about someone, you want them to be happy, and this feeling is multiplied a thousandfold when it comes to an unhappy parent, whose misery can be frightening as well as sad to a helpless or dependent young child. If your way of caring about someone is to feel what they feel—to empathize, to identify—you have far fewer defenses against that person's misery. And if you're also born with a genetic vulnerability to depression, you're that much more likely to become depressed yourself.

Although little research has been done into the role of friends in girls' depression, I think a similar dynamic applies. Highly empathic girls often feel for their peers or even for strangers as well as for their parents. Girls in distressed lower-income communities, like Susie, or in high-stress middle-income communities, like Nicola, may well pick up on the anxiety and depression of those around them and have difficulty shrugging those feelings off.[11]

A poignant example of this kind of empathy was expressed by singer/songwriter Alicia Keys, who revealed in a November 2007 *Ebony* article that she had a nervous breakdown (sounding a lot like a major depression) after her initial success. "My nature is to make sure everybody is well taken care of and happy," the article quotes her as saying. "For the past five years, I don't know when I ever said no, to the point where I became so dependable for people that they took advantage of it."[12] As a result, Keys says, she became moody, depressed, and unable to sleep. Yet she denied even to her closest friends that she was having difficulty, continuing to maintain the image of herself as a strong, nurturing caretaker (and world-famous pop star).

The crisis came to a head when a relative became sick. Keys cared for the relative, taking one day a week from her busy schedule to visit, and then collapsed when her loved one died. "For the first couple of weeks, I was wracked with grief and with guilt," Keys says.

Keys' mention of guilt is significant. According to Carolyn Zahn-Waxler, a pioneer in this field, empathic people are often laid low by their awareness of having potentially been responsible for another person's distress: the feeling of guilt. Not only does the sensitive girl feel another's unhappiness as her own, she also feels guilty for having caused that unhappiness in the first place.[13] Rightly or wrongly, an empathic girl may conclude that she is causing her already unhappy mother additional distress. "If only I weren't so much trouble," the girl might think. "If only I could make less work for Mom." Or "If only I behaved better, Mom wouldn't worry so much." Or "If only I were a more lovable person, perhaps Mom would feel happier when I tell her that I love her."

Likewise, a girl with a lot of emotional empathy might feel similar guilt toward a sibling, friend, or even a stranger. "When I got the chance to go to a better high school, I know so-and-so felt envious and sad. That's *my* fault. *I* caused that."

Again, this type of guilt is particularly deadly given the new circumstances of the Triple Bind, which require girls to compete as well as to empathize. Such guilt is a recurring theme on *America's Next Top Model*, for instance, which may be another reason teenage girls like the show so much: contestants are always having to choose between loyalties to their friends and their own longing to win. Adding insult to injury, Tyra Banks and the other judges often scold the girls in both directions, urging them to be competitive and self-focused on the one hand and inviting them to partake of "sisterhood" and cooperation on the other.

Every season, you can identify the girls who feel no empathy, who have no compunction whatsoever about pushing others out of the way in their relentless quest to be on top. You can also see girls laid low by their conflicting emotions: "My best friend just got eliminated, and since I'm still in the running, at least part of her loss is *my* fault." The winning girl wasn't able to save her friend—worse, she beat her out. If the winner empathizes with the loser's feelings of sadness, the loser will drag her down, too. But if the winner *doesn't* empathize, *doesn't* mourn the loss of her friend, what kind of a woman is she?

I've often been struck by the way a teenage girl will talk about her friends' problems as though they were her own. When I ask thirteen-year-old Madison, for example, how she's doing, she launches into accounts of the girls she knows: "Well, I'm kind of worried about Camille right now. She's pretty depressed because her folks are getting a divorce. It's especially hard for Camille because she's the kind of person who worries that everything is her own fault, you know? I try to talk her out of it, but she won't really listen. I'm also concerned about Diana, because she's on this crazy diet and I think it's making her way too tired. She thinks she's so fat—but she's *not* fat! Well, maybe a little overweight, but she should *not* be starving herself like that! Now, Vera is doing great. She's got this new boyfriend and I think he's really good for her. . . ."

Madison's insight, sensitivity, and generous nature can't be denied. But with all that talk of her friends' feelings—and, at a deeper level, overconcern with those feelings—where is the room for her own emotions? The main news that's coming into her head and heart are the ups and downs of Camille, Diana, and Vera, not the needs of Madison, whatever they may be. Consequently, if Camille, Diana, and Vera are unhappy, Madison may feel as though it's *her* failure, or at least her responsibility to make them better. If she's got a preexisting vulnerability to depression, or if she's facing many difficulties and losses in her life, she may well become depressed. Even if she's at genetically low risk for clinical depression, she may become distressed, feeling—again like Seligman's dogs—unable to affect her world. She's confused her friends' problems with her own, and either depression or a kind of learned helplessness may be the result.

THE INDIVIDUAL GIRL

A lot of the research on child development focuses on *individuation*: the process of becoming a unique individual, which is one of the key tasks of adolescence. Traditionally, boys have been seen as having more of the skills that lead to individuation: assertiveness, self-confidence, expressiveness, and commitment to one's own agenda. You can easily picture a little boy growing into himself by means of these skills: "I want orange juice, I *don't like* apple juice!" "I'm going to climb to the top of the jungle gym. I wonder if I'm strong enough to do it? I bet I am!" "Dad, I want you to take me to the amusement park, and I want to ride on the Ferris wheel; *please*, can we do that?" The boy who develops successfully learns what he likes and what he's capable of—who he *is*—by asserting himself, trying things out, expressing his preferences. By the time he's an adolescent, those skills come in mighty handy.

Traditionally, girls have been seen as more compliant, less interested in discovering and expressing their own agendas than in divining and agreeing to the wishes of adults. "What would *you* like to do today, Mommy?" "I'm a good sharer, I'll give the bigger piece to you!" "I'd like to climb up to the treehouse. Is that okay with you, Dad?" We don't yet know to what extent these differences are inborn or socialized, but certainly girls are more often rewarded for putting others' needs first, while boys are more often rewarded for asserting themselves.[14]

As girls grow up, then, they tend to have a vexed relationship with individuation skills. They may never have developed these skills, either because of their own temperament or because their families have discouraged them from doing so. ("A *good* girl asks permission!" "A good girl waits to see what *other* people might like to do!") Possibly, they have developed these skills but feel guilty or anxious about putting them to use. ("*I* know what I want, but Mom will be mad at me if I blurt it out.") Or perhaps they do use these skills but then feel excessively guilty about doing so. ("Maybe I shouldn't have spoken up so quickly. I mean, yes, I'm getting my way—but what if Dad is really upset about it?")[15]

What if individuation doesn't happen the way it should? One result is a person who perpetually tries to please others while always remaining dependent on caregivers. Also, although the term is imprecise, some psychologists believe that children who don't individuate properly create a kind of "false self": the person they think everyone wants to see. This false self is often based on an image of being good, not rocking the boat, and by definition it's at odds with the true self, which is undoubtedly not "all good" or always compliant. The conflict between the false and true selves may create the conditions for depression—a kind of vulnerability, if you will. As you can see, because girls are under greater pressure to hide their true selves, they are at far greater risk of depression—and indeed, the numbers bear this out.[16]

Certainly, in this paradigm, the Triple Bind greatly intensifies the risk. First, girls are put into an untenable situation, in which they are both encouraged to individuate and punished when they do so. ("Try your best to get to the top, but only a mean girl doesn't care about other people's feelings!") Then, in today's culture, any possible alternative identity—punk rocker, intellectual, activist, artist—doesn't let the girl off the hook from being pretty, hot, and thin; having the perfect boyfriend (or girlfriend); and striving for conventional success and mainstream achievement. That false self—the thin, pretty, successful self that nearly every role model seems to have, seemingly without sweat or effort—must always be maintained, no matter what other aspects of your self you are pursuing.

"I guess I have to look this way," the empathic, people-pleasing girl decides. "It feels empty, but it's the only way to be popular. I don't know if it's worth it to be on the soccer team: I like playing, but I don't really care so much about winning. But my coach says that only losers don't 'go the extra mile,' and I'd like to please my coach. My mom is having a hard time these days, and so is my friend Hannah. How can I be happy when they're so miserable?"

Indeed, the statements of real teenage girls echo these conflicts. Jessica, whom we met in Chapter 1, gave up tennis when she found it too competitive:

> I think it is kind of ridiculous, 'cause you can't have fun anymore—like, you can't play a sport to enjoy it. The only reason I ever played tennis was because I . . . like being active and I think [sports] are a healthy thing. Other than that, I like socializing—you know, being with my friend and making new friends . . . on the team. . . . When my coaches would be like, "You have to win . . . you have to do all these tournaments, you have to do weight training, and you have to work all summer on it," I was like, *no*!

Nicola had a similar experience with the pressure she felt playing basketball. Instead of being a pleasurable way to use her body and develop her strength, the sport became a competitive endeavor that she just wasn't comfortable with:

> I got [only] a two-week break the entire year from basketball—that's just a lot. We were traveling, we were going down to San Diego, down to L.A. to play, and like,

> with that, it was more like stressful than fun. And, yeah, the tournaments are awesome and they're fun, but when it comes back to playing in league, it's just so serious. . . . I think at the end of it, I was so sick of basketball that I didn't even want to play it. And my mentality is, "I am not good enough to play in college, so what's the point in playing in high school, it's not like I am going anywhere." I pretty much gave up on something that used to be the most important thing in my life—because I lost it.

The three conflicting demands of the Triple Bind put the empathic girl in a particularly difficult position. At best, she'll feel distressed. At worst, she'll collapse with debilitating panic, as Nicola did, or succumb to the bingeing, self-mutilation, violent behavior, depression, or suicide attempts that have created today's crisis.[17]

THE DANGERS OF RUMINATION

Another risk factor for depression is girls' tendency to ruminate: to chew over an incident or a feeling again and again in their minds, looking for a satisfying way to process it. Ironically, as with empathy, the tendency to ruminate is actually an outgrowth of girls' initial strengths.[18]

For example, girls tend to mature earlier in their use of language. During the preschool years, boys tend to be impulsive and active, whereas girls learn to "use their words" to regulate their own behavior better than their male counterparts. A boy simply climbs up onto the counter to get the candy jar; a girl is more likely to say to herself, "I *really* wish I could have that candy, but Mommy will be mad if I go up there, and besides, I might hurt myself." According to pioneering Russian psychologist Lev Vygotsky, the internalization of language—silently letting yourself know what to do and what not to do—is a key step toward self-regulation. And girls develop such language skills earlier than do boys.[19]

Likewise, starting in the preschool years, girls tend to play in smaller and more intimate groups in which they use language to work out conflicts and deepen relationships. As anyone who's ever observed girls knows, this can lead to some fairly high-level negotiating. ("What if *I'm* the princess right now and wear the fancy dress, but *you* get to wear the crown and be the queen . . . and then in ten minutes, we trade?") Boys, by contrast, tend to have more fleeting social contacts, cover a wider geographical area, and use language not to relate but rather to dominate. ("If you don't give me that ball right now, I'm going to make you wish you had!")[20] Again, girls' ability to work things out through language has long been considered an asset.

Finally, as we've seen, girls often display a greater tendency to emotionally empathize with others. For example, when children as young as four are shown a victim in distress, a girl's heart rate decelerates more quickly than a boy's: a biological indication that the girl is paying more attention to the distressed person. This awareness of others is yet again considered a sign of maturity.[21]

So language skills, relationship patterns, and empathy conspire to make girls more "prosocial": more sensitive to others' feelings and more committed to working out conflicts. Traditionally, these have been viewed as girls' strengths, especially in contrast to "antisocial" boys, whose lack of empathy can predict delinquency and juvenile violence.

It turns out, though, that the problems run both ways. True, boys lacking in empathy may become antisocial, but girls oversupplied with empathy may become depressed. That very ability to use language can turn into rumination: going over and over and over a disturbing incident, rehearing hurtful words, or mentally rehearsing a painful argument. The girl who can't let go of her pain may become overwhelmed with it.[22]

Likewise, the girl who's spent her childhood developing relationships in those small groups may become devastated by conflicts with girlfriends. Because she's developed greater intimacy with others, she's also made herself more vulnerable, a vulnerability that may be further magnified by a tendency to ruminate. "That thing Emma said to me—it really hurt my feelings! What do you think she meant? Did I say something to make her speak that way? I remember exactly what I said: 'Don't worry about the test!' How could she get upset about that? Did she think I was being sarcastic?" The longer the girl chews over the relationship, the conversation, and her own hurt feelings, the worse she feels—one form of the problem known as "impaired emotion regulation" or "inability to self-soothe." Add high levels of emotional empathy and excessive compliance into the picture—the confusion between her friend's feelings and her own and the need to avoid overt conflict—and the verbal, sensitive, ruminating girl is potentially at risk for depression, as well as eating disorders and suicidal thoughts.[23]

As you might imagine, the Triple Bind magnifies this risk yet again. These days, a girl who is trying to please the adults in her life is expected to be nice to her friends *and* to compete with them. Wanting, even needing to please and perhaps even to comfort the adults who care for her, she may feel overwhelmed with distress at not being able to fulfill two conflicting expectations: being nice like a girl while winning like a boy. The third aspect of the Triple Bind ups the ante: the girl must please both adults and peers by sustaining a perpetually thin, pretty, and sexy persona (sexy, but not slutty), and she must conform to an ever-narrower set of mainstream values, leaving her even less room to discover who *she* is and what *she* wants. As we've seen, distress is one possible outcome; bingeing, self-mutilation, violence, depression, and suicide are others, especially for girls with other vulnerabilities and risk factors.

THE MASK OF CHEER

Blaine was a bubbly, enthusiastic fourteen-year-old who lived in suburban Charleston with her single mother. Blaine's mother worked long hours as an emergency room nurse, and while she loved her job, she also struggled with the grueling work and the tendency to burn out with which every hospital nurse contends.

As a two-person family, Blaine and her mom had become quite close, with Blaine often referring to her mother as "her best friend." Blaine's mom's long work hours made time with her seem like a special prize to Blaine, who took on as many household duties as she could in order to spare her mom any extra chores. Blaine was a good student with an A- average, an enthusiastic soccer player, a talented musician (she played clarinet in the school band and was taking jazz lessons), and a popular girl with several "best friends." As far as Blaine's mom could see, Blaine was the perfect daughter: cheerful, loving, productive, happy.

Blaine's mother had struggled with depression twice before, just after Blaine was born, and in the year after Blaine's dad died. Now, in Blaine's fourteenth year, Blaine's mother suffered from another episode, perhaps brought on by perimenopausal changes. Although she managed to keep her job, she felt increasingly listless and exhausted. Many of her off hours she spent sleeping, so even more of the household responsibilities fell on Blaine.

To all appearances, Blaine came through like a trouper. On her mother's day off, she served Mom breakfast in bed. She redoubled her efforts to keep the house clean. She even did extra loads of laundry so her mother would have fresh uniforms for work. All this while she kept her grades up, stayed on the soccer team, and excelled at her music. She seemed happy, cheerful, and energetic throughout, the same bubbly girl she'd always been.

Then one day, Blaine's homeroom teacher noticed that the fashion-conscious girl was wearing long-sleeved sweaters, even though all her classmates favored short sleeves. The teacher took Blaine aside and asked her to roll up her sleeves. When Blaine reluctantly complied, the teacher saw the nicks, scars, and freshly formed scabs, evidence that Blaine had been cutting herself.

Luckily, both mother and daughter were able to get the counseling they needed. But I heard in Blaine's story the tragic echoes of so many girls, whose self-mutilation, depressed thoughts, and suicidal wishes are hidden under a mask of cheer. Blaine was the prototypical "parentified child," the girl whose main goal in life was to make her mother feel better.[24] If cheer and hard work would do the trick, Blaine was willing. But her price for compliance (and empathy for her mom) was a kind of terrifying numbness as Blaine shut off her anger, her sorrow, and her fear. Feeling that her mother's depression was taking up all the available emotional space, Blaine did everything she could to suppress her own feelings. Then she felt compelled to cut herself until she bled—just so she could feel *something*. Unable or unwilling to use her voice, Blaine acted out her feelings through her body.[25]

When the counselor asked Blaine why she felt so bad, Blaine's voice dropped to barely a whisper. "I just think it would be easier on Mom if she didn't have to take care of me," she said. "She has so many other things to worry about. She doesn't need me, too."

Psychologists and psychiatrists might say that Blaine showed *alexithymia*, a psychological term referring to the inability to express one's feelings, and often used to describe girls who mutilate themselves or those with extreme suicidal urges.[26] In a sense, alexithymia is the opposite of rumination. The alexithymic girl feels numb or has no idea how she feels, while the ruminator chews over her loneliness, her sorrow, or her anger, again and again and again.

I wonder, though, if the two conditions are not two sides of the same coin, each made worse by the power of the Triple Bind. Girls who are put in impossible situations—required to meet contradictory expectations or asked to care for people whom they don't really have the power to help—may respond either by "numbing out" or by ruminating. But in both cases, like the animals in *Wicked*, they have already gotten the message that nobody's listening. What's the point of articulating feelings when they won't be heard? And how *can* a girl articulate her critique of the society that asks her to do two contradictory things at the same time, all while looking pretty, hot, and thin, all while being discouraged from questioning the values of her society or the expectations of her culture?

Consider the mixed messages we explored in the previous chapter, in which popular TV shows both support girls' aspirations and suppress them. Consider how hard it would be for a teenager to express her sense of confusion, anger, and helplessness in the face of such subtle, destructive messages. Psychiatric diagnoses are by definition specific to a particular individual with a unique life history and a personal set of responses. But when so many girls are cutting themselves and considering suicide, when so many girls are showing alexithymic tendencies, I have to believe there's a larger problem at stake. The Triple Bind puts our girls into an impossible position, about which it's virtually impossible to speak. As a clinician and scientist, I have struggled for years to articulate these issues and find their expression in today's pop culture; how could a teenage girl be expected to find the words?

Moreover, girl culture provides a particularly difficult challenge in the context of the Triple Bind. Girls have been taught to focus on their feelings; that's supposed to be one of their strengths. But if you can't *do* anything about your feelings—if you can't change the circumstances that are creating your anger, sorrow, or fear—then what good does it do you to know what they are? In this regard, the traditional boy, who charges across the football field oblivious to the pain he causes and the pain he feels, is far better off than the typical girl, swamped by her knowledge that everyone is suffering.

So in today's Triple Bind culture, girls face three overlapping problems. First, they're encouraged to ruminate—to get in touch with their feelings and put them into words. This may in itself constitute a risk factor for depression if a girl can't get past the feelings but instead gets stuck in them.

Second, the ruminating girl is expected to perform like a boy. But the whole reason boys *can* perform as they traditionally have is because they're trained to suppress or ignore any feelings that interfere with peak performance. Athletes and soldiers are only the most dramatic example of this; boys are routinely told to "suck it up and be a man" when it comes to any type of achievement. Girls who are expected to perform like a man but feel like a woman are truly being set up for depression, if not worse.

Third, girls are taught to ruminate, asked to perform, and then encouraged to believe that it's their own fault if they can't do both—and do both effortlessly. At best, they're given spurious solutions: shopping, dieting, and other forms of self-improvement. At worst, they're simply blamed for not working hard enough, for not expressing themselves clearly, for not "sucking it up" as the boys have always done. In some cases, the rumination and worry may shut down altogether, leading to alexithymia, numbness, and confusion.

Alicia Keys came through her crisis and wrote a gospel-inflected song about it: "Superwoman." The music aches with the pain she feels, but the lyrics maintain against all odds that she is a superwoman, as are all the women out there. No matter how discouraged or beaten down they feel, Keys sings, she and her sisters can fly, they can get home before dark, they're wearing a secret S beneath their street clothes: they are superwomen.

Teenage girls posting comments on the YouTube website get the message. One of them writes that she sang the song at her high school assembly and everybody cried—even one of the teachers. Another writes poignantly that her mother is a superwoman.

Keys summed up the song for *Ebony*'s readers. "A Superwoman," she explains, "is a woman who has incredible dreams, incredible ambitions, all the things she wants to do, but she also knows how to take care of herself."[27] Perhaps, in today's Triple Bind culture, a girl (or woman) who takes care of herself actually does need superpowers. As Blaine, Susie, Nicola, and Alicia Keys would attest, she certainly faces superobstacles.

CHAPTER 6

Bratz Dolls and Pussycat Dolls

Teaching Our Girls to Become Sexual Objects

The girls are being taken out to what they believe is a pleasant celebratory dinner. But when they arrive at the chic L.A. eatery, they discover that their hosts have a hidden agenda. The girls are to dress in fishnet stockings, garter belts, microscopic halter tops, and minuscule leather skirts and to perform an improvised "dance" solo inside a lighted box while patrons clap and cheer. This, they are told, will be the perfect test of their "confidence."

That's a scene from the spring 2007 reality series *Pussycat Dolls Present: The Search for the Next Doll*, which chronicles the top-selling pop group's efforts to find a new member. In typical reality-show fashion, the contestants are put through their paces—in this case, performing new song-and-dance routines—while one young woman is eliminated each week.[1]

The Pussycat Dolls are known for their provocative blend of innocence and raunch. Young women who seem fresh and untouched enough to appeal to the middle-school market dress like prostitutes and engage in athletic, near-pornographic dance routines that combine the vigor of an aerobics studio with the explicit gestures of a strip club. The Dolls were cited in a widely publicized 2007 research review by the American Psychological Association as one of the problematic purveyors of the new preteen sexuality, so their prostitute-cum-stripper aesthetic shouldn't come as a surprise.[2]

What *is* surprising is the way this fairly conventional version of sexual self-objectification is continually presented as the epitome of self-confidence, empowerment, and individuality. The girls are told repeatedly to "find your own voice," "express yourself," and "claim your inner power," even as they're also instructed to embody the group's hypersexual style and keep their weight down. "Sing loud, sing proud, and do everything from your heart," says Pussycat lead singer Nicole Scherzinger, while the choreographer comments snippily that one *overly* sexual contestant (a former go-go girl) dances "like a little Stripperella."

As with other aspects of the Triple Bind, the girls are given impossible, conflicting messages: *Be sexy—but not too sexy. Claim your own style—but match the group's aesthetic. Be proud and empowered—but don't talk back to the choreographer. Turning yourself into a sex object is empowering, while fitting a generic image of "sexy" will help you express your unique self. And if you want to enjoy your own sexuality, the one aspect of your life that ought to be full of pleasure and free of effort, work hard—harder than you've ever worked before.*

As on *America's Next Top Model*, some of this advice might indeed be useful for anyone planning to become a professional performer (for a fuller discussion of *Top Model*, see Chapter 1). But speaking as a psychologist who works with young people, I'm disturbed by the program's insistence that these crazy-making messages are actually good for you.

I'm not the only one to notice the contradiction. Commenting on that nightclub scene, the *Variety* reviewer wrote, "The young women initially balk when asked to do a stripper-like routine at a nightclub, as if bouncing around in lingerie is appreciably different from the attire they sport the rest of the hour. Adding to the hypocrisy, [Pussycat Doll creator and show producer Robin] Antin seeks to justify the exercise as a self-confidence test rather than what it is—lad-mag fare for those too cheap to buy *Maxim*."[3] The empowerment message isn't just Antin's fantasy, however. The pop culture magazine *Radar* asked one hundred teen concert-goers to say who had done more to empower women, the Dolls or Secretary of State Condoleezza Rice. Two-thirds of the girls chose the Dolls.[4]

How are young girls responding to this version of female empowerment? Well, some of them are trying to imitate it. Randi, for example, the free-spirited sixteen-year-old we met in the Introduction, goes to parties every weekend with her girlfriends at the houses of various friends. There's always a lot to drink, and everyone gets drunk—"a little drunk, very drunk, or super-drunk," in Randi's words—as quickly as possible.

At first, there's dancing, which Randi describes as a kind of making out set to music:

> It is sort of like you hook your leg in someone else's either from the front or behind, and then you just sort of grind to a beat if you're good. If not, you don't even worry about rhythm, and you just grind.

Then, Randi explains, you find someone to hook up with. Randi catalogues the different levels of sexual experience among her girlfriends: Two have had actual intercourse, "but they're the ones with steady boyfriends and they only do it with them." Two more don't have boyfriends but instead hook up with different guys each week, in sexual activity that stops short of intercourse but that often includes giving the guys blow jobs "so the girls are still virgins, which is very important to them." Randi and two of her other friends kiss and make out with guys, but they haven't yet gone further than that. One friend, Randi tells me, has been hooking up with the same guy every week for a few months, "but they're not, like, together or anything. They just hook up a lot." Another girl has a "friend with benefits": "They don't want to be together, but she gives him a blow job when they hook up."

I try to find out whether the girls are enjoying these sexual encounters. It's striking, for example, that the girls give blow jobs but the guys don't seem to reciprocate in kind. Randi looks at me blankly, though, and I almost have the feeling that she doesn't understand the question. None of the young women have had orgasms, she tells me, but of *course* they're having a good time: they're partying!

As I try to get a better sense of what the girls' experiences are like, Randi seems more and more puzzled. It's almost as though I were asking her whether she enjoyed any of the individual drinks she had at each party. It's fun to drink, it's fun to get drunk, it's fun to hook up—or if it isn't, if there are also hangovers and vomiting, or dizziness and nausea, or a sense of, well, boredom, so what? Hooking up is what you do.

As Randi speaks, I hear the same affectless tone that surrounds the sexual encounters described in the Gossip Girl, It Girl, and A-List book series (see Chapter 4): life is boring, and sex usually is, too, but what else is there? Although sometimes the girls in those books feel romantic passion or sexual pleasure, far more often they're just marking time. Here's one of many such passages from the Gossip Girl series:

> Blair just wanted to get it over with quickly, but Miles wanted to take his time, going over every inch of her body in a way that seemed almost clinical, like he was a dermatologist checking her skin for eczema or melanoma or something. She tried to relax and enjoy the feeling of Miles licking her instep, but they were both completely naked and she couldn't help thinking that if Miles had been Nate, they would have done it by now.[5]

I wish I could expect better experiences for Randi and her friends as they get older. But a June 2006 *Rolling Stone* article about Duke University suggests that college coeds at the nation's fifth most competitive school are equally likely to view sex as relatively joyless and impersonal, something that's part of frantic, drunken social activity rather than a source of pleasure, intimacy, or fulfillment.[6]

According to the article, girls consider it an honor to be invited to "help out" at fraternity pledge parties. Upperclassmen lead the freshmen pledges into the party room, dressed only in their boxers. Then the girls straddle the boys, calling them "babies" and making them suck on pacifiers and baby bottles full of alcohol. The girls then pour chocolate syrup and smear whipped cream on one another and make the boys lick it off. One senior fraternity man commented, "The girls are doing it as a friendship gesture for these guys, but when you think of it, it's really kind of demeaning."

Friendship? Demeaning? The real question is, are the young women having fun? If they're not—if they're only interested in pleasuring the men—then something is very, very wrong.

THE PRICE OF BEING A SEX OBJECT

I'll admit it: I've led with the most shocking stories I know because despite coming of age in the era of "free love," I am, frankly, shocked. Because I don't consider myself a prude and because I realize that teenagers are going to have sex whether the older generation likes it or not, I've had to ask myself why I'm reacting so strongly to this newest version of youth culture. After all, there *is* something empowering in a woman being able to express her sexual feelings. I'd love to think that the Doll imitators, the Gossip Girl readers, and the Duke girls think of themselves as sexy and desirable, feel empowered to ask for the kinds of sexual attention they want, and are confident about their sexual relationships in general.

But that's not what's happening at all. Instead, girls are being asked to *act* sexy while losing access to sexual pleasure and learning to despise their own bodies.[7]

The *Pussycat Dolls* program lays bare the contradiction. Each episode culminates in a highly sexualized performance from the contestants, but the prelude is scene after scene of girls worrying about their weight, their looks, their breasts. "Put on the fake boobs!" snaps the choreographer at one of the final contestants. He explains to the camera, "I know if *I* was a woman, having more up there would make *me* feel more womanly."

Or consider the episodes that center on tall, statuesque Anastasia, whom Geffen Records president and contest judge Ron Fair described as having a gorgeous, Greek-goddess body. But Anastasia worries about "stress eating," and sure enough, she has a hard time fitting into the costume they've chosen for the contestants' Vegas debut.

Yes, if you look closely, Anastasia's belly is not perfectly flat, and unlike her petite competitors, she's tall and full-figured to begin with. In fact, she's got a body similar to the Amazonian ex-supermodel Rebecca Romijn's: big breasts, an hourglass figure, long dancer's legs. But cultural standards have changed since the supermodel era, and Anastasia's body is now out of fashion. So instead of being encouraged to celebrate her stunning looks, Anastasia was pushed to feel shame for them. Instead of understanding herself as a sexual being, experiencing her own passions and desires, Anastasia was encouraged to judge herself through others' eyes. Rather than making her feel more sexual or more in control of her sexuality, the Dolls' "sexy" performances ultimately made Anastasia feel sexually inadequate and completely subject to the men who criticized her. To my mind, she and every other female viewer were being taught the opposite of sexuality and the opposite of forming a healthy identity: not to experience your feelings from the inside out, but to view your body from the outside in. In other words, she was being taught to objectify herself.

Certainly, young women's confusion of love, attraction, and empowerment is at least as old as the novels of Jane Austen, while the blurred boundaries between "sexual empowerment" and "becoming a sex object" go back two decades or more to Madonna's "Blonde Ambition." But because the new sexual look is even more explicit and because the talk of empowerment is so much louder and more pervasive, I think the confusion has reached a whole new level. How do you discover your own sexual feelings—a discovery that may well be empowering—in a culture that defines *sexy* by how closely you match a preconceived look and set of moves? How do you distinguish between having sexual feelings and being perpetually available, like the Duke girls, who let boys they've never met (let alone become attracted to) use their bodies in sexual, demeaning ways? How do you discover what makes *you* happy, what satisfies *your* needs, in such a confusing culture, when you have come to evaluate yourself primarily by the sense that you must have a particular "look"? And how do you decide how to express your own sexuality, in your own way, in your own time, when you've been exposed to girls as young as five, seven, and nine wearing thongs or boas, dressing up as older women for lingerie fashion shows, and consuming a whole set of "tween" beauty products?[8]

SEX AND THE SINGLE FOURTH GRADER

The young women I spoke with have many different values, sexual styles, and sexual histories. But in their own way, each of them echoes the sentiments of sixteen-year-old Lupe from Chapter 1: the expectations are impossible, and we don't even know what they are. It is the contradictory nature of today's sexual messages that makes them so confusing—and so disabling, particularly in the context of the Triple Bind.

As you'll recall, the Triple Bind calls upon young women to be sensitive and relationship-oriented like traditional girls, and to be competitive and achievement-oriented like traditional guys. But it also requires them to be perpetually pretty, thin, and hot; to succeed in the traditional female domain of wife and motherhood, and to accept the values of mainstream society, a set of requirements that doesn't always sit so easily with the other two. How does a sensitive, empathic girl learn to focus on her own sexual pleasure rather than on giving a guy what he wants, especially if she's supposed to be a "hottie"? How does an ambitious girl keep her grades up while staying pretty, thin, and sexy enough to please several guys or while being warm and loving enough to nurture a boyfriend? Can a girl present herself as a hot, sexy object *and* involve herself in an intimate, loving relationship? Can she be smart, empowered, competitive—*and* attract a guy? Can she reconcile her own fears, anxieties, and uncertainties with her hot image (which, remember, must be presented as effortless), or reconcile her own wish for sexual pleasure with the needs of a boy she loves? And, in a world that has so narrowed the conversation about values and definitions of success, how can she discover whether she truly wants marriage or a family or even a long-term relationship? How can she decide what sex means to her or think about what she wants it to mean?

"I wish I had in my head . . . what the system is for us," says Anya, the French major at a small, liberal arts women's college in Pennsylvania, whom we met in Chapter 3. "But I think that is part of the problem: . . . there are so many contradictory things coming at us." When I encourage Anya to name the contradictions, the words come spilling out. "I could just say random things that I've noticed," she offers.

> Kids who can't read or write because they are so young know all the words to really vulgar and demeaning songs. I hear them saying these things and they have no idea what they're saying. . . . But they know all the words and it's the most popular music right now. So, it comes at them from that level because that is the only music that they play at little kid dances and stuff. That's what they dance to. . . .
>
> Then, clothing. Clothes get tighter and tighter . . . right now the fad is just wearing skin-tight tights and then a shirt over it. Even little girls wear things that have words written on the butt, so that's where you focus. The new girl dolls that are really popular are called Bratz, and the . . . seven-year-olds and even four-year-olds want them, and they are these heavily made-up dolls. They've got these belly-button shirts and really skimpy shorts. . . .
>
> And then . . . once you get past the dolls and such . . . you get into high school, where there are girls who were labeled as, like, "easy" and nasty and stuff, but it was [both] a mark of pride and an insult. Like girls would jokingly say, "Oh,

> you're such a slut." But it's not like—it's a bad thing, but it's a good thing *because* it's a bad thing. I barely know how to articulate it because I'm too close to it.

When Anya was sixteen, she dated an eighteen-year-old guy, who, she says, was very much willing to go along with her request that they not have sex until she was eighteen. Other girls, she says, made different choices.

> One of the things that bugs me about it is I see boys expecting [sex] and I see girls using it to gain power. And I think it's—I just don't think it's a very good way to wield power. It makes me pretty uncomfortable when I see that happening. And the problem is, girls might have power then, but they lose respect, so it's just a humongous mess, so, like, I don't even know how it works. I really wish I did, it would make my life a lot easier if I could figure out what the dynamics are.

Anya's very confusion articulates the problem: *Be sexual by the time you're eight, but you're a slut if you do it with your boyfriend at sixteen—only, maybe that's a good thing? Sex gives you power, but with power, you lose respect—so maybe sex disempowers you? And please, figure all of these issues out in a context where you're expected to be sensitive and loving like a girl, ambitious and competitive like a boy, effortlessly sexy (but not slutty), and somehow able to think through these issues without any of the genuine alternatives or conversation that feminism, the counterculture, and other movements previously tried to provide.*

The Dolls' 2006 hit "I Don't Need a Man" makes the contradictions even sharper. The lyrics might almost be taken from a feminist tract, as the lead singer proclaims her independence: she doesn't need a man to feel complete, she doesn't need a ring or even a helping hand, she can buy herself the things she wants, she is even able to give herself sexual pleasure. Yet the words are sung while the Dolls primp: shaving their legs, blow-drying their hair, seductively applying lipstick, dressed in leather corsets and high heels and performing sexy, stripper-like dance moves. For whom are they primping, if not a man?

The target audience of teenage girls would have to conclude that independence consists of being so pretty, thin, and hot that any guy would have to want you—but you're so strong and independent that you can tease him, with a dance and lyrics that say "I don't need you" or "Look but don't touch." Girls may enjoy the kind of power that being sexy gives them over a man, but it is hardly the route for them to get in touch with their own desires, enjoy their own bodies, or learn what gives them sexual pleasure. Nor is it an effective way for them to develop an identity based on their own wants and needs.

And therein lies the problem. If the new sexuality were about authentic self-exploration—girls learning what satisfies them sexually and emotionally, discovering how to ask for what they want, and feeling empowered to say no when they mean no—I'd be all for it. Controversial though it might be, I would stand by the belief, as a psychologist and a responsible adult, that getting in touch with their sexuality, through understanding themselves and their needs, is basically good for teenage girls in mid- to late adolescence.

The problem is that this new sexualization actually *keeps* girls from connecting to their sexuality—or, for that matter, to any true identity. This is particularly problematic for all the girls who are dressing and behaving in sexualized ways before they've even reached menarche.

I'm not even sure that menarche is the correct boundary here, since many teenage girls need a while to connect sexual *feelings* (which generally begin around the age of nine or ten) with physical sexual *maturity* (the average age of menarche is around twelve for girls today) and then sexual *relationships* (which have an emotional component and so need to begin much later).[9] Just because a girl is physically capable of having a baby doesn't at all mean she's ready for—or even genuinely interested in—an intimate physical relationship.

But let's acknowledge for the moment that some thirteen-year-olds and maybe even younger girls are ready for some version of romantic expression: holding hands, kissing, and the like. Let's acknowledge, too, that the age of menarche has been declining. For normal-weight girls, the age of menarche has dropped, across the last century, from roughly age fourteen to roughly age twelve. Also, according to a 2007 University of Michigan study, girls who are an average of twenty-two pounds overweight have an 80 percent chance of developing breasts before their ninth birthday and starting menstruation before their twelfth.[10] So as our obesity crisis grows, even more girls will be maturing early.

But the Triple Bind culture in which we live is also doing everything it can to interest girls well before the age of puberty in buying, wearing, and promoting sexualized images. In 2003, $1.6 million worth of thong underwear was bought for girls ages seven to twelve to wear. Toy manufacturers are selling black leather miniskirts to girls under eight. A televised Victoria's Secret fashion show featured seven- to nine-year-olds modeling sexy underwear. Abercrombie and Fitch sells girls'-size T-shirts with slogans like "Who needs brains when you've got these?" And girls in the six-to-twelve "tween" market are being targeted by the makers of Bratz dolls, whose outfits include halter tops and faux-fur armlets, and whose faces were described by *New Yorker* writer Margaret Talbot as having "the sly, dozy expression of a party girl after one too many mojitos."[11] There's even a new term for overly sexualized youngsters: *prosti-tots*.

These facts are available to any reader of *Newsweek*, the *New Yorker*, and the *New York Times Magazine*, which in 2006 and 2007 devoted considerable ink to the topic of girls' sexuality. Or you could just watch TV: in spring 2007, besides the Pussycat Dolls show, you might have seen a *Boston Legal* episode on "Little Tarties" (a clear reference to Bratz dolls) or a *South Park* rerun of "Stupid Spoiled Whore Video Playset," the prescient episode that first aired on December 1, 2004. The deliberately outrageous program portrayed South Park's fourth graders mobbing Paris Hilton's new Stupid Spoiled Whore boutique and buying her Stupid Spoiled Whore Video Playset, complete with night-vision filter, a losable cell phone, play money, and sixteen hits of Ecstasy. Inspired by Hilton, the fourth-grade girls start wearing belly shirts and miniskirts and even throw a sex party.[12]

But I didn't need the media blitz to alert me to the dangers of early sexualization. I first confronted it a dozen years ago, when I walked into our initial summer program for preadolescent girls. We had established three separate classrooms in each of these programs, one for ages six to eight, one for ages nine and ten, and one for ages eleven and twelve. By this point, I'd run a number of programs for boys of the same ages, not to mention having been a young man during the sexual revolution. So I didn't expect to be surprised.

But I was. I saw not all but certainly some nine-, ten-, and eleven-year-old girls looking, dressing, and acting as though they were sixteen. I heard them using sexual language that was far beyond their years. A few of them talked about boys' bodies: hips, asses, pecs, six-packs. Even the liberated coeds I'd known in the 1970s hadn't spoken about sex like this—and these were girls who hadn't yet turned thirteen.

Some of these girls were sexually mature, with breasts, hips, and womanly figures, and they may have been among those for whom family history or other biological factors had led to early menarche. A few chose to dress and act in such a sexualized fashion that some visitors even mistook them for staff. I'll admit that it threw me for a loop, much in the way that today's cultural commentators seemed shocked to discover the same phenomenon spreading through the mainstream.

Granted, 60 percent of these girls had been referred to us for attention and learning problems, so we were already attracting girls in some form of trouble. We were definitely getting a lot of girls who'd had early experiences with boys, perhaps in response to absent fathers, and some girls who'd been sexually molested, making them all the more likely to present themselves as overly sexualized.[13]

Still, back in the 1990s, meeting those girls made a real impression on me. I could see how early they felt compelled to present themselves not as needy children but as sexy adults. I could also see the toll their efforts took. Many of them didn't even seem sexual to me—but they did look like sex *objects*.

At the time, I put these girls' self-presentations down to the high-risk lives they led. Now I see that this troubling sexualized style has become, in many ways, the cultural norm. And the crisis-level statistics we've been seeing, as well as the testimony of girls like Randi and Anya, suggest that this kind of oversexualization is simply harmful for girls.

THE SEXUAL DISCONNECT

So here's the problem: if girls pretend to be sexual before they really *are* sexual, they're going to find it much, much harder to connect to their own sexual feelings. They are also going to start to view themselves as objects. And they will be much more likely to have trouble using their brains in the service of schoolwork. Even if their T-shirts *didn't* glorify breasts over brains, I'd be concerned about how their premature sexualization interferes with adolescent development in general, and mature sexuality in particular.[14]

Let me speak for a moment as a developmental psychologist. The best-informed investigators in my field place a great deal of emphasis on the importance of kids doing tasks when they're ready—but not before. Take those early-reading programs, in which kids are taught, even drilled, to recognize letters as early as age two. These are *not* helpful boosts but may be quite damaging to a child's own innate sense of curiosity.[15] Very young children need time to explore the world on their own terms. If they get that time, they'll be ready by age four or five to sit quietly while you teach them something, and prepared at age six or seven to adapt to elementary school.

By contrast, if children are shoehorned too early into some product manufacturer's idea of what a good little learner looks like, they may learn how to imitate this image. They may even parrot back the correct answers. But their own inner connection to the joy of learning might well be lost, as will their needed preparation for such learning via creative play.

In the very same way, if a girl is made to fit a sexualized image before she's ready—whether because of sexual abuse, premature dating, media imagery, or some combination—she may indeed learn how to act the part she's being thrust into. What she won't learn, though, is the connection between sexual attitude and sexual feeling. She won't learn what it feels like to desire someone, to want to be close to him or her, to enjoy touching and being touched. She won't learn how to tell the difference between the kinds of kisses she likes and the kind she doesn't, between the sexual touching that feels good at that moment and the touching that doesn't fit her mood. She won't learn how to tap into her sexuality as a positive, empowering force—one that enables her to ask someone out, or to flirt, or to initiate the kind of sexual connection she enjoys. She may know how to *look* like she's doing those things. She may even be very good at faking them. But the connection between going through the motions and feeling the emotion will be lost.[16]

As a result, another paradoxical result of premature sexualization is *delayed* sexualization. Lots of girls, like Anya and Marcy, adopt an asexual style, seeking to avoid a sexuality they're not ready for. They can't tell the difference between "sexy" and "sex object," either, and they're perceptive enough to sense the falseness in their girlfriends' overly sexual styles—and in the culture's flagrant images of female sexuality as a full-time preoccupation. These girls may go too far in the other direction, unable to recognize the stirrings of their own desires, unwilling to present themselves as sexual beings.

I observed this, too, back in the 1990s. Beside the overly sexualized girls in my summer programs stood those tweens in baggy jeans and loose T-shirts, ignoring their hair and holding their bodies awkwardly. I watched these girls when they returned five and then ten years later for our follow-ups, and sure enough, many of them have not yet developed a sexual style with which they are comfortable. To me, this seems an injury, too, just like the oversexualization of their classmates.

Muscular and athletic, Anya struggles with defining her own sexual presentation. When we speak on the phone in December, she tells me:

> Right now . . . I am wearing a sweatshirt because it's cold, but I'm also— . . . my mom and I have had wars about this. She hates sweatshirts and she hates them because I wear them all the time. And they are pretty much all that I wear.
>
> . . . [I]t really started sophomore year of high school. . . . I wasn't even aware that I was self-conscious, just that I was. I think that I sort of dealt with these contradictory messages by saying, "Okay, I am going to value myself for my intelligence, I am going to value myself for what my friends think about me because they think I am a good friend and they think I am a good person, and I have completely ignored and put to the side guys [or] trying to attract other people, and I do that by covering myself completely." It's just easier for me not to think about that, not to have to worry about that.

Anya stresses that she's "a really happy person," an assessment borne out by her enthusiastic voice and her openness about these issues. But, she adds, "I sort of missed out on a humongous part of female adolescent growth because I completely— . . . I think I would be offended if anybody ever told me I was sexy. I think I would be horrified, because I really don't want to be that."

Why not? I ask her. And again the words come spilling out:

> I think it's because I see things in the movies, and I see girls get hurt because of that, and I see girls get demeaned because of that, and there are very few girls

> who are portrayed in a good way because of that. I don't want to be valued for that and I don't want to be demeaned for that either.

Anya explains that the current version of "sexy" just doesn't fit her body type:

> These days what's in style are long, dangly, glittery earrings, and long wavy hair that's layered, and very tall, very thin, only with strangely large breasts and a butt. And that is really not how I'm built. I'm like my dad, I am about five feet tall, I'm technically overweight but it's really pretty much just my body type. I am a little bit [overweight] but I'm not unhealthy. I exercise, I eat pretty well, but I don't have that body type and I don't feel like compensating for that with personality.

She pauses. "And I think that I would look ridiculous, too," she adds. "And I don't really want to make an idiot of myself."

Anya is confused by her own confusion. Her mother, a happily married social worker, doesn't dress in an overtly sexy way, so Anya understands that there are a lot of different ways of expressing her sexuality. Yet her mother's reassurances, coming from another era, seem almost to come from a different world.

Thus, when she heard from her mother that she herself could decide when she wanted to start presenting herself as a sexual being, Anya was skeptical. "I felt like, 'Yeah, that is a really smart thing to say,' " Anya admits. "But my initial reaction was 'I will never feel comfortable enough to do that. I'm never gonna want to do that. I'm going to want guys to like me on completely different terms.' "

What terms? I ask her.

"I want them to listen to what I say and not say, 'Oh, it's so cute when you get cause-y,' " says Anya. "Or 'It's so cute when you try to say something serious or have a stimulating conversation with someone.' I don't want them to be surprised when I do something well."

What Anya seems to be saying is that girls caught in the Triple Bind are also waiting for the boys to catch up with this new historical moment for girls, to appreciate girls' new abilities as well as their traditionally valued looks and femininity. In true Triple Bind fashion, Anya expects herself to achieve and compete like a boy. But her culture tells her that being sexual means being sexy, which seems to preclude being smart or being taken seriously.

Accordingly, Anya tells me that one "guy friend" in her major used to be attracted to her—until he found out that she knew more about French studies than he did. Now, she says, he likes her and they hang out together, but the romantic spark is gone:

> He'd always tried to flirt with me before, but after that I became completely just a friend, totally just the friend zone. He called me and he'd want to talk with me

> about problems with his girlfriend, so I became his own personal psychiatrist and movie buddy.

When pressed, though, Anya admits that the problem isn't only with the boys. She herself wonders how she could handle the demands of doing well in school *and* having a boyfriend:

> I am having a really good time at college right now, but almost to stay as focused on the classes as I want to be, I feel like if I wanted a boyfriend, the energy I would have to put into making myself attractive and open and available to the guys here would essentially be like kissing my schoolwork goodbye, and that is my favorite part of my life here. . . . I wish I didn't have to choose between schoolwork and being available to guys here, but I do.

Why? I ask her.

"Because that would mean that instead of Friday nights going to see whatever French film my French professor has told me to go see, I would have to go to the 2:00 A.M. dances that are practically orgies," she explains. "[Sex] seems like it takes a lot of energy, and it takes the time that I am usually spending writing essays and stuff."

Of course, Anya adds, her life is not all studying: she has made some wonderful women friends in college, too. But they don't take up the kind of energy that men and romance might. When asked why not, she answers, "[B]ecause with my friends usually we're watching the French film together. . . . I am sure there are some guys who like to go watch French films or whatever, but I haven't found them yet."

Of course, girls have been worrying about being smarter than guys for several decades now, not to mention the taboo against a girl beating out her guy in a sport or athletic competition. Women have been writing about the frustrations of these old-fashioned attitudes for some time as well. But in the context of the Triple Bind, such traditional attitudes become even more problematic, because girls are now expected to compete like boys in the classroom, on the playing field, and for college admissions—all while looking sexy, cute, and thin, and all while maintaining the façade of effortlessness. Expected to compete with boys in one domain while letting them win in another puts today's girls into an impossible bind indeed.

So between the suggestive music and the sexy dolls and the expectations of the boys she knows, Anya can't figure out a version of being sexual that would actually give her pleasure rather than drain her, a sexual style that would make her feel strong and complete rather than rendering one aspect of her invisible. As a result, she says, speaking of her sexuality, "I just deny that's a part of me. I just haven't figured out how to handle it yet or how I want people to see it. . . . So I wear a lot of sweatshirts."

PAYING THE PRICE FOR "PROSTI-TOTS"

Anya and Randi both have poignant stories to tell, but they're far from the only girls struggling with these issues. What happens to all the other girls who disconnect from their sexual selves, whether through over-sexualization or through delayed sexualization? What price do they—and we—pay for this aspect of the Triple Bind?

As we've seen throughout this book, today's girls are at ever-greater risk of binge eating, self-mutilation, suicide, and aggression, with the age of onset for depression dropping. As the American Psychological Association points out, that's at least partly because they've been oversexualized and, too frequently, are victims of sexual abuse. Prematurely sexualized girls are also at greater risk for sexual abuse when they get a bit older: they seem to be "asking for it," and indeed, they may be, even if they don't actually want what they're asking for. Girls who are in conflict about their sexuality—whether overly sexual or asexual—are often at greater risk for other types of self-destructive behavior, and the risk goes up if they come from families or communities that are also at risk. Early pregnancy, rape, sexual violence, and painful or abusive relationships are other common results. So are doing poorly in school, feeling unable to strive or achieve, and seeking drugs or alcohol to numb the pain.[17]

One particularly disturbing finding, from an ingenious experiment by Barbara Fredrickson and colleagues, is that when young women were asked to try on a bathing suit for fifteen minutes (alone in a dressing room, in front of a mirror) and then perform an advanced math test while in that garb, their performance was clearly worse than that of a comparable set of women who were asked to try on a sweater and then take the test wearing that. Significantly, young men's performance was largely unaffected by this same experimental manipulation—in fact, the men performed slightly better in the bathing suits! Frederickson concluded that women's body image plays a major role in the way they use their minds and memories, whereas men are relatively free of such effects.

The women in the swimsuits also showed a pattern of restrained eating when offered candy bars, more so than the women in the sweaters, and they reported more bodily shame and more "disgust" on a questionnaire they completed while wearing the swimsuits. Preoccupied with how they looked, fighting the ever-present "internal critics" who were part of their self-objectification, the women saw their performances plummet even as their shame and disgust rose.[18]

If girls' academic performance was affected by a single, brief experimental trial, how do you imagine their schoolwork suffers from the virtually constant exposure to sexy women in magazines and TV shows, on billboards and the Internet, and in movies, ads, and music videos? Clearly, the objectification of women's bodies and the installation of that ever-present internal critic has a far-reaching impact on women's abilities.

Another body of research suggests how destructive sexualized stereotyping can be for girls. Through a series of studies conducted over the past decade and a half, Stanford psychologist Claude Steele and colleagues have explored how sexual and racial stereotypes affect college students and other young adults.[19] Steele began with race, discovering that if you give African American college students a basic cognitive test, they perform differently depending on what they are told about the test's purpose. When black students were told that the exam was simply to see which items would work best on a new test, they performed relatively well. Given the same test but told that they were being tested on their academic ability, black students performed far worse. Significantly, white students performed equally well no matter what they were told.

Steele concluded that black students were aware of the stereotype holding that African Americans are less intelligent and less verbally "sharp" than white people. Afraid that they might be found stupid, the black students who thought their academic skills were being evaluated felt anxious and underperformed, through a process Steele calls "stereotype threat."

Steele and colleagues expanded these findings by performing a similar set of investigations with women. Two groups of students were given a basic math test. One group was told that the test did not reflect differences in men's and women's abilities, and in that group, both sexes performed equally well. The other group was told that the test tended to favor men, and in that group, the women performed worse than their male counterparts. (Like the white students in the initial studies, men performed equally well no matter what they were told.) In other words, when the stereotype threat was invoked, women underperformed, just as the black students had.[20]

Psychologists have come to believe that in such studies, a key mediating mechanism—the active force that determines the results—is black or female students' anxiety about fitting the stereotype for their race or sex. This anxiety interferes with working memory, causing the participants to forget things they might otherwise recall or to fail to give sufficient attention to the questions. Whether the stereotype was raised implicitly (as with the black students) or explicitly (as for the women), it had an enormous power over both groups. By contrast, the black or female students for whom the stereotype was not raised suffered from no such anxiety, and with no working memory deficits, their performances were not affected.[21] Clearly, stereotypes have the power to influence us in profound and disabling ways.

Other studies reinforce these findings. In one of them, girls (and boys) were exposed either to sexualized music videos or to videos without such content. The ones who viewed the sexualized images subsequently expressed more sexist attitudes, agreeing with the notion that women's main role was to serve men's pleasure. (Viewing the videos also made the children more likely to say that premarital sex was acceptable.) In another experiment, when female college students were shown TV commercials that stereotyped women—for example, a woman jumping for joy because of a new acne product or drooling over a brownie recipe—they later avoided math problems on an aptitude test and showed a lack of interest in vocational choices that might require math-related skills.[22] Again, the stereotypes seemed to have a hold on the girls and women who were exposed to them, inducing those who watched them to fulfill the stereotypes by avoiding cognitive challenges.

Imagine the consequences for girls today, as they are barraged with images of females who are defined solely by their sexiness. In real life, the Pussycat Dolls may be smart, well-educated, competent; who knows? But their on-screen persona is all about the sex. You can't imagine them running for president, doing brain surgery (as on *Grey's Anatomy*), or even working at a fashion magazine (as in *Ugly Betty*). Everything about their clothes, moves, and demeanor says that they are good for one thing and one thing only.

The American Psychological Association agrees, offering the following conclusion in its 2007 review: "If as the self-objectification literature suggests, girls' preoccupation with appearance ties up cognitive resources, girls will have less time and mental energy for other pursuits, limiting their future educational and occupational opportunities."[23] Oversexualized images are simply damaging to girls, in and out of the bedroom.[24] (Of course, nonsexual images of women can be damaging to girls as well, such as when women are portrayed in stereotypically feminine ways.)

Self-objectification doesn't just interfere with intellectual pursuits—it interferes with women's sexual pleasure. Studies reveal, for example, that when girls and women self-objectify—that is, when they come to view their bodies mainly in terms of how they please men—their self-esteem is low and they suffer in terms of their own sexual satisfaction.[25] A girl who is primarily concerned with how well her body fits some preconceived idea of "sexy" is going to be far less able to relax and enjoy whatever sexual experiences she chooses; she may even be less able to set limits and say no, feeling that an "ugly" girl such as herself should take what she gets and feel lucky to get it.

Thus, another damaging effect of oversexualized imagery comes through girls' dissatisfaction with and even hatred of their own bodies. Research tells us that by middle school, 20 to 50 percent of U.S. girls describe themselves as too fat, while some 60 to 70 percent of teenage girls are dieting. A quick glance at any newsstand reveals dozens of headlines about diets, weight, and which stars are looking heavy this month, so that teenage girls could easily believe that being thin is a prerequisite not just for being attractive but for being an acceptable human being. Again, girls who are worried about having ugly bodies are going to find it much harder to discover and then enjoy those bodies' capacity for sexual pleasure, let alone to assert with their sexual partners the kinds of touching they do and don't want.

But if being thin is in, so is having big breasts, even though it's biologically difficult to do both. And so, in the ultimate version of seeing sexuality from the outside as opposed to feeling it from the inside, girls eighteen and younger had 300 percent more breast implants in 2003 than the year before, while all forms of plastic surgery for this age group are going up as well. Breast implants don't make the wearer feel any more sexual: there's no sensation in those little saline packets. But they do make girls *look* sexier, in a painful testament to the increasing power of media culture. What does it say about women's experience of their own sexuality that the number of breast implant procedures has risen during the past decade, making breast jobs the number-one cosmetic surgical procedure for women?[26]

If teenage girls harbor any remaining doubts about the worth of plastic surgery, they can always look to their favorite teen celebrities, reports of whose plastic surgery can be found in every gossip magazine. In January 2008 alone, a casual glance at the newsstand would reveal reports of *Gossip Girl* star Blake Lively's nose and lip job, *High School Musical* star Ashley Tisdale's nose job, and *The Hills* star Heidi Montag's lip and breast job. Montag claims she isn't the only one on her show to have work done, asserting that "[a]lmost everyone on the show has had some kind of surgery" and wishing that the other stars would be as forthcoming about the issue as she has been.[27]

So what message do teenage girls get from this plethora of gossip? They see that the thin, beautiful, sexy women who star in their favorite shows apparently aren't thin, beautiful, or sexy *enough*; that even the stars must resort to surgery to improve their bodies and their faces.

Yet another disturbing trend involves the number of ten- and twelve-year-old girls being sexually harassed by boys, receiving unwanted sexual attention or sexual pressure and even being the victims of rape. This long-standing problem appears to have been made worse by the increasing number of media images portraying girls as sexual objects, which tends not only to make girls objectify themselves but also to induce boys to view girls primarily as sexual objects intended for their gratification.[28]

More research needs to be done, but my own sense is that this kind of harassment expresses the confusion we're seeing in the culture at large: adult women are being infantilized, invited to dress and act like little girls, even as real female children are being "adultified," dressed in sexual outfits and trained to dance, pose, and display themselves.[29] If we insist that all women are really sexy little girls, and that all women are intended to offer men sexual pleasure, then we expose women of all ages to sexual harassment.

Finally, the past few years have seen an increase in the rate of prostitution during the early to midteen years. Obviously there's no direct link between girls dressing like prostitutes (in the styles glorified by the Dolls and others) and girls actually becoming prostitutes. But both real and "fashion" prostitution are products of the same overly sexualized culture that encourages the sexual maltreatment of girls—itself a clear risk factor for prostitution.[30]

SEX AS SHOPPING: BRATZ DOLLS AND TILA TEQUILA

One of the most disturbing aspects of the oversexualization of girls is the way it plays into consumerism. Girls who are thrown into either distress or crisis mode due to the conflicting messages of the Triple Bind are encouraged by many aspects of the culture to shop their way to serenity. "Retail therapy" is promoted as the solution to hatred of your body ("Buy clothes that make you feel better about yourself"), stress ("Pamper yourself with some new face cream and a pedicure"), the desire for a boyfriend ("He won't be able to resist you in this killer outfit"), and loneliness ("Grab your girlfriends and go shopping"). Then, as girls become committed to the new oversexualized look, they have to buy the right clothes, accessories, and makeup to attain it. It's almost become a vicious circle: the more girls come to view themselves as objects, the more objects they desire to buy.

Serious studies of the effects of consumerism reveal that materialistic values are associated with lowered grades and with increased rates of teenage depression.[31] Even more alarming is the confusion of sex and shopping throughout teen-girl culture. We've already talked about the way *America's Next Top Model* offers haircuts and makeup as the avenue for self-expression and career success. Girls who want to learn about the latest sexy looks can begin by playing with Bratz dolls and their accessories, which have proven to be a consumer bonanza. MGA Entertainment, the company that produces the dolls, expected to earn $3 billion in 2007 as their product has overtaken Barbie as the top fashion-themed doll.[32] In the summer of 2007, the movie *Bratz* was released, and while box office revenues were disappointing, the company reaped further profits in other tie-ins—the Luscious Lip Phone, the Dazzlin' Disco Karaoke—not to mention conducting further promotion through short Bratz cartoons.

Interestingly, although the Bratz dolls are highly sexualized, the movie and cartoon characters are innocent and almost asexual. Instead of being interested in sex, they have a "passion for fashion." In the traditional teen-girl movie, romance with a cute guy is the driving force, but the Bratz movie is all about bonding with the girlfriends, usually at the mall.

The Bratz movie offers an interesting spin on the Triple Bind, as all the characters seem to have mastered its three contradictory demands. Each movie character (based on a doll) is ambitious and accomplished, almost frighteningly so: Chloe is a soccer superstar, Sasha a cheerleader who performs extraordinary stunts, Yasmin a journalist and singer, and Jade a math whiz and fashion designer. Their talents seem to come effortlessly—early in the movie, Jade whips up a stunning scarlet dress that turns her design teacher from a mousy woman into a glamorous diva—and of course, all the girls are also pretty and fashionably dressed.

In some ways, I was glad to see a film that valued female friendship over boys and dating. (One or two of the girls are interested in boys, but the female bonds are the strongest.) But I was also disturbed to see the ease with which each girl deployed her supersized talent. An earlier generation of movies, such as the 1980s teen films by John Hughes, portrayed teenage girls as struggling with their art: Mary Stuart Masterson's spunky drummer in *Some Kind of Wonderful,* for example, or Ally Sheedy's lonely artist in *The Breakfast Club.* Those girls might have potential, but they weren't performing at an adult level, and they spent much of the film agonizing over how to fulfill themselves. The Bratz movie makes it all seem so easy. Wouldn't a real teen or tween feel intimidated by these apparently effortless adult-level talents, just as an ordinary-looking girl would feel intimidated by the seemingly "natural" beauty and fashion?

As I thought about the film, I realized that these very insecurities may have been precisely what the film was meant to provoke, much in the way of a commercial advertisement, which seeks to create an anxiety and then offer a product to relieve it. If you're not as beautiful as the Bratz girls, go shopping. If you're not as talented as the Bratz girls, go shopping again. If you wish you were like the Bratz girls—go shopping, and then indulge in still more shopping. That's what *they* do whenever they feel blue, and it seems to work like a charm.[33]

A visit to the Bratz website makes the message even more clear.[34] You can buy products that allow you to fantasize about a career, or about stardom, or about beauty itself: there are Bratz Star Singerz and Bratz Neon Pop Divaz (buy your own headset mike to sing along), sports equipment for Bratz girls (including bikes, skateboards, skates, and jump ropes), the Bratz fashion designer kit, and the Bratz Stylist dolls. The popularity of the line even sparked a controversy when the National Labor Committee accused the company in

December 2006 of having the dolls made in Chinese sweatshops under inhumane labor conditions (the company issued a statement denying the charges).[35]

Interestingly, the Pussycat Dolls also planned to bring out their own line of dolls, and for a while they had a deal with Hasbro.[36] Hasbro backed out, however, under pressure from a group called Dads and Daughters, which argued that the Dolls were an adult group. "I think our objections made sense," said group president Joe Kelly in a posting on MTV News. "I mean, I don't think any father wants their 6-year-old daughter walking around like a sex kitten."[37]

I'm glad the dads are concerned about their daughters' premature sexualization. But the confusion of sex with shopping continues. In a provocative *New York Times Magazine* article, Peggy Orenstein explored the ways that sex, shopping, and princess fantasies are conflated for her three-year-old daughter.[38] Orenstein, who has written extensively about the pressures on middle-school girls, eloquently described the flood of products that encourage girls to identify with princess fantasies of being pretty, sweet, and beautifully dressed.[39] Orenstein welcomed the images that departed, even a little, from the traditional princess conventions, but she was also concerned about the contradictory expectations that I have identified as the Triple Bind. Citing an October 2005 survey by Girls Inc., Orenstein points out that school-age girls "overwhelmingly reported a paralyzing pressure to be 'perfect': not only to get straight A's and be the student-body president, editor of the newspaper and captain of the swim team but also to be 'kind and caring,' 'please everyone, be very thin and dress right.' "

"Give those girls a pumpkin and a glass slipper and they'd be in business," comments Orenstein. She points out that Club Libby Lu, the mall shop dedicated to the "Very Important Princess," chooses its malls based on a company formula called the G.P.I., or "Girl Power Index," to predict potential sales revenues. "Talk about newspeak," Orenstein remarks. " 'Girl Power' has gone from a riot grrrrl anthem to 'I Am Woman, Watch Me Shop.' "

If you want to see a literal conflation of sex and shopping—that is, a woman shopping for sex—check out the fall 2007 MTV series *A Shot at Love with Tila Tequila.* Virtually every teenage girl I spoke with mentioned this show, either as something that she watched or as something her friends did. I must admit, I never felt more old-fashioned or out of touch as when I viewed it; it was probably the single most striking departure from the Baby Boomer/free love/1970s culture in which I came of age.

The premise is simple: Tila Tequila (née Nguyen), the former *Playboy* and *Maxim* model who parlayed a site on MySpace into international fame, is looking for someone to love.[40] On the first episode of the show, Tila comes out as bisexual. She explains to the contestants that she therefore recruited sixteen straight men and sixteen lesbians to compete for her affections. "I never told anyone this before," Tila keeps saying—but at the very least, didn't she confide in the show's producers?

The contestants compete for "a shot at love with Tila Tequila," who asks them to bring her gifts, dress up in sexy clothes for her, and otherwise prove their worth as potential soul mates. Tila frequently kisses and makes out with the contestants on camera, often in front of other contestants, and she has all the competitors move into her fabulous mansion, where they share a giant bed. Tila presumably sleeps elsewhere until the contestants are whittled down to the final three, each of whom gets a night alone with her. The uncomfortable morning-after at the breakfast table, when Tila and her previous night's date enter together and eat with the other two, is played out again and again, just in case girls didn't get the message the first time: sex is a competition, the point of being sexy is to win the contest, and yet all of it is couched in romantic, conventional terms: "I felt a real connection," "I've come to really love her," "I know I'm the right one for her, the one who can really make her happy."

Of course, the teenage girls (and boys) who watch Tila understand that she's a media figure, not to be taken as a literal model for their own lives. But let us not underestimate the power of media in setting the standards for sexual behavior and women's appearance. A young woman named Amanda Wagner, a student at Wheaton College in Massachusetts, decided to explore these standards in the fall of 2007 when she and a few friends conducted a survey about women shaving their pubic hair. The survey was inspired when a friend of Amanda's was asked "Why don't you shave your box?" by a boy with whom she was having sex.

Amanda decided to find out who shaved, who didn't, and why not, partly because "I had conversations with my girlfriends about this topic for years now. In high school there were discussions over whether people shaved and how much. Brazilian waxes and bikini waxes and this and that."[41]

I asked Amanda what she thought about the topic. She considered for a while before replying:

> I think there is, I guess maybe, a cause and effect between porn and what women expect their bodies to be and what men expect women's bodies to be. And any woman knows that they do not look like a porn star does, but men don't really know that. And I know that, like, increasingly younger boys are seeing pornographic pictures and videos before they even see a real woman. And so I do believe that that could have an effect on the way that women feel they need to represent themselves. And a lot of the responses I got through the survey were like, "Yes, I do shave and I do it because I think it's more attractive or more appealing to the opposite sex." . . . I am sure in the back of most women's minds, [appealing to men] . . . definitely is a part of [why they shave or wax].

Listening to Amanda describe the supposed "other" reasons for shaving—both sexes' belief that it was somehow more hygienic, or that it somehow led to better sex—I couldn't help remembering Tom Robbins's groundbreaking novel *Even Cowgirls Get the Blues.* Published in 1976, at the height of the feminist movement, the story centered on a factory that manufactured "feminine hygiene products"—douches—and on the women who revolted against this effort to make them see their bodies as dirty or disgusting. "The vagina is a self-cleansing organ!" was the militant chant of the cowgirls, who were presented as playful and sexual, a living rebuke to the uptight, repressive culture that feared female fluids.[42]

The trend to consumerize women's bodies began several decades ago. One of the pioneers in identifying this phenomenon is media activist Jean Kilbourne. In her 1999 book, *Deadly Persuasion*, the culmination of two decades of talks and slide shows about the power of advertising, Kilbourne writes:

> [A]dvertising corrupts relationships and then offers us products, both as solace and as substitutes for the intimate human connection we all long for and need. Most of us know by now that advertising often turns people into objects. Women's bodies, and men's bodies too these days, are dismembered, packaged, and used to sell everything from chain saws to chewing gum. But many people do not fully realize that there are terrible consequences when people become things. Self-image is deeply affected. The self-esteem of girls plummets as they reach adolescence partly because they cannot possibly escape the message that their bodies are objects, and imperfect objects at that.[43]

I couldn't agree more. Sadly, less than a decade after Kilbourne wrote those words, the process of objectification has reached a qualitatively new level. Bratz dolls, Tila Tequila, the prevalence of pornography, and a thousand other images encourage our girls to see their bodies as yet another consumer product, one that must be shaved, waxed, and adorned with makeup to be attractive to men and, in the case of Tila Tequila, women. Apparently, even lesbian girls are learning that love is a contest where the best body wins—or maybe it's the best "connection," or the sexually freest girl, or the nicest. The terms of the competition are hard to decipher: a confusing jumble of messages that makes girls all the more determined to be "perfect," just so they're sure they've covered all the bases.

As we saw in Chapter 4, at least some girls (and women) are hungry for a cultural alternative. Maybe that's why fall 2007 also saw the debut of a show called *How to Look Good Naked.* Hosted by Carson Kressley, who first rose to prominence on *Queer Eye for the Straight Guy,* the show begins with Kressley calling upon women to celebrate their bodies, even to flaunt them. As he exhorts women to love themselves, women of all shapes and sizes emerge from the houses of a suburban street and fall into formation behind him.

They begin to strip down to their bras and panties, and then, as the camera pans up, you see their bras flying into the air. This is the lead-in to a show that every week takes a woman who hates her body and teaches her to love herself.[44]

The show always begins by encouraging the woman to undress, to love and celebrate her naked body just as it is. No weight loss tips, no discussion of "slimming" fashions—just a straight-up call for the woman to appreciate herself. Later in the episode, the woman is encouraged to wear clothes that show herself off—Marcy would have to give up her loose T-shirts and Anya would be encouraged to let go of her sweatshirt—in exchange for clothes that say, "I am a beautiful, sexual woman who is proud of my body." But the premise of the show is that every woman's body is beautiful and sexy, not because it fits an image but because it simply *is*.

Even *How to Look Good Naked* falls back upon products, however, as the women are taught to apply makeup and choose outfits that bring themselves out. In the sex-as-shopping culture, maybe that's hard to avoid. No matter how good you look naked, sooner or later, you have to get dressed. And once you do, you'll have to fight long and hard to keep from turning your body into an object.

CHAPTER 7

The Wired Child

How Cyberculture Interferes With Girls' Identities

Megan Meier was a thirteen-year-old girl who lived in Dardenne Prairie, Missouri, a small, friendly community where all the neighbors knew one another and the children tended to play together.[1] Megan was outgoing and sociable, known among the neighborhood kids as a fearless and generous little girl who loved to laugh and who took it upon herself to lead a blind classmate from class to class at school.

Megan also struggled with self-hatred, believing that she was too fat, and she had a lifelong battle with depression. In third grade, Megan told her mother that she wanted to kill herself, and a psychiatrist prescribed Celexa for depression, Concerta for attention-deficit disorder, and Geodon to help stabilize her mood. After that, although her mother says she still obsessed about her weight, Megan seemed to do well throughout elementary school.

Then, like many girls, Megan began to flounder in junior high. In eighth grade, her parents transferred her from public school to Catholic school, which seemed to liberate Megan from her focus on appearance. According to her mother, thirteen-year-old Megan was "not paying attention to her hair as much, not worrying about undereye concealer."[2] The move also coincided with the cooling of a friendship with a girl across the street, who was hurt and upset by what she saw as Megan's abandonment.

Previously, the girls had been quite close. In fact, when Megan was twelve, the two of them set up a secret MySpace account together, complete with a flashing *Playboy* bunny icon. Megan's parents discovered the account through a cousin and shut it down. Eventually, the friendship ended, and Megan moved on.

She hadn't moved on from her love affair with MySpace, however. For several weeks, she begged and pleaded with her parents to let her return to the site. In September 2006, they finally agreed to let her open a new account.

The Meiers tried hard to be responsible parents, and they made the account conditional on several restrictions. They wanted the account to be private, which meant that other kids could send messages to Megan only if they'd been accepted by her as a friend. Anyone who clicks onto the MySpace home page can view a member's site, if they can find it; while public sites can be contacted by anyone, private sites can receive messages only from people who have been specifically accepted by the member. Thus, Megan's parents made sure that they could approve both the content—the words and images that Megan posted on her page—and the friends who could communicate with Megan through her account. Most importantly, one of her parents was to be in the room whenever Megan was on the site.

Soon after she joined the site, Megan received a "friend request" from a sixteen-year-old-boy named Josh Evans who had seen her site. To continue the communication, Megan would have to add him to her approved list of friends. Reluctantly, Megan's parents agreed to let her communicate with Josh, but they warned Megan that if he wrote anything obscene or out of line, she'd have to delete him.

Megan and Josh began to correspond, and Megan was ecstatic. "You're my beautiful princess," Josh wrote to Megan one day after seeing a picture of her in a tiara.[3]

Then, after about a month of this steadily growing online relationship, Josh sent an angry message: "I don't like the way you treat your friends, and I don't know if I want to be friends with you."

Megan wrote back in confusion. When she didn't hear from Josh again that day, she panicked, writing message after message to try to clear things up. The next day after school, she ran to the family computer in the basement. Her father was upstairs taking a nap after an early shift, but her mother was home, so Megan went online. Then Megan's mother had to take Megan's sister to a dentist's appointment, so she told Megan to get off the computer.

Megan didn't. When her mother called from the dentist's office, she heard Megan crying over the phone. Her mother called again twenty minutes later, and Megan still was distraught. When her mother arrived home, Megan was still in front of the computer, even more upset. The messages from Josh had sparked other messages from various online friends. As the online firestorm continued, Megan called one girl a slut, and the girl responded with matching insults. Someone called Megan fat. Megan replied that she was now skinny. Megan's father says he later discovered a final message from Josh, saying, "You're a shitty person, and the world would be a better place without you in it."[4]

Megan's mother tried to reason with her daughter, but Megan ran upstairs, bumping into her father on the way. Twenty minutes later, Megan's mother went up to check on her daughter and found her hanging in the closet, suspended from the new belt they'd just bought at Old Navy—dead.

The tragedy was painful enough, but it got far worse when Megan's family discovered that there *was* no Josh Evans. The boy was a hoax, concocted by the mother of Megan's "abandoned" friend—the family's neighbors across the street. Some other people were also involved, including an eighteen-year-old girl who worked for the neighboring family and the teenage daughter of another neighbor. Megan had killed herself because of a fight with a boy who didn't exist.

CYBERCULTURE AND THE TRIPLE BIND

Megan's story embodies many of the grievous ways in which the new cyberculture interacts dangerously with the pressures of the Triple Bind. First, of course, was Megan's preoccupation with her weight and appearance. Megan's elementary school worries about being too fat offer eloquent testimony to the extent to which girls must achieve that "thin, hot, and pretty" look earlier and earlier, with ever more unrealistic standards for both beauty and thinness.[5] Megan's ongoing obsession with her weight and looks—especially given her early-appearing depression and her attention deficits—made her more than usually vulnerable to both rejection by a boyfriend and the cruel teasing of teenage girls.[6]

Then there were Megan's efforts to negotiate premature sexualization. At twelve she was barely old enough to have a boyfriend, let alone to be looking for sex. Yet she'd chosen a *Playboy* bunny icon for her first MySpace account, further evidence of the ways that even preteens feel obliged to present themselves in sexual terms they can't fully understand. At thirteen, Megan was fond of Pink, the Victoria's Secret loungewear line, which includes a free stuffed dog with many purchases. *New Yorker* writer Lauren Collins called it "a tender contradiction: the girl who wants both a stuffed animal *and* a Miracle Bra."[7] As we saw in the previous chapter, the overly sexualized culture of the Triple Bind makes it harder than ever for teens to manage the transition from little girl to sexually mature adult while forming a secure identity.

Moreover, the Triple Bind exacerbates the teen-girl culture of relational aggression: teasing, insults, competitiveness over looks and boys, and all too often downright bullying. We'll look more closely at both relational aggression and outright violence in Chapter 8. A bit later in this chapter, though, we'll consider how the Triple Bind is fertile ground for the particularly intimate form of aggression known as cyberbullying, in which e-mails, instant messages (IMs), blogs, and websites are the medium for what can seem like cruel, relentless harassment that follows girls right into their bedrooms.

Indeed, although some of the initial fears that the Internet would usher in a whole wave of sexual exploitation may have been exaggerated, studies conducted in 2007 reveal that for some teens, online sexual solicitation is real, with the most threatening forms experienced by girls: everything from suggestive comments in online chat rooms to actual efforts by sexual predators. Moreover, this online victimization is specifically associated with depression and substance abuse, above and beyond the effects of other forms of "offline" victimization (abuse, witnessing violence) that the girls in the studies might also have experienced.[8]

Finally, there's the ephemeral, deceptive, yet all-encompassing nature of cyberculture itself. If you've never seen a MySpace page, I encourage you to go to the site (www.myspace.com) and check it out. You'll see a basic Web page with links allowing you to search for a particular person or to browse the site according to gender, age, relationship status, and interest. A user, for example, might ask for profiles of single women ages eighteen to twenty-one who are seeking dates and relationships (you can also identify yourself as interested in "networking" or as looking for friends). You can't search blindly for anyone younger than eighteen, but MySpace does accept members as young as fourteen, so you can look for someone by typing in her screen name or other information that you might have about her. MySpace basically runs on the honor system, with no effective means of enforcing its restrictions and no guarantees against possible imposters, such as a middle-aged man who pretends to be a teenage girl.[9] (Facebook, which has become more popular than MySpace, operates in a similar way.)

Your browse request will turn up a page full of photos. Click on any one, and you'll access that person's MySpace page, with its own graphic background (black with neon symbols is a favorite look), photos of the member (girls favor sexy poses and smiling, happy shots, often with their boyfriends), and various kinds of information, including favorite music and movies, slogans and quotes, links to the member's blog, and questionnaires, such as "What kind of drunk are you?" or "What does your favorite drug tell you about yourself?"

An adult who browses through the various pages may question the presentation: Is this girl *really* as hip as she's making herself out to be? Is this guy *really* as sensitive, or as tough, or as cool? Does this boy *really* have all the sexual experience he's implying? Does this girl *really* have such a happy life?

A teenager, though, might be impressed if not overwhelmed by the plethora of mature-looking, sexy, and experienced young people, and might well take the statements, photos, and overall impression at face value. It's hard enough for teenagers to realize that their friends and fellow students are not always strictly honest, and harder still to see through the illusions of cyberculture. The all-encompassing nature of the electronic universe makes it that much more difficult to defend against: all too easily, even an adult can come to feel that *everybody* looks like this, dresses like this, thinks like this. The isolated user might easily conclude that she is not only lonely and left out but genuinely ostracized from the human race (or the most desirable segment of it), thoroughly disqualified from ever belonging—or ever being happy.[10]

At the same time, there's something dysphoric about cyberculture: page after page of people who consider suicide their best option; who cut, burn, or bruise themselves and display the photos proudly; who starve themselves into anorectic thinness and eagerly share advice on how you can achieve the same results. A girl who wandered into that portion of the World Wide Web might also conclude that suicide, self-mutilation, and eating disorders are normal, acceptable responses to the pain and loneliness felt by far too many teens and tweens.[11]

Whether the view is positive, negative, or somewhere in between, the emotional experience of cyberculture is often the same: the sense of being overwhelmed with words, images, and, these days, sound (many teenagers put their favorite music up on their pages). A girl trying to figure out her own identity, or her own responses, might easily feel swamped: by happy, pretty people; by miserable, self-destructive people; or simply by a hermetic, noisy culture that makes it hard to hear herself think. Combined with the pressures of the Triple Bind—the sense that whatever else a girl does, she must also always be sexy, thin, and incredibly successful and that she has very little room to question the dominant values of society—cyberculture can make it seem daunting indeed to create an authentic identity.

Despite the frequent loneliness of being home, alone, and online, cyberculture is also an extremely public environment. Had only her cyberboyfriend been involved, Megan might have been able to weather the "breakup." But the sense that so many other people were pulled into her private drama, calling her names and criticizing her actions, was clearly one blow too many.

Megan's dreadful sense of being watched and judged, even hated, is the flip side of girls' use of the Internet to publicize their lives. Watch any group of teenage girls today—at home, at a party, at the mall—and you'll see them snapping picture after picture on their digital cameras or, often, on their phones. These images make their way right onto the Web, on the pages of social networking sites, or perhaps on the girl's own website, blog, or e-mail. In the Triple Bind culture of self-objectification, girls turn themselves instantly into images, meant to be viewed from the outside in, actively inviting viewers to watch, judge, admire. Experience itself becomes an object to display. (For more on self-objectification, see Chapter 6.)

As we saw in Chapter 2, some people are born with fewer biological and psychological resources to resist stress, and Megan seems to have been one of those people: most girls wouldn't respond to her situation by killing themselves. But many would become depressed or anxious, and many more might respond by bingeing, injuring themselves, or simply ruminating over the situation, as Megan did, while becoming increasingly distressed. (For more on the relationship between girls' rumination and depression, see Chapter 5.)

Cyberculture has many gifts to offer our girls. But all too often, it's an aspect of the Triple Bind that can become deadly—in Megan's case, literally so.

A WIDER WORLD ON THE WORLD WIDE WEB: THE POSITIVE SIDE OF CYBERCULTURE

Before I continue to criticize cyberculture, I want to pause and point out that the Internet is undoubtedly a wonderful invention; hardly an original thought, but seemingly at odds with much of the other material in this chapter. Girls became the fastest-growing segment of Internet users in the 1990s, primarily for relational activities: e-mail, IMing, and chat. (Boys use it mainly to play video games and download music.)[12] And indeed, for many girls, the Internet can be a godsend: a way to stay connected to their friends; an opportunity to get information that may be hard to find in their daily lives, especially about sexual matters; a chance to express themselves through blogs and perhaps to meet people who share their interests through websites, forums, and chat rooms. For the girl who loves rock climbing or is fascinated by snakes or wants to know more about becoming a biochemical engineer, the Internet can be a lifeline, a way to remind herself that the often narrow worlds of middle school and high school are *not* the borders of her universe. For the girl looking to meet either boys or girls who look at life the way she does, the Internet can seem like a tremendous open window on a whole new world.

Sharon Mazzarella edited *Girl Wide Web*, a 2005 collection of articles that speak eloquently about these possibilities.[13] Essays explore the ways girls conduct activism online, challenging media images of women, for example, or using the Internet to find information they can't get elsewhere. For those of us concerned about the constricting effects of the Triple Bind, especially the way it seems to preclude alternative identities and to demand that all girls conform to its impossible expectations, we can welcome the way the Internet occasionally offers girls new images of female identity and new possibilities for discovering community. After all, a virtual community may be better than none, as for the girl who joins a forum or chat room on a topic that interests her. Sometimes, too, the virtual becomes the real, as when girls discover friends or dating partners through online services, or learn about community groups that they can join live and in person.

But, sadly, a number of the essays in Mazzarella's collection conclude that the more things change, the more they may stay the same. Despite the great possibilities for a wider set of visions to emerge in the cyberculture, there is a depressing tendency for the types of commercial, consumerist, hierarchy-preserving, and numbing messages to take precedence in today's wired world, through a near-constant barrage of messages and images that prevent rather than encourage true exploration and identity formation. Moreover, as Megan Meier's family learned, the new electronic culture enables a whole new set of problems, not least of which is the brand-new phenomenon of cyberbullying.

CYBERBULLYING: INTIMATE AGGRESSION

Cyberbullying can take many forms. In Megan's case, an adult and some teenage girls joined in an elaborate hoax, but most of the abuse came from real girls whose screen names (and perhaps also real names) Megan knew. Even in that case, however, Megan had the sense unique to cyberculture of being flooded by abuse in her own home, the all-encompassing feeling that she had no safe space, nowhere to hide from the insults. To a tween or teenage girl, being barraged by criticism online can feel truly overwhelming, creating the sense that "everybody" is upset with you or that "everybody" knows your shameful secrets.[14]

Compared to traditional bullying, which is usually confined to school or the neighborhood, cyberbullying may seem even more powerful precisely because it can invade parts of your life you once considered private. No space and no time are protected: threatening e-mails or insulting IMs can arrive at any hour of the day or night. You can wake up to a mailbox full of angry words, or hear the IM tone beep throughout your evening's homework. Thanks to the miracle of electronics, cyberbullying can continue twenty-four hours a day.

Even as it intrudes upon your intimate, private spaces, cyberbullying may also extend to the farthest reaches of the globe. Cyberbullies can start websites that anyone with an Internet connection can access. They can post blogs read by people around the world. They can generate information about you—true, false, or some mixture of the two—that remains accessible online long after you and your bullying classmates have left middle school. The sensitive, imaginative teenage girl who is aware that material posted online is available to anyone and that it can never be changed may feel crushed indeed.

This was the experience of Keisha, a bubbly fourteen-year-old who suddenly became quiet and withdrawn. Luckily, Keisha's mother immediately noticed the change in her normally cheerful daughter and pressed her child to open up. During a long, painful talk, Keisha finally explained. A group of girls at her school had targeted Keisha—even now, Keisha wasn't quite sure why—and they'd started barraging her with hundreds of harassing e-mails. The e-mails came at all hours of the day and night, from several weird e-mail addresses. They said things like "You're such a slut" and "Nobody likes you" and "You're so fat, it's disgusting—especially in that purple outfit you wore today."

Some of the e-mails talked about things Keisha supposedly did with her girlfriends, calling her a lesbo and including some explicit Photoshop-altered pictures. Some of the e-mails were supposedly from Sean, a boy Keisha liked, talking about how repulsive he found her. Some of the e-mails went even further, saying, "Nobody will ever love you, even after you grow up" and "Why don't you just kill yourself?"

Keisha had borne up surprisingly well under the initial barrage. She was pretty sure Sean himself hadn't written any of the e-mails, and she took comfort in the fact that only a few people besides herself had seen them. But then the girls had started a website that featured secret cell-phone photos taken while Keisha showered in the school locker room.

"I know it's just these dumb girls in my class," Keisha sobbed, finally giving way to her tears. "But now there's a website! Anybody who Googled me could see it! Sean could see it. When I go to college, everybody will see it. It's just up there forever and I'll never be able to get rid of it."

Unlike Megan, Keisha was a sturdy, self-possessed young woman who was able to find some perspective on her painful situation. Luckily, too, Keisha's mother was able to work with the school principal to put the cyberbullies on notice. Announcements of the school's zero-tolerance policy for bullying were made both at a school assembly and at a PTA meeting, and Keisha's mother spoke at both, declaring her willingness to go to the police if the culprits were ever discovered. Although no parents or children ever came forward, the harassment somehow stopped. (For support in responding to cyberbullying, see Resources.)

But cyberbullying continues around the country. And as more children continue to go online, it's getting worse.

Certainly, online activity among young people is increasing by leaps and bounds. The Pew Internet and American Life Project reported in 2005 that 94 percent of teens ages twelve to seventeen had used the Internet at some point, with 87 percent reporting current use (up from 73 percent in 2000). Over half of teens (51 percent) reported daily usage. Some 64 percent of teens used instant messaging (which many now prefer to e-mail), with half of that group reporting that they used it every day.

The movement to the online world occurs most rapidly during the transition to middle school, and especially so for girls, who continue to have a higher level of engagement with online technologies than boys throughout high school. Even kids ages eight to twelve are getting into the act: Nielsen reports that 35 percent of tweens own a cell phone, and 20 percent use instant messaging.[15] With so many children plugged into the cyberworld, the potential for cyberbullying increases.

In fact, cyberbullying has become an increasingly widespread problem, with ever more severe consequences. A 2006 survey of 935 twelve- to seventeen-year-olds across the nation revealed that 38 percent of girls who go online say they've been bullied, compared to 26 percent of boys. The harassment took such forms as threatening messages, e-mails forwarded without consent, embarrassing photos posted without permission, and the spreading of rumors. Focus groups conducted by the Pew Project likewise detailed the gruesome and demeaning extremes in which "e-thugs" might engage, including accusations of sexual orientation, taunts of weakness, and compromising pictures broadcast far and wide by perpetrators hidden safely behind their own computer screens.[16]

According to a 2003–4 nationwide student survey by i-SAFE, an international Internet safety education group, an incredible 58 percent of all children report that someone has said mean or hurtful things to them online, with four out of ten saying that it happened more than once. In many cases, "mean" and "hurtful" rise to the level of bullying: 42 percent of all U.S. children have been bullied while online, with one in four students saying that it happened more than once. More than one-third of all kids have been threatened while online, with one in five saying that it happened more than once. And more than one-fifth of all students have received mean or threatening e-mails or other electronic messages. Significantly, more than half the students that i-SAFE surveyed (53 percent) admitted that they themselves had said something mean or hurtful to another person while online, with more than one in three saying that they had done it more than once. In an endless cycle of cyberviolence, the bullies are often the formerly bullied, hiding behind secret identities and cyberanonymity as they try to release their shame and helplessness by harassing somebody else.[17]

This secret electronic world is often hidden from parents and other caregivers: some 58 percent of the students surveyed said they'd never told any adult about their hurtful online experiences. Reading this figure, I'm struck by the poignancy of Megan's experience. Even though she showed her mother the messages she'd been getting and sending, she took no comfort in her mother's response. When her mother saw that Megan had defended herself from the "fat" insult by saying that she was skinny now, the mother's response was understandably to ask Megan why she was defending herself in those terms. Megan's mother was trying to encourage her daughter not to view "fat" as an insult and "skinny" as a defense. Instead, Megan got upset.

"You're supposed to be my mom," Megan said. "You're supposed to be on my side!"[18] That's when Megan ran up the stairs. At that moment, all Megan could see was that she was being attacked and she had to defend herself. From her teenage perspective, her mother couldn't possibly help or understand. Despite the presence of two loving parents in the house and despite her mother's almost always standing beside Megan at the computer, Megan felt totally alone. Clearly, her deepening depression was making her view the world in black-and-white terms. But it didn't help that cyberculture had, by that point, become more real to her than her own family.

Certainly, for many teenagers, peers trump parents.[19] But cyberculture has widened the gap. Teenagers' MySpace or Facebook pages are a domain with which most parents aren't familiar, and there teens meet people their parents will never know and have conversations that no adult will ever overhear. In the separateness of this other world, teens and tweens are suddenly thrown into situations in which they must negotiate complicated social relationships without any help from parents or other caregivers. The transition into autonomy is already a fraught aspect of early adolescence; cyberculture ups the ante.

Parry Aftab, a lawyer who pioneered investigation into cybercrime, says that part of the power of cyberbullying comes from the magnetic pull of the online world. As young people struggle to cope with their new autonomy, their need for friendship and belonging is greater than their fear of bullying. "In middle school, kids don't get a chance to know who you really are," Aftab says. "There's a need, and social networking sites are important."[20]

As a developmental psychologist, I see her point. A key component of the middle school years is the sense of isolation, as children begin to push past their families into the wider world, often with a great deal of insecurity, uncertainty, and shame. They want independence, but they're not quite ready for it. In a TV and Internet culture that portrays children as behaving in an adult fashion, socially as well as sexually, tweens and young teens have an even harder time figuring out what they can and can't handle.

One key way for children to work through these issues is by comparing themselves to real-life peers: *Is Janie allowed to date yet? Can Brandi pick out all her own clothes? Does Latisha feel weird about boys, the way I do? Does Monique hate those girly outfits too?* Children need to know that they're not the only ones at sea as they encounter all the core issues of adolescence: independence, sex, identity. Sure, they could just turn off the computer, but the relief of having friends to help them negotiate these issues must far outweigh the fear of cyberbullying.

The conflicts are further sharpened by the Triple Bind. As we've seen, girls feel stuck in a "girl world" of relationships even while they're also told to join the "boy world" of competition, achievement, and winning—and they're not given any cultural alternatives that might allow them to escape into a truly different perspective. As a result, girls must now compete with one another on all levels: not just about boys and looks, but for grades, athletic victories, and college admission. But many girls can't give themselves wholeheartedly to the contest because they depend upon their friends so much, not to mention the cultural messages that competition is unfeminine, that nice girls put other people first, and that ambition is a very unattractive quality, at least for women. Such messages are all the more confusing because they coexist with an apparently quite different one: you can be sexy, skinny, popular, *and* a winner.

So we've got lonely, confused, and competitive girls; we've got a Triple Bind culture that offers them no real alternatives to its mixed messages; and we've got a new form of bullying (a kind of competition) that doesn't require anyone ever to see a victim's face. It's no accident that as girls have entered cyberculture, they've turned to cyberbullying as well.

THE CYBERCULTURE OF SELF-OBJECTIFICATION

There's another way that cyberculture plays into the Triple Bind: through its illusion of a hermetically sealed universe that contains every one of life's possibilities. I don't want to exaggerate here. For many kids, the cyberworld offers true diversity, ways to find friends, peers, and alternative communities that might allow some escape from the pressures of the Triple Bind. It may well be a way to forge a real identity, to meet other teens with alternative views of the world, and to create a vision of how things could be.[21]

But to a troubling degree, cyberculture also reinforces the message of mainstream culture: everyone is pretty; everyone is sexy; everyone is thin—and anyone who doesn't fit those standards is a loser. If a girl sees dozens of sexy, skinny teenagers on TV, she can at least remind herself that they are actresses or celebrities, not "real" people. But what about all those "ordinary" girls with their blogs and their MySpace or Facebook profiles? They can't all have doctored photos. They can't all be lying about their social lives. Can they? It's all too easy for a lonely teenage girl to feel like she's the only loser in the world. Cyberculture has reinforced the feeling that there's no way out of the Triple Bind.

In a February 12, 2006, cover story in *New York* magazine, Emily Nussbaum chronicled the ways cyberculture has changed young people. The first change she noted was to my mind the most significant: "They think of themselves as having an audience."[22] Nussbaum gives an account of Xiyin Tang, a Columbia University student who in fifth grade created two online periodicals. One year later, she was distributing her online journal to two hundred readers. "Even so," Nussbaum writes, "she still thought of this writing as personal."[23]

Tang went on to publicize various aspects of her life online, with a special focus on posting various types of photographs. "To me, or to a lot of people, it's like, why go to a party if you're not going to get your picture taken?" she tells Nussbaum, who adds that media researcher Danah Boyd has dubbed this phenomenon "invisible audiences." Nussbaum explains:

> Since their early adolescence [these young people have] . . . learned to modulate their voice to address a set of listeners that may shrink or expand at any time: talking to one friend via instant message (who could cut-and-paste the transcript), addressing an email distribution list (archived and accessible years later), arguing with someone on a posting board (anonymous, semi-anonymous, then linked to by a snarky blog). It's a form of communication that requires a person to be constantly aware that anything you say can and will be used against you.[24]

Sound familiar? The Triple Bind culture already invites girls to view themselves from the outside in, to see themselves as constantly on display, to present their looks and emotions and abilities and their very selves as objects for the gratification of boys (or, in some cases, girls), or the nurturing of friends, or the reassurance of parents, or the dazzling of college admissions committees. Cyberculture intensifies this process, so that even a journal becomes not a private space in which to explore your feelings but a public space in which to present yourself to others. A blog or online journal feels personal but is really public. E-mails sent to friends seem intimate but can be shared with dozens of others at the push of a button. Instant messages sent on the spur of the moment to a single, trusted friend can become public documents circulating for weeks among people you barely know. It would be easy for a vulnerable girl to conclude, as Megan did, that there's no way out. It would be easy for any girl to respond, as so many do, with depression or self-harm.

It would be easy, too, for even sturdy, resilient girls like Keisha to feel distressed, beleaguered, or simply sad as they resist—but sometimes just barely—the power of cyberculture.

THE CULTURE OF BUSY-NESS AND THE DANGERS OF MULTITASKING

There is yet another way in which cyberculture intersects with the Triple Bind, and that is through multitasking: the process of doing several tasks at once, usually with electronic equipment. Talking on a cell phone and sending text messages while shopping, driving, or doing homework are only some of the most common examples, not to mention flipping back and forth between online homework and e-mail, IMs, and other Web pages.

Teenagers are particularly prone to multitask. The December 2006 report of the Kaiser Family Foundation on multitasking, for example, begins with a quote from a seventeen-year-old boy: "At this very moment, I am watching TV, checking my email every 2 minutes, reading a newsgroup about who shot JFK, burning some music to a CD, and writing this message."[25] The report informs us that in 1999, 16 percent of time spent interacting with electronic media was multitasked, while by 2006, that figure had shot up to 26 percent. Some 49 percent of students in grades seven through twelve consume some other form of media while they watch TV; 62 percent multitask as they read; and 63 percent do more than one task while sitting at the computer, presumably hopping between IM, online homework, and various websites, all while music is playing in the background and perhaps as they also talk on the phone. One seventeen-year-old in the study was quoted as saying, "I get bored if it's not all going at once."[26]

In an essay from the November 2007 *Atlantic Monthly*, novelist Walter Kirn decried the whole notion of multitasking as contributing to what I have called the culture of busy-ness (see Chapter 3). Railing against the whole notion of multitasking, he wrote:

> *Multitasking* . . . begins by giving us more tasks to do, making each task harder to do, and dimming the mental powers required to do them. It finishes by making us forget exactly how on earth we did them (assuming we didn't give up, or "multiquit"), which makes them harder to do again.[27]

Kirn is referring to the recent discoveries by neuroscientists of the ways our brains try to cope with doing two or more tasks at once. For example, two UCLA studies have shown the potential problems of multitasking for our ability to remember and ultimately use most effectively what we've learned. In the first investigation, people in their twenties were asked to sort index cards under two different conditions: in silence, and while keeping track of specific tones from a series of random sounds. The subjects were able to do the card-sorting task equally well under both conditions, but differences emerged when they were asked to remember the *content* of the cards. In the silent condition, subjects remembered the content much better than those who had been asked to multitask. When subjects' brains were also occupied with listening to and trying to track the musical tones, the subjects became unable to remember what they'd read.[28]

The researchers used functional neuroimaging (a method of viewing the brain's activity with an MRI) to conclude that when subjects were performing only a single task, they utilized the hippocampus, the part of the brain that is essential for turning our learning into long-term memory. Consequently, the subjects remembered the information on the cards they sorted. The second task, though, involved the striatum, a brain region that performs rote or repetitive work, such as tracking musical tones. This brain region appeared to "compete" with the hippocampus, causing problems with remembering the primary sorting task.

In the second study, college students performed a different memory task: on a computer screen they saw a Mr. Potato Head figure wearing some combination of bow tie, glasses, mustache, and hat. They had to learn which combinations of these features were associated with his preference for chocolate versus vanilla ice cream—a novel learning task, to be sure. Here, students had not only to remember but also to predict the figure's subsequent preferences, based on their memory of which features had been linked with his earlier ice cream preferences. As in the first study, some subjects did this while trying to remember tones, while others did it silently.

The dual-task subjects had a harder time learning the task initially, but they showed improvement with repeated tries, becoming able to figure out the combinations of Mr. Potato Head's features even while also trying to track the tones. Researchers concluded that multitasking may make learning initially harder, but many people can still learn.

But the dual-task subjects had real problems when they tried to predict which flavors Mr. Potato Head would prefer on *new* trials. In other words, they had problems in translating their memory into new performance and in flexibly using what they'd learned.[29]

In daily life, of course, we need not only our memories but also the ability to apply what we've learned to new situations. The researchers speculated that when learning is multitasked, people may not "own" the information as single-task learners do, holding it in reserve to apply to new situations or allowing it to shape their other experiences of learning or performance.

Thus, the student who needs to memorize dates for a history exam may be able to do the job efficiently while listening to music, checking e-mail, and seeking the latest sports scores. She may even get just as good a grade on the pop quiz as the student who studies in silence. But when the multitasker comes upon the dates she's memorized in a different context, she may be less able to link two disparate events together, less able to speculate, for example, about how the 1972 Watergate scandal and the 1972 antiwar protests were related. The more focused, alert memorizer, on the other hand, may be more able to integrate her past and future studies, using her learning flexibly and with deeper understanding.

Many scientists, myself included, are concerned about the implications for young people who multitask. After all, their brains are still developing, and we know that brains develop optimally only by being used well. Possibly, young people are training their brains to do more things at once than we adults are capable of—which is certainly not a bad thing. But it's also possible that they are depriving their brains of the conditions for deeper learning and more flexible applications of that learning.

I am even more concerned about how the relentless culture of busy-ness and the 24/7 culture of entertainment affect a young person's ability to ponder, reflect, and imagine. One of the greatest injuries of the Triple Bind, it seems to me, is the way that alternative—and potentially more authentic—identities are precluded. Girls are taught that being sexy, thin, and successful are bottom-line requirements, no matter what activities they engage in, no matter what feats they achieve, no matter what relationships compel them. They are also given the message that the dominant culture is all there is—that no political, artistic, or social movement could possibly challenge mainstream notions of success or achievement. The relentless stream of images from cyberculture and the endless flood of tasks and entertainment from electronic media may come to take up all the available space, depriving girls of the silence and creative time they need to reflect on their own values, identities, and desires.

I don't know whether Megan Meier's story would have been different if she hadn't spent her afternoons in the family basement, e-mailing friends on MySpace and flipping through the various Web pages she found online. Would her sense of herself have developed differently if she'd spent more hours with actual friends instead of virtual ones? Did she need time she never got to take long, quiet walks, or to dream and speculate over a book, or to write in a journal that would have been truly private? Did she have access to a culture that offered other images of female beauty and female achievement, other life paths that might have sparked her imagination or reassured her of her worth?

Cyberculture takes up so much of teenagers' mental and emotional space, it's hard to know how it affects their sense of themselves and their world. Girls with preexisting vulnerabilities, such as Megan clearly had, may be drawn to cyberculture to escape some of their pain and isolation. But do the worlds they experience online deepen their feelings of disconnection? As we've seen throughout this book, girls are succumbing to life stresses earlier and earlier, and with ever more extreme distress. True, up to three-fourths of our teenage girls will make their way to adulthood without developing a clinical disorder, though even they must be affected by the wall-to-wall culture of multitasking and endless entertainment. But for vulnerable girls such as Megan, cyberculture is almost certainly more dangerous.[30]

IDENTITIES FOR SALE: CYBERCULTURE AND CONSUMERISM

In the July 31/August 7, 2006, edition of the *Nation*, columnist Patricia J. Williams wrote a provocative essay about her experience joining Facebook and MySpace. Williams, a law professor, was disturbed by what she saw as an increasing trend of young people to eschew the activism of *her* youth for greater absorption in online activities. She was also disturbed by the way students maintained their online activities even during class. Ostensibly, she writes, students are taking notes and checking sources,

> but always a part of their heads, a slab of their faces, an ear or an eye, is sucked into those powerful machines. You can see them receding—heads, necks, arms, torsos disappearing into the fog. Sometimes I just want to pull them out by their feet and manacle them to their chairs.[31]

When Williams joined the social networking sites, she was struck by how commercial they were. Participants, she discovered, were asked to classify themselves by their interests, and all too often, "interests" took on a consumerist cast: what products you like to buy, what kinds of entertainment you consume, what brands you felt defined you. Williams points out that media magnate Rupert Murdoch owns MySpace. She considers how much information about individuals is stored on MySpace, information that could help a corporation identify potential customers and develop new markets, and remarks, "If I was a data miner, I'd be in there every day."

Many of the themes we've considered throughout this book come together in cyberculture: the way any person, no matter who she *really* is, can create an online persona of any age, sex, or appearance, suggesting that identity is infinitely malleable and detachable, with no authentic connection to a real self. Or the way ads and entertainment news sit side by side with political coverage and thoughtful essays, suggesting that every idea or work of art is just another cultural object to consume and that every person is just another potential consumer whose every preference is logged and stored. Or the way meaningful community—face-to-face interaction with others who share your values and beliefs—is confused with virtual communities, people who may sign the same online petitions or click the same online buttons but who don't really participate in your life.

Cyberculture also furthers the illusion that everything is an object and everything is for sale. Girls can buy clothes, makeup, and diet aids online. Or they may simply look at pictures of hot, pretty, thin girls. Or they may click on a movie's website—such as the one for the Bratz movie (see Chapter 6)—and buy any one of a number of the Bratz products. Or play a game. Or correspond with other fans. Or post a comment. Or even participate in a conversation, as those who post comments respond to one another. On the surface, these activities may seem different. But in the all-encompassing consumerist cyberculture, buying and writing and presenting oneself—and objectifying oneself, and being entertained—all begin to seem like a seamless web, all conducted alone, at home, in front of a computer screen.[32]

"The powerful thing about online is that everything happens inside your head," remarked an Internet-savvy friend who provides tech services for a law firm.[33] She suggests that this "internalized" quality of electronic communication is why online "flames" and verbal battles can become so heated so quickly. The argument seems to be happening not outside you but within you, and perhaps that's another reason why Megan Meier responded so intensely. Surely Megan would have suffered had she endured three or four hours of real-life bullying and insults. But would that have seemed as overwhelming, as all-encompassing, as her online experience, through which she must have felt as though those angry, critical voices were all somehow happening not outside her but within her?

Most of teens' time online isn't spent being cyberbullied, of course, but rather in reading, shopping, downloading music, and viewing Web pages that are likely to be lined with ads. In such a world, a teenage girl might easily feel that her job was not to create her own authentic identity but rather to craft a persona that she could present (or even sell) to the world. Self-objectification and consumerism—defining yourself by what you look like and what you purchase—might come to seem like the most efficient ways to craft that persona.

Exhausted by their endless round of activities, demoralized by the relentless need to produce, teenage girls may turn for some relief to their online world, which seems to offer entertainment, friends, and the social connections they so desperately need. Sadly, that online world may leave them with even fewer resources to resist the Triple Bind.

CHAPTER 8

See Jane Hit

The New Culture of Violence Among Teenage Girls

- September 2007: A high school student in Tampa, Florida, is kicked and punched by three girls. A fourth takes photos that she later posts on MySpace.[1]
- October 2007: A thirteen-year-old girl comes forward about a fight in a Cincinnati-area middle school. Katelind Lewis was attacked by another girl when she was twelve but didn't report the incident until several months later, when video of the fight was posted on YouTube. Katelind remembers that she was punched and beaten, but she's forgotten most of the fight because she blacked out partway through. On the video, you can hear the shouts of other girls encouraging her attacker.[2]
- December 2007: Some twenty to thirty teenage girls fight outside a mall in Independence Center, Missouri, in a brawl so severe that a security officer is injured while he and his fellow officers use pepper spray and Tasers to break up the fight. "Dozens of Girls Fight, Possibly over Boy," reads the news headline.[3]

Is violence increasing among teenage girls? That question, apparently so simple, is actually the focus of a great deal of recent controversy among policy makers, researchers, and the general public.

Certainly, an online search for the words "girl fight" or "violence by girls" turns up a number of news stories like the three cited above (not to mention several sites where you can watch home videos of "girl fights" as entertainment). Certainly, too, many news articles appeared in 2007 claiming that girls were becoming more physically aggressive, a view persuasively expounded by psychologist James Garbarino in his 2006 book *See Jane Hit*, in which he cited a number of statistical sources.

According to Garbarino and others, the upswing in female violence was the indirect result of the feminist movement and Title IX, the federal program beginning in the 1970s that mandated equal federal funding for boys' and girls' sports. Empowered by feminism and set free on the playing fields, girls suddenly had permission to use their bodies, display their strength, and act in their own defense.

Yet these positive developments had their downside. After decades of increases, boys' violence slowly declined during the 1990s, by many counts, but girls' aggression rose precipitously. Garbarino and others celebrated girls' new empowerment but expressed alarm over their new rush to violence.[4]

Some researchers have taken issue with this conclusion. Meda Chesney-Lind and Joanne Belknap analyzed official crime statistics and concluded that what has changed is not girls themselves but the way we view them.[5] Before the 1970s, these investigators point out, "everybody knew" that girls could not be violent; it simply wasn't in girls' nature. When the occasional violent female entered the legal system, no one knew how to identify or treat her: she simply defied expectations of how females could behave. If her violence was in self-defense against male violence (especially sexual assault or domestic abuse), it was often tagged as mental illness, a view poignantly expressed in Marge Piercy's groundbreaking 1976 novel, *Woman on the Edge of Time*, in which women guilty of little more than fighting to defend themselves are labeled pathologically violent and incarcerated in a mental hospital.[6]

As the feminist movement flowered, as Title IX took hold, and as TV's spate of violent female superheroes began to appear—including such programs as *Xena: Warrior Princess, Buffy the Vampire Slayer,* and *The Powerpuff Girls*—the cat was out of the bag: girls *could* be physical, athletic, and competitive, and they could be violent as well, in self-defense perhaps, or in defense of others, but also in the pursuit of delinquency and destruction. As female violence became more visible, police departments, social service agencies, schools, and courts hurried to relabel girls with a range of problems as violent. Suddenly, the number of girls charged with assault went way up.

But have girls really become more violent? Chesney-Lind and Belknap contend that they have not, or at least not nearly as much as researchers and the media have claimed. These investigators argue that girls who become involved in domestic violence—fighting with a sibling or defending themselves against physical or sexual abuse at home—are now hauled into court on assault charges. Likewise, "status offenses" (e.g., running away, often in response to sexual abuse; or being a "teen in need of supervision," a legal designation in some states) have in many jurisdictions been recategorized as assaults. And schools' new zero-tolerance policies boost the figures still further, as discipline problems once handled by school authorities are now being dealt with by the legal system.

In other words, a girl who several decades ago might have been treated by a social service agency or disciplined by a school principal has more recently been branded as "violent" and charged with assault. Hence, the statistical jump in girls' violence, which Chesney-Lind and Belknap believe to be substantially artificial.[7]

I can add that during this same period, women and girls who formerly would have been hospitalized—either because they really were mentally ill or because their violence was labeled as "deviant"—have now been increasingly placed into juvenile hall or jail. As the deinstitutionalization movement gained force during and after the 1970s, the vast majority of mental hospitals were shut down, so that people with mental disorders, who once would have received treatment, are now simply being locked up. Among these are more women and girls than previously, at least partly because of the kind of relabeling that Chesney-Lind and Belknap describe.[8]

But it would be a grave mistake to think that violence among girls does not exist. In the words of Chesney-Lind and Belknap, we must "avoid both the denial and the demonization of girls' violence."[9] And instead of criminalizing girls for resisting the sexual and physical harassment and assaults of their fathers, stepfathers, brothers, and classmates, as the researchers pointedly state, we must address the oppressive contexts that produce girls' aggression.

Are girls engaging in physical violence more often? An authoritative piece of evidence suggests they are. The 2001 surgeon general's report (commissioned in the late 1990s by the Clinton administration in response to the Columbine school shootings) found significant numbers of girls who identified *themselves* as violent offenders. Based not on official statistics but on girls' own accounts, the gap between boys' and girls' performance of seriously violent actions decreased markedly between the early 1980s and the late 1990s, with between 16 and 32 percent of girls saying that they had committed a serious violent offense—one that could or did produce serious bodily injury—by the age of seventeen.[10]

What to conclude? There is no doubt that Chesney-Lind and Belknap have revealed systematic distortions in official statistics on assault. Still, it is impossible to overlook the self-report statistics from the surgeon general's report and the wide array of evidence cited by Garbarino and others, including official statistics, adult reports of youth behavior, and additional self-report information. Both my reading of the literature and my own experience convince me that the upswing in female aggression is not a myth, even if some official statistics can be deceptive. Girls' violence is real, and it's almost certainly increasing. And, like all the other aspects of the crisis we've explored in this book, we must look to the Triple Bind to help provide some understanding for what's behind this alarming trend.

GIRLS PLOT—BUT THEY ALSO HIT

There are two major forms of female violence. One is relational aggression, which is conducted through words, social alliances, rumor-mongering, and other forms of emotional manipulation. The other is physical aggression: blows, punches, kicks, and the use of weapons.

Most of us are far more used to associating girls with relational aggression than with the physical kind. "Girls plot, boys hit," goes the saying. The 2004 movie *Mean Girls* (based on Rosalind Wiseman's 2002 nonfiction book, *Queen Bees and Wannabes*) made public what a lot of females have always known: teenage girls have lots of ways to torment one another without seeming to be "mean." Or as Elaine put it on one memorable episode of *Seinfeld*, "We just torture each other until somebody develops an eating disorder."

Wiseman was a pioneer in popularizing the notion of relational aggression.[11] However, much of the important underlying research was done by Nicki Crick, now at the University of Minnesota. Along with a number of other scientists, Crick helped develop methods to determine how girls, who are never as physically aggressive as boys, retaliate against, gang up on, or exclude their peers. Whereas boys tend to resolve conflicts by confronting or hitting, often recovering relatively quickly and moving on, girls—with their advanced verbal skills and their intimate familiarity with tight-knit relationships—devise elaborate, diabolical, and often cruel ways of social manipulation to exclude disliked peers; to get even with girls who are seen as competitors (often for boys); and to create social networks with harshly drawn boundaries specifically intended to exclude other girls.[12]

Female victims of such relational aggression are often quite wounded by such actions. And female perpetrators often find themselves in similar kinds of trouble, academically and socially, as the boys who are prone to commit physical aggression.[13]

Yet it is not at all clear that relational aggression is the exclusive province of girls. Boys also know how to gang up and torment each other, even if they often lack the verbal panache and subtle cruelty that teenage girls have turned into a fine art. And if boys know how to plot, girls definitely know how to hit.[14] They have learned from sports, from boys, from the media, and from the culture at large that physical aggression is increasingly an option.

Still, when we consider physical violence, boys and girls show some definite differences, as well as some striking similarities. Some of the most interesting data come from the famous Dunedin study that we first considered in Chapter 2.

The Dunedin project, you might recall, is a lifelong study of all the children born in Dunedin, New Zealand, during a single twelve-month period in the early 1970s. Using the Dunedin figures, and summarizing from a large array of additional research on aggression, psychologist Terrie Moffitt (now at Duke University) identified two types of antisocial children. First there are those whose aggressive actions begin to cause problems during their preschool years. Despite changes in their aggressive behavior as they grow up—from tantrums to fights to assaults to robbery—the members of this first group never really seem to stop being violent.

Second, Moffitt identified those relatively peaceable children who become antisocial only once puberty hits. These troubled kids tend to back off from aggression once they reach mid- or late adolescence—though they are likely to suffer the consequences of their aggressive actions well beyond their adolescent years.[15]

Moffitt believes that the first group—the so-called early starters—includes about 5 percent of all boys but only 1 percent or fewer of all girls. Because this group's violent behavior occurs so early, researchers have come to believe that it results from powerful influences apparent in the first years of life, including genetic risk; a difficult style that seems to spring from temperament; poor attachment to parents and other adults; early cognitive deficits, often in verbal abilities; and a range of family pathology and problematic child-rearing styles.[16]

Because so few girls exist in this category, it's nearly impossible to do systematic research on them, but their very rarity is probably an important clue. Girls' superior verbal skills, empathy, compliance, and attunement to relationships may help protect them from developing into violent children. Consequently, only a tiny fraction of girls—presumably those with severe deficits in these "girl skills," along with other serious risk factors—actually begin the early-starter pattern of aggression and violence.[17]

Intriguingly, the second group of children, the ones who become delinquent only during adolescence, is far more gender-balanced. In the Dunedin study, the ratio of boys to girls in this group was about 1.5 to 1.[18] Clearly, adolescence sets off aggression, violence, and antisocial behavior among both girls and boys. Yet girls seem to have a violent style all their own, even if researchers can't quite agree on exactly what it is.

One view is that violent girls have different goals than their male counterparts. Boys and men tend to be territorial, asserting their turf. Girls, on the other hand, are socialized to be caring and nurturing, expressing aggression mainly in the home or in the context of relationships. In this view, girls use violence mainly to protect themselves or younger siblings from sexual or physical abuse, or to express the pain of failed romantic relationships. And indeed, much of girls' fighting is directed toward other girls, often over boys, issues that come to the fore during adolescence.[19]

Another view is that girls become aggressive for many of the same reasons that boys do, but that certain risk factors are especially important for females. A great deal of evidence suggests that several variables—sexual abuse, poverty, early puberty, boys' influence, and a lack of bonding to school—are especially likely to predict aggressive behavior in girls, with girls in this category seeming especially susceptible to the often antisocial boys whom they tend to select as their boyfriends.[20]

Perhaps a girl who's been sexually abused becomes violent in self-protection. The line between self-defense and aggression then becomes blurred as the girl responds violently both to actual or perceived attackers and to targets on whom she can take out her own pain. As for poverty, girls who grow up in extreme social deprivation may be left with little purpose except to fight for their turf, their boyfriends, and any sense of dignity they have left. In this case, their violence becomes their only claim to personhood. With respect to early puberty, researchers have found that this factor predicts antisocial behavior and delinquency—but mainly when girls attend co-ed schools.[21] Antisocial boys may prey upon (and serve as negative role models for) these newly maturing, vulnerable females, roping them into a life of violence. And regarding school, when girls fail to identify with achievement goals, it may become easy for them to get swayed by antisocial influences.

But poverty, abuse, early maturation, and a lack of academic identification aren't enough to explain the recent upswing in girls' violence. For greater understanding, we must look to the Triple Bind.

EMPATHY, DESPAIR—AND *BUFFY THE VAMPIRE SLAYER*

One of the key gender differences that's emerged with regard to violence and aggression is the ultimate fate of the violent person. A boy who's aggressive and/or delinquent is statistically likely to remain on that path. Although there are always exceptions, the most violent adolescent boys will probably progress to a life of antisocial behavior, partner abuse, and (often) substance abuse.

A violent girl, in contrast, faces a far wider set of possibilities, what is known in my field as a "multifinal" set of outcomes. True, they're all negative, but at least they're more varied than boys' fates tend to be: early pregnancy, continued relationship problems, depression, suicide, anxiety, and somatization disorders (the tendency to express psychological conflicts through seemingly mysterious physical ailments).[22]

To me, the varied outcomes for violent girls suggest that no matter how aggressively a violent girl behaves, she is still struggling with the Triple Bind: trying to be good at girl stuff, such as relationships; trying to be good at boy stuff, such as winning; and trying to remain perpetually (and effortlessly) pretty, thin, and hot. The impossibility of achieving these contradictory demands may well lead to violent frustration, even as it also creates depression and anxiety and keeps many girls feeling hostile, isolated, and unable to create satisfying relationships.

Picture for a moment today's prototypical violent girl. Because she's reached early puberty, premature sexualization sets her up for unwanted attention at the very least, and perhaps also for sexual harassment, abuse, or rape. As a female in the Triple Bind culture, she's encouraged to view herself as an object, not to mention the likelihood that others—boys, men, and other girls—will tend to objectify her as well. She's competing with other girls, often over lovers but perhaps also as part of girls' relational aggression, in which cliques and loyalties become the pretext for enormous cruelty. Significantly, this girl is twice as likely to be depressed as her male counterpart, suggesting both that she's despairing under the weight of this objectification and that she's tormented by her greater tendency to empathy and compassion. She commits violent acts, yes, but then she's far more likely than a violent boy to feel remorse or guilt, uncomfortable emotions that she must work ever harder to shut down.[23]

The conflicts that young women may feel over their violent behavior are poignantly expressed in the popular TV series *Buffy the Vampire Slayer*, a program that achieved near-cult status among teen and tween girls when it aired from 1997 to 2003. As I reviewed the twenty-first-century literature on girls and violence, I was astonished to discover that, in a way, *Buffy* had arrived there first: the show's two most violent female heroines, Buffy and Faith, were portrayed in terms eerily reminiscent of what researchers have been finding and are continuing to discover.

The show's premise is a potent one reflecting the new developments for girls and women that have also enabled the Triple Bind. In the fantasy world of the program, Buffy is a teenage girl who has been mystically chosen to slay vampires and other demons who threaten humanity. We can view Buffy as a creation of the post–Title IX world: she's able to stand up for herself and others, she's physical and athletic, and she acts as a leader among the mixed-gender group that fights with her.

But Buffy also struggles with a double bind, finding it painful to cope with two conflicting sets of demands: being good at looks and relationships (like a girl) while remaining athletic, ruthless, and dominant (like a boy). Like the real-life girl who defends herself and perhaps her siblings from abusive adults, Buffy is proud of her role as Slayer, which requires her to protect the weak. Like a real-life gang member, Buffy also sees her role in social terms, using her strength to protect "her" gang (humans) against the bad guys (vampires and demons). And like any good leader, Buffy works hard to maintain her authority even as she also seeks to be receptive and responsive to the people she leads.

Clearly, Buffy's strength, heroism, and leadership come at a cost. She's frequently disturbed by the sacrifices her role entails and its conflict with traditional female activities. How can she be both a Slayer and a cheerleader or prom queen (roles she competes for in the show's early seasons)? How can she find a boyfriend who accepts that she's stronger and more of a leader than he is? How can she escape the stigma that follows her from her old school, where her vampire-slaying led to the burning of the school gym, causing Buffy to be labeled as delinquent? Because Buffy kills only to protect her family, community, and humanity in general, her violence has a contradiction at its very heart. How can she reconcile her compassion and empathy with her responsibility to kill those who are genuinely evil?

Buffy often risks being overwhelmed by these conflicts. She feels isolated from her non-Slayer friends and from her beloved mother, who is nurturing and supportive but who for most of the series has no idea of Buffy's Slayer status. In one plot line, Buffy is forced to slay a "good" vampire boyfriend who turns bad, but who magically becomes good again the moment before Buffy slays him. Agonizing over the pain she causes and the loss of her love, Buffy becomes depressed. (Recall that in girls, aggression and depression co-occur far more often than they do in boys.)

Yet a nurturing mother, a reliable father figure (a male mentor sent to train and guide her in her slaying duties), and a loyal group of friends help Buffy combat her depression and keep her violence within socially useful bounds. Like the real-life girl who receives the mentoring and emotional support she needs, Buffy is able to escape the worst consequences of her violence.

Perhaps more importantly, and in crucial contrast to the conditions of the Triple Bind, Buffy is sustained by an alternative set of values. She's able to forgo both conventional female success (cheerleading, popularity) and conventional male success (good grades, college admissions) in the service of a higher goal: saving the world. Unlike girls caught in the Triple Bind, Buffy sees herself not as a consumer but as a crusader, an important member of a dedicated community. Time and again, Buffy strays from these values, and every time, the program demonstrates, she risks losing both her identity and her life. The program argues relentlessly that a girl's (and boy's) only salvation is to become part of a group and an endeavor that are larger than herself.

Buffy's fellow Slayer, Faith, is not so lucky: she lacks both mentorship and a sense of community, and these lacks are her downfall. A second Slayer who appears later in the series, Faith is virtually a prototype for the girl whose violence locks her into a downward spiral of delinquency.

Throughout the season in which she first appears, Faith struggles with a painful combination of empathy and violence. Although she enjoys killing demons in a way that Buffy never has, she's also capable of compassion and guilt. Her longing for relationship and intimacy is at odds with her need to protect herself through a kind of physical and emotional invulnerability. She also envies Buffy, as the two girls vie for position within Buffy's group of friends.

Faith copes with these conflicts by developing an ever-greater commitment to violence, coupled with a crippling depression. As a metaphor for this condition, Faith eventually falls into a coma, paralyzed by her inability to reconcile her aggressive responses with her guilt, empathy, and longing for love.

In sociological terms, Faith's background includes virtually all of the real-life risk factors found for violent girls. She comes from an impoverished, violent neighborhood: the show actually identifies it as South Boston, known as a struggling Irish American community. Like many depressed girls, Faith had an alcoholic mother, witnessed violence at an early age (demons killed her Watcher, the male mentor who was supposed to protect her), and was left isolated as a teenager.

Without Buffy's support network, Faith develops a kind of toughness that tends to isolate her further. Unlike Buffy, who is ambivalent about her Slayer powers, Faith actively enjoys slaying: she shows us what a thrill it is to be the strongest and most dominant, the one who holds over others the power of life or death. Whereas Buffy's early sexual relationships are tender and romantic, Faith's are shown to be aggressive and quasi-violent. In one memorable episode, she seizes an inexperienced boy and takes complete charge of the sexual act, which is portrayed more as an outlet for her post-slaying excitement than as any expression of real feeling.

At first, Faith reserves her violent responses for demons and vampires, much like the girl who acts out only against those who would abuse her or her siblings. But her pleasure in violence leads to trouble when Faith gets carried away and accidentally kills a human. Overcome by a guilt she cannot express, Faith becomes increasingly violent and isolated. Betrayed or misunderstood by the adults who are supposed to protect her (she discovers that one of her Watchers is only using her for selfish ends), Faith eventually allies with a bad guy, an older male demon who treats her lovingly while encouraging her to commit still more violent acts.

No matter how violent she becomes, however, Faith yearns for meaningful relationships and becomes depressed without them. At one point, she connects with Buffy in a dream, giving Buffy the information she needs to slay Faith's evil protector. In another episode, she switches bodies with Buffy, trying out Buffy's life as a "good girl," sleeping with Buffy's new boyfriend, and eventually, imitating Buffy's heroism. Sent to prison for her transgressions, Faith returns in the show's final season, redeemed, repentant, and ready to take her place in the larger community of girls dedicated to saving the world: a poignant testimony to the way that violent girls also struggle with empathy and a longing for relationship.

Although the crisis of the Triple Bind didn't fully emerge until the twenty-first century, the slightly earlier *Buffy* offers powerful evidence for the kinds of pressures that eventually produced the statistics we've been seeing. Girls in *Buffy* are torn between their traditional female allegiance to relationships and empathy even as they're called to act in ways that were once reserved for boys: displaying their physical strength, fighting in active combat, taking charge of dangerous situations with little regard for their own feelings or those of others. Unlike post–Triple Bind TV shows, *Buffy*'s creators also evince a deep commitment to modeling alternative ways that girls can relate to the mainstream culture. Buffy's best friend, Willow, is presented as dowdy and unfashionable, yet she later finds a cool boyfriend and revels in her own sexuality. Later still, she becomes a lesbian, and her girlfriend, Tara, while presented as attractive, is heavier than most conventional TV heroines (a fact that caused considerable controversy on the many websites and message boards devoted to the show). Cordelia, the show's Queen Bee character, is presented as a prisoner of her need for popularity and conventional beauty, a struggle that continues when she leaves *Buffy* to become a regular on *Angel*, a popular spin-off.

Viewing past episodes of *Buffy*, I'm struck by how modestly even the sexy teenagers dressed, by today's standards, and at how many efforts were made by creator Joss Whedon and his team to portray a variety of female identities and looks. As recently as ten years ago, girls were given far more ways to articulate and contend with conflicting demands and expectations. Today's TV programs—even those with an avowedly progressive agenda—seem to take the cultural imperatives so much more for granted.

Buffy also articulates repeatedly the solution for the Triple Bind I discuss in Chapter 9: finding a community of friends and colleagues to join with in a larger purpose—in the show's case, literally saving the world. Time and again, Buffy and Faith founder in their isolation, only to be saved when they find community or nearly destroyed when they reject it. The series finale transforms the show's very premise: instead of Buffy and Faith being unique in their special Slayer identities, they become part of a worldwide community of Slayers, with all girls given the potential to discover their hidden gifts. Moreover, the show explicitly rejects consumerism: the apocalyptic final conflict also destroys the town mall. For violent girls as for all who struggle with the Triple Bind, the solution lies in overcoming the pressures to objectify oneself and others—through shopping and excessive focus on appearance as well as through violence—connecting instead to a more authentic self, a greater purpose, and a larger world.

VIOLENCE AND EMPATHY: ALESIA'S STORY

Buffy, of course, presented a fictional world, but one of the real-life girls who participated in my summer research camps reveals the connection between empathy and violence with even greater poignancy. Alesia was the miniature raging bull I referred to in the Introduction, a bright but troubled African American girl who'd been diagnosed with severe ADHD in early childhood. Big, solid, and tough-looking, Alesia seemed almost male in her "don't mess with me" persona. She'd frequently lock eyes with another student across the room, her challenging stare almost inviting the other girl to throw the first punch. If the other girl didn't, Alesia well might, often with disastrous consequences. "This camp was the first thing I didn't get kicked out of," she told me once: her violent behavior and out-of-control aggression had led to her expulsion from everything from school to Girl Scouts.

Yet there was something about Alesia that was also very solid. You could tell that she had a sense of right and wrong, a kind of integrity that could be counted on. And though she was certainly one of the roughest girls in the camp—getting into fights in which she'd gouge, punch, and battle with no holds barred—somehow nearly everybody liked her. She was tough, yes, but she wasn't a bully: she'd never pick on the littler kids, never do more than tease them in a friendly way. One of the key characteristics of a psychopath is his or her early *lack* of empathy, often expressed as a tendency to exploit and torment younger, weaker children (and animals).[24] Alesia wasn't like that at all; if anything, she stood up for the smaller girls when *other* people bullied them. When we did sociometric assessments periodically during the program—in which each girl would privately rate each of her classmates—Alesia turned out to be one of the most popular girls we had.

As with all the girls in our summer program, we stayed in touch with Alesia, and so we had the pleasure of seeing that she finally seemed to find her way. Her father was probably the most important reason: although he was a struggling single father caring for four children, he somehow always found time to listen to Alesia, always found the patience to cope with his demanding daughter. "You have to find a way of disciplining her without hitting her," he told me once. "That's the main thing. Get her under control—help her control herself—but you can't hit her. That doesn't teach her anything."

Alesia dated guys for a while and then became involved with a young woman, a sweet, quiet girl who doted on Alesia, who was devoted to her in return. This girlfriend, JJ, was also a calming influence on Alesia, offering the big, tough girl a chance to soften up and show her vulnerability.

When Alesia was a teenager, her father moved them from their rough, urban Bay Area neighborhood into a quieter community in Austin, Texas, where an understanding aunt served as a mentor. Alesia enrolled in the public high school and soon became a star soccer player. Six feet tall and solid, she *looked* like an athlete, and the field was one place where her size worked in her favor. Her involvement with JJ continued and, despite the strains inherent in any long-distance relationship, the two remained close.

But Alesia's struggles weren't over. Back in San Francisco, she and two older brothers had been members of a gang. She'd only been in Austin for a short while when she was approached by gang members there, and somehow—she would never tell me how—she became involved with them. She quickly gained the respect of the other members (all boys), and when the leader, her best friend, was shot and died, the gang's leadership passed to her.

Think for a minute what this tells us about how times have changed. Alesia not only joined an all-male gang, she was accepted as its leader. Think, too, about the contradictions in gender roles that her situation reveals. Alesia was strong and physical as a boy is supposed to be, but she was also empathic and caring, as befits a traditional girl. (She was also conventionally concerned with her appearance: whenever I saw her, she was decked out beautifully in matching colors, a sort of Gap version of gangsta.) Though she had considered leaving the gang, when her dying friend asked her to take over its leadership, she didn't feel she could refuse. "He was my *boy*," she tells me. "Was I supposed to just ignore him?" Her responses exemplify the paralyzing conflicts of the Triple Bind: to fulfill what she saw as her obligations—obligations born of a womanly sense of duty and relationship—Alesia would have to step into a male role; indeed, one of the most dangerous and problematic of male roles, leader of a band of violent guys.

For a while, Alesia's life continued along two tracks. As a star soccer player, she was being recruited by a number of local colleges, a positive result of the Triple Bind, as girls' sports have evolved to the point where some African American *women* can view sports as their route to upward mobility.

At the same time, though, Alesia was running the gang she had inherited. She used her leadership position to make changes that again point to her "female" empathy: under her guidance, the gang became more of a defense organization than a collection of troublemakers. The group took on an almost religious overtone, vowing to help and protect others in their community. "We weren't looking to start anything," Alesia explains. "Someone wanted to mess with us, they'd find trouble, but we wouldn't start it." Like a real-life Buffy, Alesia tried to mediate between her (traditionally male) sense of honor and her (traditionally female) feelings of empathy, between her (male) role as leader and her (female) role as nurturer.

Eventually, Alesia managed to extract herself from the gang and focus on her studies, her sports, and the prospect of going to college. A few schools were interested in her, and the prospect of an athletic scholarship seemed very real.

Alesia also continued to display an unusual degree of empathy and interest in helping others. "She was always bringing people into the house all the time," her father tells me. "She had a good friend who was due to have a baby any day, and she told that girl to bring the baby over to our house. The girl had nowhere to live herself, no family to take her in, and Alesia actually offered to adopt the baby. I asked her, 'What are you talking about?' She said, 'Dad, when she gets her life back together, she can take the baby back.' I said, 'How are you going to go to school and take care of a baby?' She said, 'I can do it, I can manage somehow.' I had to make her promise she wouldn't."

Although the girl with the baby never came to live with Alesia and her family, some of Alesia's other friends did. "She takes in people like wounded puppies," her father says, torn between exasperation and pride. When I ask Alesia why she focuses so much on helping others, why she finds it so difficult to focus on herself, she shakes her head. "My heart's too big" is all she'll say.

Alesia's blend of empathy and violence continued to cause problems for her. At one point, the younger brother of someone in Alesia's former gang was kidnapped by the member of a rival gang. Although Alesia was no longer a member, the rest of the gang turned to her in this time of crisis, testimony again to the dual roles she had played so successfully. Asked to lead a rescue mission to retrieve the frightened child, Alesia didn't know how to say no.

"Why didn't you just hang up the phone when they called?" her father asked her later. (Alesia had always been honest with her father about everything, including her gang membership.) "You know you didn't have to go."

"There's just no way I couldn't have gone," Alesia insisted. Perhaps part of her was responding to the excitement of jumping into a car and attempting a daring rescue of a child in distress, a thrill traditionally reserved for men. But more important, certainly, was her own sense of obligation to her fellow gang members and her wish to protect a child.

Certainly, male gang members evince the same type of loyalty and protectiveness. But because girls are more often socialized to be empathic and focused on relationships, I believe the conflicts were even sharper for Alesia and that she found it even more difficult than many boys might have to resist the call for help.

The gang's effort was successful, but Alesia's feelings about the event were mixed, to say the least. She did manage to free the kidnapped child, but when a rival gang member threatened her and the boy with a knife, Alesia was nearly killed. The whole experience scared the hell out of her, and once again she tried to dissociate herself from her former friends.

Then she encountered a seemingly insurmountable obstacle: she severely tore her thigh muscle during a game. The doctors promised her a full recovery, but for a long while, she couldn't play, and she couldn't physically get to school. Although doing all the required work at home, Alesia couldn't attend the labs for her science course, and despite her and her father's repeated pleas, the school wouldn't give her credit for the classes, meaning that Alesia wouldn't be able to graduate on time—and wouldn't be eligible for the scholarships she was being offered.

Both Alesia and her father attribute the high school's decision to race. "They let other girls make up their work that way," Alesia's father says. "But they take one look at my daughter, and all they see is a criminal."

Even these problems didn't derail Alesia. She found a small local college that agreed to admit her after she had made up her work over the summer. She planned to present this news to her father as a graduation present. Her injury healed, Alesia returned to school, expecting to earn her last few credits over the summer.

But once again, Alesia's past, and her empathy, caught up with her. A member of her former gang came to her high school, looking for a male student he was supposed to knife. Alesia somehow learned of his visit and intervened, talking the guy down from his violent intentions and convincing him to give her his three-inch knife. From Alesia's point of view, she had saved her friend. But when another student reported the incident, the school's zero-tolerance policy came into play: Alesia was expelled for carrying a weapon.

Alesia's father confirmed her daughter's version of this story, and based on everything I know of both of them, I believe it. Alesia saw herself as trying to save her friend—but the school saw just another violent black girl.

Alesia's father wanted her to attend an alternative school that was willing to take her in after the expulsion. But Alesia was afraid to go there. "The kids that are there actually *did* knife people, they actually *do* all those things people think I do," she tells me. "I don't want to be there. It's scary." As of this writing, she is planning to return to San Francisco, hoping to finish school there.

As I think about Alesia's story, I'm struck by how many different factors played a role in her violence. Certainly poverty, her neighborhoods, and her school were all important. So was her ADHD, which as we know contributes to impulsive behavior.[25] When one former gang member said, "We gotta get this guy," Alesia didn't stop to think: she just jumped in the car and went. When another gang member showed up at her school, Alesia jumped in to rescue him, too, with no thought for her own safety or future as she convinced him to give her his knife.

But surely Alesia's empathy is also a key part of the picture—her vivid sense of what might happen to the kidnapped child she went to rescue or the troubled young man she helped turn away from a dreadful act. If you look at Alesia today, you'll see a young woman who, like her fictional counterparts on *Buffy*, is trying to craft a new kind of female role: the compassionate leader, the strong girl, the athlete with a heart. You'll also see a young woman who struggles with the demands of looking pretty, thin, and hot: although Alesia doesn't fit the conventional standards of beauty, she's very fashion-conscious. Yet as a large black woman, she has to deal with society's contradictory messages about how she's supposed to look. Even though society's standards for beauty have widened to include women of color, with fashion icons such as Tyra Banks leading the way, such women are still often slender, light-skinned, and ultrafeminine, nothing like the broad-shouldered, dark-skinned Alesia.

Like a girl, Alesia puts others first. "My daughter is a good girl," her father tells me, "but she makes some very bad choices. I wish she'd learn to be a little more selfish." But like a guy, Alesia also uses her strength to get what she wants; and like a teenager, she struggles with a world that seems to have no place for her, no role that fits her young, black, female self. Her resilience, determination, and commitment to others is remarkable: despite all the obstacles she has encountered (including the ones she's created for herself), Alesia remains loving, optimistic—whole. But as she struggles to create her own identity and determine her own values, I wonder how she'll find a place within the increasingly narrow confines of the Triple Bind.

VIOLENCE AND THE TRIPLE BIND

When we considered the other aspects of today's crisis—depression, eating disorders, self-injury, suicide—we could see a direct link between these disorders and the Triple Bind. Girls were torn between female roles, male roles, and the painful lack of cultural alternatives, and they responded by bingeing, cutting themselves, or succumbing to a depression that they otherwise might have been able to withstand.

Girls' violence, on the other hand, seems linked to the Triple Bind not directly but indirectly. As the culture continues to objectify women, portraying them as ever more sexualized objects (even while also presenting them in ever more diverse and powerful roles), both boys and girls are cued to view girls as objects, too. But now when boys *treat* girls as objects, when they harass or attack or even insult them, the girls are fighting back. And when their longing for relationship and intimacy isn't satisfied by the increasingly consumerized, impersonal culture, girls have new license to express their frustrations not only against their own bodies, through bingeing, cutting, and suicide attempts, but also through the bodies of others. If we are to address the root causes of girls' violence, then we must come to terms with the Triple Bind.

CHAPTER 9

Is There a Triple Bind Solution?

So now we've seen how the Triple Bind and its impossible expectations have created a crisis among our teenage girls: unprecedented levels of bingeing, self-mutilation, and self-reported violence; a falling age of onset for depression; and a disturbing spike in girls' suicide rates. We've seen that during our current era of almost limitless opportunities for girls, biological and psychological vulnerabilities can interact with cultural and social pressures to trigger these devastating outcomes.

We've also examined how the Triple Bind creates distress for all girls, even those without such risks and vulnerabilities. We've explored how increased consumerism and sexualization (especially sexual objectification), along with cyberculture and the culture of busy-ness, increase the pressure for all our daughters, intensifying the sense that there's no way out. And we've seen how the very qualities that can serve as girls' greatest strengths—empathy, verbal skills, thoughtfulness, and sensitivity, especially when paired with risk factors such as trauma or a depressed caregiver—can also become their greatest weakness.

As we saw in the Introduction, exposing our daughters to the Triple Bind is like confining them for several hours a day in a room full of cigarette smoke: producing distress, perhaps, and some lingering symptoms, but an experience that the majority of our daughters can survive. For our most vulnerable girls, though, the Triple Bind is truly deadly, a potent reminder of just how toxic our social environment has become. These vulnerable girls are our canaries in the coal mine, the girls who are the first to succumb to the pressures that threaten to undermine and perhaps destroy their sisters. That's why the first story I want to tell you in this chapter is that of Marisol, whom I view as a kind of object lesson in just how dreadfully we may be failing the next generation.

Marisol's story may seem unusual, even extreme. But I believe that what happened to her is the power of the Triple Bind writ large. And as you read her story, remember that a shocking proportion of our daughters have fallen victim to substance abuse, a sense of deep emptiness, and even selling their bodies.[1] If we can come to terms with Marisol's tragedy and that of girls like her, we may be able to see the enormity of what's at stake.

MARISOL'S STORY: THE CANARY IN THE COAL MINE

Marisol's biological mother gave birth to her daughter when she was only nineteen. During her pregnancy, the young woman used alcohol, cocaine, and perhaps other drugs as well, which probably contributed to Marisol's early diagnosis of ADHD and perhaps also to her long list of other problems: learning disabilities, discipline problems, eventual alcohol abuse, bouts with the law—the works.[2] By the time Marisol was eight she had lived with her biological mother as well as with several foster families and in a group home. We don't know exactly how many parental figures were involved in her life, nor do we know whether she was abused (though she may well have been).

Eventually, Marisol and her younger sister were taken in by her grandmother, who raised her lovingly. It seemed that at last, Marisol might have found a safe haven, a place to become the child, the teenager, and the woman she had it in her to be.

Still, young Marisol was a handful. Lanky and wild, she approached life with a kind of desperate intensity that makes perfect sense when you consider her background but that unfortunately tended to alienate her from many of the adults who might otherwise have offered a helping hand. Her attitude put off many of her peers as well, leaving Marisol isolated and often lonely.

At our girls' summer program, where I met her when she was nearly ten, Marisol would often suddenly take it into her head to run off. That was common with many of the girls, who felt a deep need to test our boundaries—and their own.

But Marisol's flights were different. She'd start running as though trying to elude a predator, wild-eyed and deeply emotional. When one of our staff people would catch her, she'd begin thrashing, screaming, and scratching. If Alesia, whose story is in Chapter 8, was a miniature raging bull, Marisol was like a wounded hawk, terrified and skittish. The staff person would struggle to hold her (one of them still has scars as a result) until Marisol finally collapsed, trembling violently and sobbing inconsolably. It wasn't a normal temper tantrum, for sure, but the acting out of some kind of grief and fear that ran very deep indeed.

For a while, though, Marisol thrived. After she completed our program, she lived with her grandmother and attended a public school near Portland, Oregon, where the family had settled. She did her best to please the adults who cared for her, doing her chores, going to church. She wanted to do well in school—but she wasn't sure what it meant to be smart. She wanted to have friends—but she wasn't sure that other girls were all that trustworthy. As she grew into adolescence, she wanted to be loved and cherished—but in her experience, guys gave her attention in exchange for one thing and one thing only.

Only during her late-adolescent follow-up visit did Marisol reveal to us that during the summer she was eleven, a neighbor boy had raped her several times. Given that experience, as well as her other risks and vulnerabilities, it is not surprising that things began to fall apart for Marisol as she hit early adolescence. She experimented sexually, was arrested several times, and eventually, at age sixteen, ran away to Seattle with a friend who promised to help Marisol build a new life in a new city. When the friend moved on, Marisol went to live with a guy she'd met who got her to have sex with him and his friends in exchange for money and a place to stay. When she told us about it at one of our follow-up visits, she didn't call it prostitution. She just said she had to have sex in order to get the things she needed—and that the guys told her she was bad at it.

Eventually, her grandmother managed to get Marisol to come home. We all hoped that the Seattle episode signified that she'd hit bottom. She entered a residential treatment center where she got help with her alcohol abuse and her behavior generally. She started to come to terms with how difficult it was for her to accept love, kindness, or caring; how she'd had to be so strong and indifferent early on that now it was almost more than she could bear to soften and open up.

"What do I have besides my looks and my body?" she told us when she finally came back. "That's who I am—that's what I can count on."

Eventually, Marisol left the treatment facility and settled in at her grandmother's house. She made solid friends at her new high school, studied hard, and began to think of college. I spent some time with her, during a follow-up visit, discussing the merits of the West Coast's fine public universities versus some private midwestern colleges in towns where Marisol had spent a few early years of her childhood. It looked as though Marisol had finally managed to escape her demons.

But the damage inside her had not been healed. On the one hand, she'd speak as a prospective college student, discussing SATs and evaluating the merits of early-decision programs. On the other hand, at a deep level, she continued to feel that she could do no better than her midadolescent sense of being hollow and used.

The day before her twenty-first birthday, Marisol stole cash from her grandmother and booked a one-way flight back to Seattle. Without warning—without even a note—she returned to the haunts from several years before and took up her old life of turning tricks and using drugs. Her story ends abruptly: the family's efforts to find her have proved unsuccessful, and neither friends nor family nor any of our staff have heard from her since.

Most girls don't end up like Marisol. Certainly, most girls from middle- and upper-middle-class homes do not. Yet Marisol has something to teach us about the pressures of the Triple Bind.

Part of Marisol's emptiness had to do with the fact that she didn't know what to wish for. She couldn't imagine herself in any traditional social identity: teacher, executive, mother, wife. She saw careers in all-or-nothing terms that were eerily reminiscent of the upscale girls I knew: if you couldn't make it to the top, you were a loser; if you couldn't have it all, you couldn't have anything. She saw boys as either Prince Charmings who would save her or as hounds who would use her—again, eerily reminiscent of more affluent girls. Like so many of the girls I had encountered, from all communities and walks of life, Marisol looked at the world of pop culture and electronic media, and she didn't see anyone she could be or even wanted to be.

Marisol faced problems that many of us will never know. Her problems had appeared early in her life and doubtless reflected genetic vulnerability, her mother's prenatal drug use, the grievous lack of a consistent early caregiving environment, and, later, the sexual exploitation she experienced. But I don't see her story as some kind of unthinkable extreme. Instead, I see her as the canary in the coal mine, the girl whose foundations give way under pressure sooner than those of more robust girls, but whose collapse gives us valuable information about what kinds of pressures are out there. Like weakened dams or levees that crack under the pressure of floodwaters earlier than their more solidly constructed counterparts, Marisol's conflicts, uncertainties, and defeats have something to tell us about what the rest of our daughters are facing.

"I JUST FEEL EMPTY": GIRLS WHO FEEL LIKE OBJECTS

The words that haunt me when I think about Marisol are the four she used to repeat in a flat, affectless voice: "I just feel empty." A healthy child should feel full of herself, bubbling over with new discoveries about who she is and what she can do. A healthy teenager feels, perhaps, overflowing: the possibilities of who she might be and what she might become seem almost painful in their abundance. With so many different paths to take, especially in these days of unprecedented opportunities for girls, how do you know what suits you best, which social and emotional and career choices are the most authentic expression of your developing identity?

But Marisol didn't feel that way, and neither do many of the better-off girls I know. To them, the Triple Bind and its impossible expectations conspire to make them feel not full but empty, not waving but drowning in a sea of contradictory demands. *Who am I really?* the growing adolescent is supposed to ask. But to Marisol, as to so many of her middle-class counterparts, that question can't be heard amidst the welter of competing voices insisting that girls should be nice and obedient and sensitive, that they should be tough and ambitious and competitive, and that they should be pretty and thin and hot—all at the same time.

Indeed, to Marisol as to so many other girls, *Who am I really?* has almost no meaning. She has lived too long not as a person with needs and wishes and feelings but rather as an object who tries as best she can to view herself from the outside in, shaping herself to the demands of an impossible environment.

Instead of *Who am I really?* the words that rang in Marisol's soul are *I am so lonely, I can't imagine another way to do it*, and *I can't imagine another way to be.* Trying to steel herself to resist the impossible demands and the contradictory expectations, Marisol couldn't concern herself with achieving the fullness of her potential or discovering the depths of her identity. Instead, she sought to become hard, impervious, invulnerable—a crueler version of self-objectification, perhaps, but very much related to the stories of the better-off girls who crack under the pressure: girls such as Megan Meier, who felt rejected by a nonexistent boyfriend and attacked by girls whom she knew mainly as words on a screen (see Chapter 7); or Nicola Cooke, who panicked and collapsed under the weight of not only her own sorrows and anxieties but also those of her classmates and family and friends (see Chapter 5). Trying to craft an identity that could withstand the pain of being misrecognized, Marisol tried not to expand and deepen her core self but instead to amputate huge portions of it, again resembling better-off girls like Randi, who seeks sex with no hope of love or even pleasure, or girls like Anya and Marcy, who actively suppress their sexual selves.

When I imagine Marisol's internal monologue—the story she has told herself in order to survive—I hear a girl trying to stay afloat in a sea of loneliness, a world that seems full of people who at worst want to use her and who at best want her to meet standards that make no sense to her. Her grandmother was certainly loving, but whenever Marisol tried to speak about the pain she'd suffered growing up—from the adults who'd cared for her and from the neighbor boy—her grandmother told her to put it out of her mind, to concentrate on her future. The older woman was only doing what she thought was right, but perhaps she also couldn't bear to hear Marisol's story, couldn't stand to know how much the little girl had suffered and was suffering still.

I've seen too many middle-class parents, shocked to discover that their daughter was cutting herself or bingeing or had even considered suicide, who have echoed elements of this kind of response. "But my daughter was so happy," they insist in bewilderment, never realizing how they may have missed the deeper currents that threaten to overwhelm their children. The cultural pressure for our teenage girls to be nice *and* ambitious, competitive *and* sensitive, attractive *and* modest serve as a kind of silencing, an unconscious but powerful insistence that girls listen not to their own pain and desire but rather to the messages of too many busy, stressed-out adults who can barely attend to their own needs, let alone those of their daughters.

I feel directionless, think too many of these middle-class girls. *There's this world swimming around me, five hundred channels on the television and the infinite space of the Internet, but none of it seems to resemble me or my life . . . and yet that's all there is. There's so much I'm supposed to be good at—but what does it have to do with me? My parents need me to be happy and successful—but that's not the way I feel, even though I'm getting close to straight As and my coach says he's proud of me. I don't feel good unless I look the way I'm supposed to look. I have sex, but I don't feel desirable*, or *I cover up my sexuality, but I don't feel safe*. And so, like Marisol, too many of these middle-class girls echo the same refrain: "I just feel empty."

LIFE ON THE BORDER

There is a long tradition in the social sciences and humanities of using psychological diagnoses as metaphors. W. H. Auden's Pulitzer Prize–winning poem, "The Age of Anxiety," signaled the post–World War II generation's preoccupation with overwhelming anxiety, anticipating the actual rise in anxiety among U.S. children that has occurred over the past fifty years.[3] In 1979, Christopher Lasch wrote of the culture of narcissism, in which a preoccupation with the self and its development took precedence over a connection to the larger world, again reflecting a larger social trend.[4]

As both a clinician and a scientist, I'm often uneasy with this broader application of terms that were initially developed to explicate specific, painful conditions that needed to be understood so that they could be treated. Diagnosis-as-metaphor too often distorts the meaning of the original psychological term, not to mention the way it frequently slights the dire pain of those who suffer from the clinical condition.

And yet I find myself reaching for a similar metaphor to illuminate the injuries of the Triple Bind. When patients come to a therapist complaining of feeling empty, the diagnosis they receive (if the emptiness is combined with impulsivity, instability, and lack of emotional control) is often *borderline personality disorder*: the condition of feeling like an object.[5]

There's a lot of controversy in my field over the whole notion of borderline personality disorder, which, like depression, is twice as common among women as among men. Some clinicians feel that the term is a kind of sexist version of antisocial personality disorder, which is at least twice as common among men. In both cases, the disorders are marked by an inability to see other people in a whole and integrated way.[6] If you have antisocial personality disorder, a fundamental lack of empathy may lead you to see other people as objects to be used or exploited. If you have borderline personality disorder, on the other hand, everyone becomes objectified in a different way: either the hero who's going to save you or the villain who will destroy you, your ideal love or your cruelest betrayer. But people aren't real human beings with flaws and strengths and agendas of their own. You feel like an object, and so you see others as objects, too, whether all good or all bad.

People with antisocial personality disorder often act out with aggressive gestures against the world. A person with borderline personality disorder may be subject to rage, but she is more inclined to act out against herself, in self-sabotage, misery, and self-mutilation. (In fact, cutting is one of the classic symptoms of borderline personality disorder.)[7] Again, the self-injurer sees her body not as a living organism but as a kind of object, inert and lifeless until it can be forced to respond.

Both disorders are also frequently related to early experiences of abuse, in which caretakers who ought to have been trusted and beloved were, in fact, betrayers who took advantage of a child's vulnerability and dependence. Indeed, being physically abused is a clear risk factor for later aggression, just as being physically and sexually abused is a risk factor, in girls and women, for the development of borderline personality disorder.[8] This early betrayal can indeed lead to a sense of emptiness. The world seems loveless, barren, and devoid of hope, and the individual similarly feels empty: unlovable, worthless, a person who got no love or protection because, she believes, she probably didn't deserve it.

Feeling unable to become a loved and loving person, the girl at risk for developing borderline personality disorder strives instead to turn herself into an object: someone who can please others, perhaps, or someone who can remain invulnerable to their betrayal, neglect, or abuse. Trying to rid herself of the sorrow, rage, and hopelessness that threaten to overwhelm her, she begins a lifelong chorus of those haunting words: *I just feel empty.*

When I speak of Triple Bind girls in terms of this diagnosis, when I compare Megan and Marcy and Anya and Nicola to Marisol, I'm speaking not clinically but metaphorically. I don't believe that the former four girls were abused or even neglected. I haven't formally treated any of them—I never even met Megan Meier—but from what I know, if they have ever suffered from clinical conditions, borderline personality disorder is probably not among them.

Yet in another sense, all of today's girls struggle with the same underlying "condition," which at one extreme can produce a diagnosis of borderline personality disorder: the condition of being turned into an object. The culture that demands self-objectification—the endless preoccupation with appearance; the relentless need to appease teachers, coaches, and colleges; the continual allure of consumerism; and the endless noise of cyberculture—is precisely the culture in which all our daughters live, and within which they must somehow try to craft workable identities that can bring them into adulthood. At a cultural level, our daughters are asked to focus not on how they feel but on how they look, not on how they learn but on how they perform, not on what meaning they have created in their lives but on what college they can get into and what success they can achieve.

Ideally, adolescence is a time to begin what Viktor Frankl has called the search for meaning, the life purpose that enables you to say: *I know who I am, yesterday, today, and tomorrow. The world may be hard, it may be full of loss, but I believe in myself and what I'm doing—and that belief can carry me through the hard times, can allow me both a sense of purpose and a sense of joy.*[9]

Instead, too many of our young people are speaking in terms that would be all too familiar to Marisol: *I feel empty. What is the next task I can undertake? What is the next sexual experience I can seek? What is the next entertainment I can find? What is the next thing I can buy, to fill myself, stimulate myself, numb myself . . . to hold off this emptiness and the loneliness that surrounds it?*

In that sense, Marisol is indeed our canary in the coal mine. Her extreme vulnerabilities, her extreme pressures, and her extreme distress are the Triple Bind writ large, the culture of self-objectification and impossible expectations that threatens to undermine our daughters.

RESILIENCE AND STRENGTH

How can girls resist the pressures of the Triple Bind? This is a complex question that deserves a complex answer. So let's begin with a concept that has taken on increasing importance among researchers in psychology and that is now almost a buzzword in the general culture: the notion of *resilience*.

Resilience has been of interest to a great many researchers, clinicians, teachers, and advocates, who seek to understand how an at-risk child can nonetheless emerge as strong, optimistic, and successful. Resilience seems to be the result of both the child's innate qualities and of certain types of relationships. Together, these internal and external factors may combine to produce unexpectedly good outcomes in the face of high vulnerability, risk, or stress.[10]

When scientists first addressed this problem several decades ago, they began by focusing on the "invulnerable" child, seeking ways to identify these apparently sturdier children and trying to determine which factors created the surprising strengths that they showed and their seemingly mysterious ability to overcome the odds. Initially, they looked for inborn qualities, assuming that a young person was inherently either vulnerable to risk or immune to it.[11]

Now we see things somewhat differently. We realize that resilience is not an entity, to borrow from the work of Carol Dweck, but rather an ongoing dynamic. Although there may be biological or inherited factors involved, resilience is also the result of identifiable family, social, and community processes that may propel young people to better-than-expected outcomes in some or even all areas of their lives.[12]

The factors that promote resilience are not mystical entities that mysteriously elevate doomed children to spectacular success. In the words of my colleague Ann Masten, a psychologist at the University of Minnesota, the important processes are a kind of "ordinary magic," qualities and relationships that may be found throughout our culture. Although helpful for all young people, these factors may hold crucial benefits for children and teenagers who also have several strikes against them.

What are the elements of this "ordinary magic"? Among personal characteristics, the most important seem to be an orientation toward the future, high motivation, and at least a modicum of positive self-regard. As for relationships, high-quality connections with caregivers or other adults—a teacher, a coach, an extended family member, a neighbor—can be a hugely important protective factor.[13]

As we've seen, the soul-destroying, disempowering messages of the Triple Bind are toxic to all girls, not just those at high risk or with vulnerabilities for mental disturbance. True, high-risk girls like Marisol are the most likely to develop clinical disorders in response to the Triple Bind. But virtually every girl in our society is affected by this cultural problem, and therefore every girl needs to develop her own capacity for resilience, to resist the Triple Bind's messages, and to forge her own particular strengths and identity.[14]

So what can we do to promote competence for all of our daughters? How can we foster a sense of purpose and motivation in the face of the relentless consumerism, objectification, and emptiness produced by the Triple Bind?

Perhaps our greatest hope for helping teens overcome the malaise that envelops both them and the culture at large lies in creating with them a sense of community, a commitment to something greater than themselves, helping them connect to a larger world of fellowship, of shared purpose, and, often, of social action. The usual protective factors that researchers have found to foster resilience—effective parenting; connection with other adults if parents are not available; safe neighborhoods; and a young person's motivation, intelligence, and sense of humor—are certainly important.[15]

But I believe that we need to look at resilience in social terms as well as personal ones. Throughout my decades of experiences as a researcher and clinician, I've seen time and time again how healing—indeed, how lifesaving—it can be for young people to connect to a broader and deeper purpose; to become part of a community of people who can "get outside themselves" to work toward a common good; to join a world that is larger than clothes, looks, and grades.

To demonstrate the power of community, I'd like to share with you one of the most inspiring stories I know, of a girl named Lily Gordon who reached beyond herself to discover such a larger world. Lily points the way to what we might hope for our daughters, even as we also seek to transform the culture that puts them at risk.

LILY'S STORY: CLAIMING A WIDER WORLD

As of this writing, Lily Gordon is a thirteen-year-old girl living in Berkeley, California. Yet her world extends far beyond the borders of her private school or her middle-class neighborhood into a global community. Lily's mother is a colleague and friend in my department, a clinical psychologist who directs our Psychology Clinic, specializing in training our graduate students in all aspects of the psychotherapeutic process. Lily's father is a high-level technical writer. Their older daughter, Rachel, is an enthusiastic, successful student at Columbia University who plans on following her mother into the field of clinical psychology.

Lily, however, was different. She always had a special intensity, a kind of stubbornness that can be associated both with high-achieving kids and with children suffering from ADHD. Her family worried about her during her toddler and preschool years, wondering whether the intensity would serve her well or become a problem that would require treatment.

Lily continued to be a handful as she grew older. Once, when she was seven, she and a friend weren't ready to leave the park at the end of the afternoon. Thinking to teach them a lesson, Lily's father got in the car and drove away, expecting to find the two children, chastened and obedient, when he returned a few moments later. Instead, Lily decided to find her own way home, and she and her friend set off, on foot, for what turned out to be a hike of almost four miles. Stopping frequently to ask directions and reversing a bus route that Lily had stored in her memory, they somehow managed to return to Lily's neighborhood before either their parents or the police could track them down. That's the kind of determination that spells trouble, or greatness—or both.

When Lily entered middle school, therefore, many close to her were especially concerned, knowing all too well the pitfalls that early adolescence holds for many girls and the plethora of obstacles that can derail even the happiest and best-adjusted teens and tweens. As a child, Lily had been a tomboy, playing sports with her many "guy friends" and hanging out with her "really good girlfriend." But what would happen to her when she entered the world of clothes and boyfriends and sex and dating?

In fact, Lily herself remembers the transition to middle school as a somewhat traumatic time, when she "kept being scared of the big kids . . . just like, I didn't want to mess up around them."

Then, at a school event, Lily heard about a friend's trip to Africa. Lily was jealous—but she also felt guilty.

> I was, like, "Well, look at my life, and these kids are talking about how they are walking miles to school and I'm like driving up in my $40,000 Volvo, like, complaining when I have to take a bus with other kids."

So when Lily was about to turn eleven, she decided to hold her birthday party for charity. Even now, she questions her motives.

> I wanna say like that it was this heroic thing, . . . like "It was 'cause I knew it was for the good of the people," but I honestly don't think it was that. I think . . . obviously I really did care about the people, but I think that a lot of it was that I just felt so guilty having the life I had. And I am sure in the back of my mind I was like, "I'll get a bigger party if I do it for charity."

As Lily was trying to decide what to do with the money she planned to raise, she learned that some of her best guy friends were planning to visit Tanzania with their families, and that one of them, a boy with African roots, was collecting money for school supplies for the children there. Lily decided that the $1,200 she eventually raised at her party would be donated to their cause.

"It was, like, not exactly like a big deal," she recalls. "[I]t just seemed to me like something nice that I could do. . . . I had no idea how much it would change my life."

A woman from the organization that had received the money contacted Lily and her family. She told them that Lily had done so much for their group that now Lily needed to visit Africa herself.

> So from that time we started planning going to Africa with them next summer. We started taking Swahili lessons and getting really involved. . . . [That] piece of my life that is so important started. . . . [N]ow that I look back, I can't imagine life without it. . . .
>
> This is really sappy, but I think [that trip] really made me who I am. . . . It made me . . . see that if people don't help each other, we're not going to get anywhere. Like, it's really not fair that my life is so perfect and beautiful, and these people are happier than the people who live around us, and they have nothing. There is such a cultural difference and we could learn so much from each other.
>
> A lot of it I feel . . . has made my values and [shown me] what I want to do with my life. When I was little I remember just thinking, I want to make a lot of money and live in a big house, and I decided my mom was going to be my maid. So now when I see the life that [the people in Tanzania] . . . lead and how happy they are, when I grow up I want to be there all the time and help these people and all the people I can. Because not only does it give me a really fulfilling feeling on the inside; my little deed and little fun summer can help change their lives.

I am so struck by Lily's words that I have to pause for a moment to take them in. "How does it feel knowing you can change people's lives?" I ask her. Lily answers immediately.

> It's like the most ecstatic happy feeling, when you give that little kid food or when you see the smile, you have done so much for them. If I gave my friend here a chocolate bar they'd be like "No, thanks." But if I gave a kid a chocolate bar there—the generosity and that feeling of happiness—it shows them a whole new idea of what if all the people in the world shared. You can see how little things there make so much of a difference compared to little things here.

As Lily continues to reflect on her experience, she invokes the idea of a wider world, which she says can allow girls to open their horizons in a whole new way.

> People, depending on how long they have known you, perceive you in really different ways. If you open up your world and make it bigger, I believe you can be more of yourself, and there are more people to accept you. If you just live in your school or just live in your small community it is really hard to show your whole self. Sometimes there are people at a bad point in their life and who are not going to accept you. The best thing you can do is believe in yourself and help them. Once you step outside of that little area you are in, you will find people who think what they don't think is cool, actually is cool.

It seems to me that Lily has found a kind of antidote to the Triple Bind. But that doesn't mean she's immune to its pressures.

> I act different around . . . different [people]. . . . I am not trying to act two-faced, but the different things that I am interested in and the different things that I care about come out when I am around different people. Around my soccer coach—who I really look up to and I really want her to like me—I'll talk about soccer more . . . [and the] more athletic things I do . . . because I am trying to fulfill her expectations . . . and . . . because like I really want her to be happy with me. But around my friends I talk about boys more, or I'll talk about what clothes I want or stuff like that. Around my guy friends I will talk about sports more, and around my teachers I'll talk about what they're interested in. So you . . . cope with [the expectations] by showing the different pieces of yourself to different people who really want to see that part. And it's not that you are . . . ashamed of any part of who you are, or . . . being something you're not. You are just kind of spreading out who you are among different interactions.

"That sounds like why it is so important to have many worlds rather than just one world," I comment.

"Yeah," Lily says with a nod. " 'Cause then you can end up being more of yourself."

> I know that a bunch of the girls at my school . . . don't have enough of an open world, and that's a reason they are not as confident—not necessarily confident, but I don't feel they're necessarily being the whole person that they are. . . . And I feel like . . . that confidence of being who you are comes from all of the acceptance, so the more experiences you have, the more . . . likely that you'll get more accepted by people for the different parts of you. You can feel more comfortable with those parts of you.

What about girls who don't feel so comfortable? I ask her.

> A lot of girls dumb themselves down around boys because they think that is the cool thing to do. I hear girls struggle a lot with intelligence and good grades be-

> cause they feel like being smart isn't going to make boys like them, so they will be really smart in class, and then suddenly they will come out and [be] twirling their hair and trying to be the stereotypical girl you see on TV. A lot of times my guy friends say they will flirt with those girls but they don't respect them. Those girls end up getting hurt because they get in relationships where the guy doesn't really care about them.

In Lily's experience, girls feel a lot of pressure to have a first boyfriend. "As soon as you have had one you are in a safe zone for a couple years," she explains. "As long as when someone asks if you had a boyfriend, you can say, 'Oh, yeah.' Then you are clear, because that pressure is only to have *one*."

It's not always easy getting that first boyfriend, however.

> I definitely know a lot of boys who are intimidated if the girl is a lot smarter than they are. . . . I feel like a lot of girls feel that they shouldn't be athletic. I don't think boys think of it as much of a bad thing, unless they feel really intimidated by the girl, like if she is way better than him at something. . . . But there are boys that don't really care if you are better than them—just some boys [care]. . . . I definitely know girls who compete with all the boys, but, like, batting the ball bad and pretending they are uncoordinated. And then when they play against girls in basketball, they will be fine. And also I know girls who really hate sweating around boys, so they try not to work hard.

And though a girl must have had at least one boyfriend, she isn't necessarily allowed to be sexual. "No one actually has sex in my grade," Lily says. "That is social suicide for a girl."

> They'd get called a slut and a ho, and your friends would be like "Why'd you do it?" And they'd probably have to . . . [come] up with an excuse like, "[He] took advantage of me" or something like that. . . . People, by their reactions, don't think it's that bad when [girls] are like, fifteen or sixteen and above.

But despite Lily's fluency in the social customs of her school, she herself seems remarkably immune to outside pressures. Nor does she talk about her life in the anxious, frustrated tone I have heard from so many teenage girls, who listed all the expectations they faced and then told me how impossible those expectations were. Lily seems not overwhelmed but energized—not drowning but waving. And when I ask her how her life would be different if she hadn't gone to Africa, she responds in terms that seem to integrate both caring and striving, both the girl world of relationships and the boy world of accomplishment: "I always have a focus: 'I want to achieve this' [raising money for Africa]. So me doing this work is something I can achieve."

FREEING OURSELVES FROM THE TRIPLE BIND

Lily Gordon is a living example of how getting outside yourself—opening yourself to a wider world of involvement and a broader community—can help to get beyond the dizzying expectations of the Triple Bind. Such opening up certainly helped Lily to channel the huge charge of energy that she had been carrying since her earliest years. Her perspective on herself, her family, and her world has been immeasurably broadened and deepened through her involvement in Africa.

Lily is not the only girl who's been nourished by her participation in a wider world. Melinda, whom we met in Chapter 2, stands as an example of how the connection to community can help a girl combat the pressures of the Triple Bind, even when she's shadowed by a family history of depression. Anya, who appears in Chapters 3 and 6, plus Amanda, also in Chapter 6, draw inspiration from their understanding of feminism, which connects them to a larger community of women and enables them to see their problems in social as well as personal terms. All of these girls have been lucky in coming from families who encouraged their sense of "world citizenship," helping them to create identities that look outward as well as inward.

The real question for all of us, then, is how our girls can get to the place where they can overcome personal risk factors as well as the self-objectifying and self-defeating culture of the Triple Bind. Some teens are simply too self-absorbed to make such a leap into commitment and a broader world; others, suffering from early experiences of abuse or vulnerability, are too impaired; still others never have a real chance to connect to wider issues and concerns, perhaps because each day is a struggle for mere survival. And all too many affluent youth can't seem to transcend the banality, consumerism, and deadening qualities of the Triple Bind. That means it's up to us, the adults, to undo the bind and work with our youth to create a new culture.[16]

Certainly, resilience has many roots, and most people doing scientific work in this area focus on personal qualities or family interactions. We know, for instance, that for some at-risk children, there are factors that can mitigate the risk: being born with a calm temperament; receiving firm but loving parental care; or, when an intact family is not in place, having a quality relationship with a caring, mentoring adult outside the home.[17] As it happens, Lily didn't have the easiest of temperaments: in fact, her mother considered having her evaluated for ADHD when she was still a preschooler. On the other hand, her family is a paragon of a warm yet structured environment, they could always afford to send Lily to good schools, and Lily herself has shown great judgment in her choice of friends. Girl by girl, these things make a difference.

But going beyond the personal factors that are usually believed to promote resilience, I believe that it was ultimately Lily's dedication to a purpose well beyond herself that helped not only to promote her membership in a "community of the world" but also to limit the kinds of paralyzing rumination and self-hatred that afflict all too many girls. How freeing it is to place your energy into something wider, deeper, and more important than incessant worries about looks, clothes, and pleasing others. Melinda, Anya, and Amanda also discovered this sense of freedom, and they all benefit from their connections to a larger community.

IS THERE A TRIPLE BIND SOLUTION?

So we come again to the most crucial question of this book: is there a Triple Bind solution? I believe there is, or at least that there can be, although I know our culture will need to change a great deal if we are to enable more girls to develop the sense of community that Lily has found: their own versions of involvement and commitment, their own deeper sense of themselves.

But we can't simply wait for the culture to transform itself; we must also attend in the short term to our girls in need. Here, then are some modest proposals for how we might address the Triple Bind, in hopes that these beginning thoughts will inspire others to come forward with new plans and actions:

- *For the girls who are most in need, getting competent and sensitive clinical help is essential.* Recall Nicola Cooke, whose story we learned in Chapter 5. An exuberant, high-spirited girl, Nicola fell prey to anxiety and depression, and she suffered far too long before her condition was properly diagnosed and treated. Perhaps in another culture, Nicola would have escaped the disorders for which her family history seems to have predisposed her. But in our culture, she did fall ill—and she needed treatment that was far too long in coming. Becoming sensitive to what our teenage girls need and ensuring that they have the help of caring professionals is crucial for girls in crisis.
- *Parents need to help their children focus on self-discovery far more than on mere achievement.* As we saw in Chapter 3, the research of such scholars as Suniya Luthar indicts parents' overfocus on achievement and excessive criticism as the key culprits behind anxiety, depression, and other disorders, especially for upper-class youth. When a child feels that her parents value not her self but her achievements, she may strive ever harder to perform. But she's also prone

to many of the disorders we've considered, acting out her distress through bingeing, self-injury, violence, or suicide attempts, even as she's overtaken by anxiety and/or depression. As we work to transform the culture, we can work to transform ourselves, being careful not to succumb to the overwhelming social messages of insisting on top grades, top teams, top everything all the time.

On a practical level, parents can lobby their children's schools for an appropriate amount of homework, help their children choose a reasonable number of extracurriculars, and make sure that whatever else may be sacrificed to their children's schedules, sleep is not. Speaking as the parent of three sons, I'll be the first to acknowledge that doing so is not easy. But I do think it's necessary, and that we have to be willing to make the attempt.

- *We can all work to provide teenagers with organizations and activities that help them engage in their communities.* There are lots of ways teens can participate in the larger society, if only we're willing to let them try. Certainly, teenagers can form their own organizations, inside and outside of school: women's groups, gay-straight alliances, environmental groups, civil rights organizations. Teens can also participate in the work of established organizations: political parties, churches, activist groups, organizations that fight the stigma of mental illness. Adults who enjoy their own meaningful work can mentor interested teens or find other ways to help teenagers become active. Workers at an animal-rescue shelter, for example, might welcome teenage volunteers or might appreciate teenagers who try to raise community awareness for the more humane treatment of animals. Musicians and actors can help teenagers create plays and songs about the problems they see and the solutions they long for. School officials, parents, and interested adults can find creative new ways to help teens discover the saving grace of community.
- *We need a renewed women's movement to help our daughters identify today's "problem with no name"—the Triple Bind.* Having seen the extraordinary impact of 1970s feminism, I believe we now need a movement that will speak specifically to the needs of young women and girls, so they can take advantage of the opportunities that the previous generation fought to give them. Such a movement could help young women resist the constant barrage of objectification, the deadening consumerism, and the culture of busy-ness (and, ultimately, emptiness) that surrounds today's teenage girls.

As I was making my final revisions to this chapter, I happened to catch sight of the March 2008 cover of *Interview* magazine, featuring actress Ellen Page, star of the film *Juno*. I'd looked to Page as an exemplar of possibilities for young women, a symbol of the kind of alternatives that have been erased in so many domains but that somehow continue to emerge despite the larger pressures of the mainstream culture. I particularly appreciated Page's *New York* magazine interview, cited in Chapter 4, in which she invoked rock singer Annie Lennox as an example of a woman who resisted her own culture's pressures to present herself in conventionally feminine terms.

So there was Page on the cover of *Interview*, dressed in Annie Lennox–like drag: a man's dark suit, narrow tie, and white shirt. But there she was, too, with bright-red lipstick and pants unzipped, her thumb hooked through the waistband of her matching bright-red underwear. The photograph had done what I would have thought was impossible: turned Lennox's subversive look into yet another sexually objectified pose. And sure enough, while the interview chronicles Page's appreciation for 1970s punk heroine Patti Smith, another woman who tried to resist the demands of conventional femininity, the illustrations show Page in the latest designer fashions by Gucci and Miu Miu, a kind of *America's Next Top Model* for indie film stars. Even the young actress who champions alternatives for girls had fallen prey to the relentless consumerism and objectification of teen-girl culture.[18]

So resisting and then undoing the Triple Bind are no simple tasks. Yet the undertaking is of crucial importance. Although most girls will escape adolescence without falling prey to the crisis-level statistics we've been seeing, all of our daughters are affected by the crisis that surrounds them. And as the statistics spike and the crisis grows, we truly don't know whose daughter will be next. We must look to the message of our canaries in the coal mine, and to the inspiring stories of girls like Lily, to recall both the urgency and the hope of our endeavor.

CONCLUSION

Coming to Terms With the Triple Bind

Working on this book has been an extraordinary journey for me. I began it as a scientist focused on the clinical condition of ADHD, working with a number of troubled girls in the San Francisco Bay area. I have emerged with a far broader perspective on the enormous promise of today's teenage girls but also on the enormous risk to our entire current generation of daughters. It's been a humbling experience but also an inspiring one, because I've come to see that all of my life experiences have played a part in helping me to name this crisis and, I hope, to address it.

I know from my own experience that being concerned with wider issues has made all the difference in my ability to find purpose, meaning, and joy in my life. Even though my family, teaching, and research have always been important to me, it took many years for me to overcome my deeply ingrained resistance to revealing my father's struggles with mental illness.[1] Indeed, once established, the pattern of keeping silent—and failing to admit or acknowledge the difficult realities of many family and social situations—can become a real habit, and a pernicious one. Silence tends to breed more silence, while the underlying issues never get dealt with.

Once I began to talk and write about my dad's experiences—and mine—I became freer in a number of ways: to address why mental illness continues to be stigmatized so grievously, to add personal experience to my teaching and lecturing, and to come to terms with why I am so deeply committed to the science of psychology and to the implementation of that science to improve the lives of others.[2] Ever since I became invested in a wider world and a deeper community—spanning scientists, clinicians, family members, advocates, and individuals coping with their own mental disorders—everything I now do has become more meaningful and more energizing: playing and talking with my sons, teaching and mentoring my students, performing research, running a department, and, finally, writing this book.

In fact, when you're really connected with what you're doing, community seems to grow almost of itself, often from the most surprising quarters. People are eager to connect with others who seem to experience a deep meaning and involvement in their own lives. As I have become more connected to my own true self, I've therefore been able to connect more deeply and meaningfully to others. Every day is a source of new energy, new contacts, and a deeper sense of commitment.

It is hard to describe the inspiration I feel from having a purpose and a sense of true meaning in my work and family life. Connection and commitment make the day-to-day struggles, the petty grievances, and the sometimes mind-numbing hassles melt away very quickly, especially when I sense a real connection between what I'm doing and a larger set of meaningful objectives.

But I come to these issues and my renewed dedication as a middle-aged man with a family and career, and a network of friends and colleagues to support me. I am not a girl approaching her teenage years, with the incredible promise as well as the undeniable peril that lie ahead. It is up to all of us to create the conditions that will open up our daughters (and our sons as well) to truly see the world around them—and then to engage with that world rather than becoming preoccupied with the many empty features of the current cultural landscape. It is up to us, as well, to recognize that when our children and adolescents, of either gender, become afflicted with mental disorders, their struggles are real and deserving of the best treatments we can provide.

Finally, it is up to all of us to see that being real with our daughters (and sons) about the things that truly matter is our ultimate task as parents, caregivers, and authorities. Those topics include real-life pain and struggles; triumphs large and small; family relationships; and the pursuit of independent goals. They also include ideas that truly engage the mind, activities and actions that challenge society's relentless objectification and consumerism, and an insistence on authentic expression. What better task could there be for us adults: to transform a Triple Bind into a rich set of opportunities?

RESOURCES

AGGRESSION AND VIOLENCE

Books

Barkley, Russell A., and Arthur L. Robin. *Your Defiant Teen: 10 Steps to Resolve Conflict and Rebuild Your Relationship* (New York: Guilford, 2008).

Coloroso, Barbara. *The Bully, the Bullied, and the Bystander: From Preschool to High School—How Parents and Teachers Can Help Break the Cycle of Violence* (New York: HarperCollins, 2003).

Simmons, Rachel. *Odd Girl Out: The Hidden Culture of Aggression in Girls* (Orlando, Fla.: Harcourt, 2002).

Wiseman, Rosalind. *Queen Bees and Wannabes: Helping Your Daughter Survive Cliques, Gossip, Boyfriends, and Other Realities of Adolescence* (New York: Three Rivers Press, 2002).

Websites

Center for Disease Control and Prevention, Injury Center
www.cdc.gov/ncipc/dvp/YVP/default.htm
Information page by the CDC about youth violence prevention.

National Youth Violence Prevention Resource Center
www.safeyouth.org
A federal resource for communities working to prevent violence committed by and against young people.

Organizations

SAVE: Students Against Violence Everywhere
National Association of SAVE
322 Chapanoke Road, Suite 110
Raleigh, NC 27603
866-343-SAVE
Fax: 919-661-7777
www.nationalsave.org

The Ophelia Project
718 Nevada Drive
Erie, PA 16505
888-256-KIDS, 814-456-5437
Fax: 814-455-2090
www.opheliaproject.org

CYBERBULLYING

Books

Goodstein, Anastasia. *Totally Wired: What Teens and Tweens Are Really Doing Online* (New York: St. Martin's Press, 2007).

Kelsey, Candice M. *Generation MySpace: Helping Your Teen Survive Online Adolescence* (New York: Marlowe, 2007).

Kowalski, Robin M., Susan P. Limber, and Patricia W. Agatston. *Cyber Bullying: Bullying in the Digital Age* (Malden, Mass.: Wiley-Blackwell, 2007).

Melton, Barbara, and Susan Shankle. *What in the World Are Your Kids Doing Online? How to Understand the Electronic World Your Children Live In* (New York: Broadway, 2007).

Willard, Nancy E. *Cyberbullying and Cyberthreats: Responding to the Challenge of Online Social Aggression, Threats, and Distress* (Champaign, Ill.: Research Press, 2007).

Websites

National Crime Prevention Council
www.ncpc.org/cyberbullying
A crime-prevention website with information about cyber-bullying.

Stop Bullying Now
stopbullyingnow.hrsa.gov
The Stop Bullying Now! website is partnered with the Health Resources and Services Administration (HRSA) and more than seventy other organizations to increase awareness about bullying. Cyberbullying information can be found under *What adults can do → All about bullying → Cyberbullying.*

Stop Cyberbullying
www.stopcyberbullying.org
A program of Parry Aftab and the Wired Safety Group, with detailed information about cyberbullying.

Organizations

i-SAFE Inc.
5900 Pasteur Court, Suite 100
Carlsbad, CA 92008
760-603-7911
Fax: 760-603-8382
www.isafe.org

Wired Safety
www.wiredsafety.org

DEPRESSION AND SUICIDE

Books

Bornstein, Kate, with Sara Quin. *Hello Cruel World: 101 Alternatives to Suicide for Teens, Freaks and Other Outlaws* (New York: Seven Stories Press, 2006).

Emmons, Henry, with Rachel Kranz. *The Chemistry of Joy: A Three-Step Program for Overcoming Depression Through Western Science and Eastern Wisdom* (New York: Fireside, 2006).

Pipher, Mary. *Reviving Ophelia: Saving the Selves of Adolescent Girls* (New York: Ballantine, 1994).

Websites

American Psychological Association
www.healthyminds.org/multimedia/teensuicide.pdf
Includes information about teenage suicide.

Helpguide.org
www.helpguide.org/mental/depression_teen.htm
A nonprofit source of information on mental health and related topics.

Organizations

American Foundation for Suicide Prevention
120 Wall Street, 22nd floor
New York, NY 10005
888-333-AFSP, 212-363-3500
Fax: 212-363-6237
www.afsp.org

Depression and Bipolar Support Alliance (DBSA)
730 N. Franklin Street, Suite 501
Chicago, IL 60610-7224
800-826-3632
Fax: 312-642-7243
www.ndmda.org

SAVE—Suicide Awareness Voices of Education
8120 Penn Avenue S., Suite 470
Bloomington, MN 55431
952-946-7998
www.save.org

EATING DISORDERS

Books

Costin, Carolyn. *The Eating Disorders Sourcebook* (Lincolnwood, Mass.: Lowell House, 1996).

Martin, Courtney E. *Perfect Girls, Starving Daughters: The Frightening New Normalcy of Hating Your Body* (Glencoe, Ill.: Free Press, 2007).

Mendelsohn, Susan J. *It's Not About the Weight: Attacking Eating Disorders From the Inside Out* (Lincoln, Neb.: iUniverse, 2007).

Herzog, David B., Debra L. Franko, and Patti Cable. *Unlocking the Mysteries of Eating Disorders (Harvard Medical School Guides)* (Columbus, Ohio: McGraw-Hill, 2007).

Websites

Eating Disorders Online
www.eatingdisordersonline.com
Resource for information about eating disorders. Discusses anorexia, bulimia, binge eating disorder, compulsive overeating, overexercising, and more.

National Institute of Mental Health—Eating Disorders
nimh.nih.gov/health/publications/eating-disorders/complete-publication.shtml
Information from the NIMH on eating disorders.

Something Fishy Website on Eating Disorders
www.something-fishy.org
Dedicated to raising awareness and providing support to people with eating disorders and their loved ones. Discusses a wide variety of topics related to eating disorders.

Organizations

National Association of Anorexia Nervosa and Associated Disorders
P.O. Box 7
Highland Park, IL 60035
847-831-3438
www.anad.org

National Eating Disorders Association
603 Stewart Street, Suite 803
Seattle, WA 98101
800-931-2237
www.nationaleatingdisorders.org

Klarman Eating Disorders Center—McLean Hospital
115 Mill Street
Belmont, MA 02478
617-855-2000
www.mclean.harvard.edu/patient/child/edc.php

GAY, LESBIAN, AND BISEXUAL ISSUES

Books

Boston Women's Health Book Collective. *Our Bodies, Ourselves: A New Edition for a New Era* (New York: Touchstone, 2005).

Kaufman, Gershen, and Lev Raphael. *Coming Out of Shame: Transforming Gay and Lesbian Lives* (New York: Doubleday, 1996).

Stevens, Tracy, and Katherine Wunder. *How to Be a Happy Lesbian: A Coming Out Guide* (Asheville, N.C.: Amazing Dreams Publishing, 2002).

Websites

The Bisexual Resource Center
www.biresource.org
An international organization providing education about and support for bisexual and progressive issues.

In the Life
www.inthelifetv.org
Documentary stories from the gay experience.

Lambda Legal
www.lambdalegal.org
Making the case for equality.

Organizations

GLSEN: Gay, Lesbian, Straight Education Network
90 Broad Street, 2nd floor
New York, NY 10004
212-727-0135
Fax: 212-727-0254
www.glsen.org

Matthew Shepard Foundation
301 Thelma, #512
Casper, WY 82609
307-237-6167
Fax: 307-237-6156
www.matthewshepard.org

PFLAG: Parents, Families, and Friends of Lesbians and Gays
1726 M Street, NW, Suite 400
Washington, DC 20036
202-467-8180
Fax: 202-467-8194
www.pflag.org

Triangle Foundation
19641 West Seven Mile Road
Detroit, MI 48219-2721
313-537-7000
Hate crime reporting: 877-787-4264
Fax: 313-537-3379
www.tri.org

SELF-HARM, CUTTING, AND SELF-MUTILATION

Books

Alderman, Tracy. *The Scarred Soul: Understanding and Ending Self-Inflicted Violence* (Oakland, Calif.: New Harbinger Publications, 1997).

Linehan, Marsha M. *Skills Training Manual for Treating Borderline Personality Disorder* (New York: Guilford, 1993).

Strong, Marilee. *A Bright Red Scream: Self-Mutilation and the Language of Pain* (New York: Penguin, 1998).

Turner, V. J. *Secret Scars: Uncovering and Understanding the Addiction of Self-Injury* (Center City, Minn.: Hazelden, 2002).

Websites

Cornell Research Program on Self-Injurious Behavior in Adolescents and Young Adults
www.crpsib.com/whatissi.asp
Shares the latest information researchers have discovered about self-injury.

S.A.F.E. Alternatives: Self Abuse Finally Ends
www.selfinjury.com
A website with resources on self-injury.

Youthline
www.youthline.org
A confidential phone line for young people that provides information, resources, and support.

Organizations

ASHIC: American Self-Harm Information Clearinghouse
315 Maynard Avenue S., Suite 12
Seattle, WA 98104
206-223-9657
www.selfinjury.org

National Education Alliance for Borderline Personality Disorder (NEA-BPD)
P.O. Box 974
Rye, NY 10580
914-835-9011
www.borderlinepersonalitydisorder.com

ACKNOWLEDGMENTS

This book reflects the efforts of a number of wonderful people.

My agent, Janis Vallely, saw the potential for a book that far transcended my work on girls with ADHD and other psychological conditions. She is skilled, savvy, wise, and insightful; her vision, determination, and wisdom led to this entire project.

Random House senior editor Jill Schwartzman has been encouraging, energetic, intelligent, and on top of every detail throughout the entire process. How fortunate to have such a vibrant, intuitive, and talented editor!

Rachel Kranz, my coauthor, gives meaning to the words *gifted*, *sensitive*, *tenacious*, and *literate*. This book is the result of intensive conversations with Rachel, repeated attempts to find just the right phrase or nuance, her lengthy West Coast journey, her incredible interviewing skills with a number of the girls who are presented in these pages, her deep insights related to getting underneath scientific facts and theories, and her wealth of knowledge about popular culture and media. In all respects, this work is a truly collaborative writing effort.

Several staff, colleagues, and friends at Berkeley were enormously helpful in getting many aspects of the research and raw materials ready. First and foremost, senior research assistant Adriana Nevado was instrumental in obtaining a host of reference materials and in coordinating focus groups and individual interviews with a number of the girls whose words appear in these pages. She has been tireless and inspirational in her efforts. Senior research assistant Suzanne Perrigue assisted skillfully in the research process as well, showing ever-greater insights the further the book progressed. Christine Zalecki, Ph.D., with whom I have worked for many years, provided deep insights about a number of the interviewees and about underlying psychological and cultural processes in girls. Andrea Stier, M.A., was an invaluable source of information about Internet "connections" and girls' dynamics. Samantha Fargeon provided valuable consultation as well.

Thanks to the rest of my lab at Berkeley: Mario Aceves, Beverly Chang, Jenny Diamond, Jenna Gelfand, Tate Guelzow, Fred Loya, Andy Martinez, Ben Mullin, Liz Owens, Erika Swanson, and Alan Vitolo.

I could not have assembled the material herein without the support of the National Institute of Mental Health, which has awarded me research grants for many years; the Department of Psychology and the Institute of Human Development at UC Berkeley; and—most of all—the families, girls, and staff members who have so generously contributed to my summer research programs, treatment studies, and longitudinal investigations.

For all of the girls who provided raw material for the interviews quoted in these pages, whether they remain anonymous or whether they are identified by name: thanks from the bottom of my heart. It is your words and your experiences that make this material come alive.

To Notre Dame High School—Belmont and particularly to Phyllis van Hagen: thanks for all you did to help us reach out to teenage girls. And to the ladies of the Girl Panel: thanks for sharing your wonderful stories.

To all of my scientific colleagues whose work is cited in the extensive notes (and to so many more, for whom space limitations precluded citations): my eternal gratitude, for it is through wise and deep science that the forces predicting both healthy and unhealthy adjustment in our next generation will be understood.

To Ellie Siegel, Sophie Siegel-Warren, Tim Cusack, Chris Gullo, Karen Szczepanski, and Bea, Wendy, Laura, Elizabeth, and Christina Kranz—many thanks! This book is richer for all of your insights.

My wife, Kelly, has been a source of wisdom, support, and love throughout all phases of this project, and many other projects as well. Thanks and love, Kel.

To Jeff, John, and Evan: you are the future, go for it!

NOTES

Introduction: Girls in Crisis

1. There are no clear-cut boundaries between patterns of behavioral and emotional problems that are classified as disorders and those that lie just below the threshold for a diagnosis. As a result, official counts of children and adolescents who are diagnosed with mental disorders are highly likely to underestimate the actual suffering involved for extremely large numbers of youth and their families. See Peter M. Lewinsohn, Hyman Hops, Robert E. Roberts, John R. Seeley, and Judy A. Andrews, "Adolescent Psychopathology: I. Prevalence and Incidence of Depression and Other DSM-III-R Disorders in High School Students," *Journal of Abnormal Psychology, 102* (1993): 133–144. Although the majority of adolescent girls make it through their teens without major disturbance, an alarming number suffer from clinical conditions. The main contention of this book is that the increased rates of several disorders and the decreased age of onset for depression are related to the combination of forces signaled by the Triple Bind. These forces are also making it increasingly difficult for any girls in our society to thrive, even if they are not prone to suffer from a mental disorder.

2. Authoritative sources confirm that 15–20 percent of girls exhibit a lifetime prevalence of major depression by their late teenage years, with depression defined as at least two weeks' duration of a list of highly impairing symptoms related to depressed and irritable mood, distorted thinking, poor sleep and appetite patterns, diminished interest and pleasure in usual activities, low energy, poor concentration, feelings of worthlessness, and, all too often, thoughts of suicide. See Dwight L. Evans and Martin E. P. Seligman, "Introduction," and Commission on Adolescent Disorder and Depression, "Defining Depression and Bipolar Disorder," in *Treating and Preventing Adolescent Mental Health Disorders: What We Know and What We Don't Know*, ed. Dwight L. Evans, Edna B. Foa, Racquel E. Gur, Herbert Hendin, Charles P. O'Brien, Martin E. P. Seligman, and B. Timothy Walsh (New York: Oxford University Press, 2005); and Constance Hammen and Karen D. Rudolph, "Childhood Mood Disorders," in *Child Psychopathology,* 2nd ed., ed. Eric J. Mash and Russell A. Barkley (New York: Guilford, 2003).

On the high end of estimates, in a community sample in the Pacific Northwest, the prevalence of major depression in females by the end of adolescence was 24 to 32 percent; see Lewinsohn et al., "Adolescent Psychopathology." More conservatively, Jane Costello and colleagues estimated that between the ages of nine and sixteen years, 12 percent of girls exhibited some form of depressive disorder: E. Jane Costello, Sarah Mustillo, Alaattin Erkanli, Gordon Keeler, and Adrian Angold, "Prevalence and Development of

Psychiatric Disorders in Childhood and Adolescence," *Archives of General Psychiatry, 60* (2003): 837–844. (By age eighteen or nineteen, this figure would undoubtedly have been higher.) Also, Ronald Kessler and Ellen E. Walters, "Epidemiology of DSM-III-R Major Depression and Minor Depression Among Adolescents and Young Adults in the National Comorbidity Survey," *Depression and Anxiety,* 7 (1998): 3–15, found that the lifetime prevalence of major depression in fifteen- to eighteen-year-olds was 14 percent, with another 11 percent showing minor depression—for a review, see Karen D. Rudolph, Constance Hammen, and Shannon E. Daley, "Mood Disorders," in *Behavioral and Emotional Disorders in Adolescents: Nature, Assessment, and Treatment*, ed. David A. Wolfe and Eric J. Mash (New York: Guilford, 2006). Because this latter estimate includes boys and girls, however, a rate of around 20 percent of major depression for adolescent girls—who show twice the rates of depression as boys from midadolescence onward—would be accurate. See also Kate Keenan, Alison Hipwell, Jeanne Duax, Magda Stouthamer-Loeber, and Rolf Loeber, "Phenomenology of Depression in Young Girls," *Journal of the American Academy of Child and Adolescent Psychiatry,* 43 (2001): 1098–1106. Overall, a rate of 15–20 percent for girls is based on sound evidence.

3. Completed suicide is still relatively rare in adolescents. Yet because of the vastly improved health conditions for children and adolescents in the modern era, which have eliminated many of the fatal diseases that used to claim lives, suicide is actually the third leading cause of death among adolescents and young adults (after car accidents and homicides); see Mitchell J. Prinstein, "Introduction to the Special Section on Suicide and Non-Suicidal Self-Injury: A Review of Unique Challenges and Important Directions for Self-Injury Science," *Journal of Consulting and Clinical Psychology,* 76 (2008): 1–8. Youth suicide rates went up threefold between the 1950s and late 1980s. After a decline between the late 1980s and the turn of the twenty-first century, data from 2003–4—the last years for which good figures are available—were published in September 2007; see Centers for Disease Control and Prevention, "Suicide Trends Among Youths and Young Adults Aged 10–24 Years—United States, 1990–2004," *Morbidity and Mortality Weekly Report, 56 (35)* (September 7, 2007): 905–908, retrieved from www.cdc.gov/MMWR/preview/mmwrhtml/mm5635a2.htm. For girls ages fifteen to nineteen, the rate of completed suicide went up by 32 percent; for girls ages ten to fourteen years, there was a huge 76 percent increase. These provocative data were highly publicized: see, for example, CBC News Canada, "Suicide Rates Among U.S. Teenage Girls at 15 Year High," retrieved from www.cbc.ca/health/story/2007/09/06/suicide-girls.html. For a review see David B. Goldston, Stepanie S. Sergeant, and Elizabeth M. Arnold, "Suicidal and Nonsuicidal Self-Harm Behaviors," in *Behavioral and Emotional Disorders in Adolescents: Nature, Assessment, and Treatment*, ed. David A. Wolfe and Eric J. Mash (New York: Guilford, 2006).

Among reasons for this sudden rise, experts from the Centers for Disease Control noted the huge pressures endured by girls in young adolescence, especially those entering middle school—a contention that I share in this book (see Chapter 3). Another reason may be the warnings now placed on SSRI medications (i.e., Prozac and related agents), because of concerns over side effects (including a temporary increase in suicidal urges) when young people begin to take these medicines. However, Robert Gibbons and colleagues have found that, county by county across the United States, *higher* rates of prescriptions of SSRI medications are associated with *lower* rates of suicide for adolescents. The increased warnings related to such medications in youth, which began in 2003 and resulted in lowered prescription rates, may have contributed to the increase in child and adolescent suicides; see Robert D. Gibbons, Kwan Hur, Dulal K. Bhaumik, and J. John Mann, "The Relationship Between Antidepressant Rates and Rate of Early Adolescent Suicide," *American Journal of Psychiatry, 163* (2006): 1898–1904; and Robert D. Gibbons,

C. Hendricks Brown, Kwan Hur, Sue M. Marcus, Dulal K. Bhaumik, Joelle A. Erkens, Ron M. C. Herings, and J. John Mann, "Early Evidence on the Effects of Regulators' Suicidality Warnings on SSRI Prescriptions and Suicide in Children and Adolescents," *American Journal of Psychiatry, 164* (2007): 1356–1363.

More generally, it has been reported that 9 percent of high school students have made a suicide attempt within the past year, with many more having given serious thought to suicide. See Centers for Disease Control and Prevention, Web-Based Injury Statistics Query and Reporting System (WISQARS), retrieved from www.cdc.gov/ncicp/wisqars; and Evans and Seligman, "Introduction." Girls attempt suicide more than boys, so this figure is undoubtedly even higher for adolescent females. Even for "tweens" (ages nine to thirteen years), more than 20 percent of students had seriously considered attempting suicide, and 15.7 percent had made a specific plan to attempt suicide. And adolescent girls report alarmingly high rates of suicidal thinking, with one in three high school girls revealing that they had thought about suicide in the past two weeks. For these data, see Centers for Disease Control and Prevention, "Life's First Great Crossroads—Tweens Make Choices," May 2000, retrieved from www.cdc.gov/youthcampaign/research/PDF/LifesFirstCrossroads.pdf.

4. With respect to self-injurious behaviors, definitions vary and estimates are hard to come by, especially because of the shame and secrecy surrounding such behavior patterns. Self-injury goes by a variety of terms: *self-harm, self-mutilation, cutting, parasuicide, non-suicidal self-injurious behavior, self-attack, symbolic wounding,* and others. It ranges from mild and extremely common behaviors such as nail biting to far more serious actions such as cutting marks into one's skin, exhibiting extremely poor self-care, burning oneself, or head banging. Self-harm is distinguished from suicide attempts in that the individual in question is attempting to release herself from deep internal pain and to ward off intolerable feelings but does not wish to die. Still, self-injurious behavior results from several different motivations, and there is clearly a link between self-injurious behavior and risk for actual suicide attempts; see Jayne Cooper, Navneet Kapur, Roger Webb, Martin Lawlor, Else Guthrie, Kevin Mackway-Jones, and Louis Appleby, "Suicide After Deliberate Self-Harm: A 4-Year Cohort Study," *American Journal of Psychiatry, 162* (2005): 297–303, and Matthew K. Nock and Mitchell J. Prinstein, "Contextual Features and Behavioral Functions of Self-Mutilation Among Adolescents," *Journal of Abnormal Psychology, 114* (2005): 140–146. The emotion regulatory function of self-harm after abuse and trauma is emphasized by Tuppett M. Yates, "The Developmental Psychopathology of Self-Injurious Behavior: Compensatory Regulation in Post-Traumatic Adaptation," *Clinical Psychology Review, 24* (2004): 35–74.

Although no viable comparisons with earlier eras are available, most authors contend that rates of serious self-injury are decidedly on the increase in recent years: Amelio A. D'Onofrio, *Adolescent Self-Injury: A Comprehensive Guide for Counselors and Health Care Professionals* (New York: Springer, 2007); Lori Goldfarb Plante, "Helping Adolescents with Self-Injurious Behavior: Cutting in Developmental Context," in *Mental Disorders of the New Millennium,* vol. 1: *Behavioral Issues,* ed. Thomas G. Plante (Westport, Conn.: Praeger, 2006). It is unclear whether girls show higher rates than boys, yet females who end up in the emergency room for self-harmful behaviors are at higher risk for subsequent suicide attempts than males; see Cooper et al., "Suicide After Deliberate Self-Harm," and Mark Olfson, Marc J. Gameroff, Steven C. Marcus, Ted Greenberg, and David Shaffer, "National Trends in Hospitalization of Youth with Self-Inflicted Injuries," *American Journal of Psychiatry, 162* (2005): 1328–1335.

Moderate to severe levels of self-harmful behaviors are found in a wide range of adolescents, estimated from 14 to 39 percent: see D'Onofrio, *Adolescent Self-Injury*; Kristin L. Croyle and Jennifer Waltz, "Subclinical Self-Harm: Range of Behaviors, Extent, and

Associated Characteristics," *American Journal of Orthopsychiatry,* 77 (2005): 332–342; Elizabeth Lloyd-Richardson, Nicholas Perrine, Lisa Dierker, and Mary L. Kelley, "Characteristics and Functions of Non-Suicidal Self-injury in a Community Sample of Adolescents," *Psychological Medicine,* 37 (2007): 1183–1192; and Prinstein, "Introduction to Special Section." D'Onofrio contends that this phenomenon has reached "epidemic" proportions, as evidenced by an explosion of reports of self-injurious behavior in teens, but the actual extent of such an increase is, again, unknown.

5. Regarding aggression and violence, between 2 and 9 percent of adolescent girls meet criteria for "conduct disorder," a diagnosis that includes both nonviolent and violent patterns of antisocial behavior; see American Psychiatric Association, *Diagnostic and Statistical Manual of Mental Disorders, 4th edition, Text Revision* (Washington, D.C.: Author, 2000). Boys are far more likely than girls to show physical aggression and other "externalizing" behavior from the preschool years through puberty, and males display more physical violence than females throughout life. Yet girls come close to catching up to boys in terms of many forms of aggression and antisocial behavior during adolescence; see Stephen P. Hinshaw and Steve S. Lee, "Conduct and Oppositional Defiant Disorders," in *Child Psychopathology*, 2nd ed., ed. Eric J. Mash and Russell A. Barkley (New York: Guilford, 2003). The exception is interpersonal violence, which still remains predominantly a male phenomenon.

Still, national estimates from self-report data indicate that somewhere between 16 and 32 percent of girls through age seventeen have committed at least one serious violent offense, severe enough to have caused bodily injury; see U.S. Department of Health and Human Services, *Youth Violence: A Report of the Surgeon General* (Rockville, Md.: Author, 2001). A book-length source regarding the increase in physically aggressive behavior patterns in girls across the past decade is James Garbarino, *See Jane Hit: Why Girls Are Growing More Violent and What We Can Do About It* (New York: Penguin, 2006). See also Martha Putallaz and Karen L. Bierman, eds., *Aggression, Antisocial Behavior, and Violence Among Girls* (New York: Guilford, 2004), and Marlene M. Moretti, Candice L. Odgers, and Margaret A. Jackson, eds., *Girls and Aggression: Contributing Factors and Intervention Principles* (New York: Kluwer Academic/Plenum, 2004).

Overall, in terms of an aggregate "count" of aggression and violence in teenage girls, a conservative 10 percent is clearly warranted, not to mention the high rates of relational aggression (exclusion, rumor-mongering, defaming of reputations) exhibited by girls, noted in Chapter 8.

6. Chesney-Lind and Belknap provide evidence that, across the past several decades, girls' potential for aggression and violence has finally been recognized. In a form of overreaction, however, a number of delinquent acts in girls have become criminalized, which is a key determinant of the seemingly sharp increases in rates of assault and violence in females. Thus, the category of "assault" has become a convenient designation for girls who may not, in fact, be as violent as boys. In short, the closing of the gender gap in violence may be somewhat mythical (see Chapter 8). See Meda Chesney-Lind and Joanne Belknap, "Trends in Delinquent Girls' Aggression and Violent Behavior: A Review of the Evidence," in *Aggression, Antisocial Behavior, and Violence Among Girls*, ed. Martha Putallaz and Karen L. Bierman (New York: Guilford, 2004). On the other hand, self-report statistics, as opposed to criminal records, reveal high levels of violence in girls, as reported in U.S. Department of Health and Human Services, *Youth Violence.* Overall, boys remain more likely to commit violence outside the home than girls, although girls have shown at least some degree of closing the gap. Furthermore, girls' and women's rates of partner violence are clearly higher than what would be believed on the basis of predominant stereotypes of females; see Chesney-Lind and Belknap, "Trends in Girls' Delinquent Behavior,"

and George Archer, "Sex Differences in Aggression Between Heterosexual Partners: A Meta-Analytic Review," *Psychological Bulletin, 126* (2000): 651–680.

7. Around 3 to 5 percent of adolescent girls exhibit the eating disorders of anorexia nervosa (involving major weight loss through various means of restricting food intake or burning calories, mediated through an intense fear of fat and distorted body image plus loss of menstrual periods), bulimia nervosa (involving both binges and means of purging, such as self-induced vomiting, use of laxatives/enemas/diuretics, or excessive exercise), or binge eating disorder (involving binge eating patterns without purging). See Eric Stice and Cynthia Bulik, "Eating Disorders," in *Child and Adolescent Psychopathology*, ed. Theodore Beauchaine and Stephen P. Hinshaw (Hoboken, N.J.: Wiley, 2008), and G. Terence Wilson, Carolyn Block Becker, and Karen Heffernan, "Eating Disorders," in *Child Psychopathology*, 2nd ed., ed. Eric J. Mash and Russell A. Barkley (New York: Guilford Press, 2003). Recent evidence reveals an increase in binge eating disorder, as noted in James I. Hudson, Eva Hiripi, Harrison G. Pope Jr., and Ronald C. Kessler, "The Prevalence and Correlates of Eating Disorders in the National Comorbidity Survey Replication," *Biological Psychiatry, 61* (2007): 348–358. This study focused on a nationally representative sample of adults, so its relevance to adolescents may be questioned. Still, key findings were that the prevalence of binge eating disorder was over 3 percent, that this condition was associated with obesity and with marked impairment, and that it has increased in prevalence in recent years, presumably because of the current "epidemic" of obesity. In short, binge eating disorder appears to be on the rise.

Wilson and colleagues, in "Eating Disorders," highlight that most investigations *underestimate* the prevalence of eating disorders, given the reluctance of many symptomatic individuals to participate in research investigations or disclose their problems and given the stringency of the diagnostic criteria in the official diagnostic guidelines, known as the *DSM-IV*; see American Psychiatric Association, *Diagnostic and Statistical Manual.* Finally, and discouragingly, prevalence rates for subthreshold forms of eating disorders, such as obsessive dieting, distorted body image, and/or hatred of one's body size, are far higher. Indeed, rates of dieting among adolescent girls are estimated at 60 and 70 percent, as reported by James D. Lock and Daniel le Grange, "Eating Disorders," in *Behavioral and Emotional Disorders in Adolescents: Nature, Assessment, and Treatment*, ed. David A. Wolfe and Eric J. Mash (New York: Guilford, 2006) (see also Evans and Seligman, "Introduction"). Such concerns begin at young ages: over 40 percent of girls before age nine wish to be thinner, and over half of nine- and ten-year-old girls report feeling better about themselves when dieting: see Margo Maine, *Body Wars: Making Peace with Women's Bodies: An Activist's Guide* (Carlsbad, Calif.: Gurze Books, 2000). Clearly, excessive concern with body size and weight is far more prevalent than are clinical-level eating disorders per se.

8. The overall figure of 25 percent across the conditions of interest (depression, suicide, self-harm, eating disturbance, and aggression) is well supported, as indicated in the previous notes and as explained more in Chapter 1. It may actually be an underestimate, if rates of adolescent depression, self-harm, and violence are as high as some contend. Several general issues regarding how to estimate and combine the prevalence of psychological/psychiatric disturbance should help to clarify how I arrived at this figure.

First, although many studies are based on those teenagers who have been referred to clinics, such referred samples are not representative of the general population; see Sherryl H. Goodman, Benjamin B. Lahey, Brooke Fielding, Mina Dulcan, William Narrow, and Darryl Regier, "Representativeness of Clinical Samples of Youths with Mental Disorders: A Preliminary Population-Based Study," *Journal of Abnormal Psychology, 106* (1998): 3–14. Compared to youth in the general population who meet criteria for a disorder, clinical samples are more likely to be white and wealthier and to show greater levels of co-occurring disorders. Representative samples are essential for prevalence estimates, and I cite reports of these herein.

Second, there is an important difference between "point prevalence," signifying the number of individuals who have the condition at a given time, and "lifetime prevalence," the number who have had the condition up to a certain age. I feature the latter herein.

Third, there is great variability in the prevalence estimates from current studies, because there is still no national-level study of the rates of child and adolescent mental disorders, and because existing investigations utilize different measures of psychological disturbance, take place in disparate geographic locations, often use relatively small samples, and employ different timeframes for recall of past problems. I have focused on the middle range of prevalence estimates rather than the upper-bound figures in some reports.

Fourth, even in representative community samples, most youth who have a mental disorder have at least one other condition, an occurrence known as *comorbidity.* It makes sense, for example, that depression and suicide would be closely linked. Yet depression and aggression/violence also show a substantial overlap—as do eating disorders and many other forms of self-harm. See Adrian Angold, E. Jane Costello, and Alaattin Erkanli, "Comorbidity," *Journal of Child Psychology and Psychiatry, 40* (1999): 57–87. The important implication is that prevalence rates for different disorders cannot simply be added up to get an overall estimate, because this would involve the double counting of those girls who have more than one condition. Throughout, I have taken care to avoid such overcounting.

Note that bipolar disorder, attention-deficit/hyperactivity disorder (ADHD), anxiety disorders, and substance abuse problems are not even included in the statistics above. And whereas adolescent boys have traditionally showed higher rates of substance abuse than girls, this is no longer the case, because girls' rates of substance abuse are rising; see Sandra L. Brown and Ana M. Abrantes, "Substance Use Disorders," in *Behavioral and Emotional Disorders in Adolescents: Nature, Assessment, and Treatment*, ed. David A. Wolfe and Eric J. Mash (New York: Guilford, 2006).

Overall, the figure of 25 percent or more is no exaggeration. Even when taking into account comorbidity—for example, subtracting out the overlap between depression and violent behavior, which is likely to be a third of each category; or the strong overlap between self-harm and eating pathology, which appears to be a substantial proportion of each category for girls—the rates of 15–20 percent for major depression, a fraction of 1 percent for completed suicide but as much as 10 percent for attempted suicide, 3–4 percent for eating disorders, 10 percent for violence, and 15 percent for self-harm add up to indicate that at least a quarter of adolescent girls can be seen to suffer from one or more of these conditions.

Finally, the rates of several of these conditions may well be growing. Evans and Seligman made this point explicitly in 2005 in their "Introduction": "What is especially alarming is that the prevalence . . . has been on the rise over each successive generation. Certain changes over time in the nature of adolescence, and the environments that adolescents find themselves in, may be responsible for these observed increases in the prevalence of psychopathology in adolescence" (p. xxvi). Such environments are the focus of this book.

9. For discussion of categorical versus dimensional perspectives, see Theodore P. Beauchaine, "Taxometrics and Developmental Psychopathology," *Development and Psychopathology, 15* (2003): 501–527; Andrew Pickles and Adrian Angold, "Natural Categories or Fundamental Dimensions: On Carving Nature at the Joints and the Rearticulation of Psychopathology," *Development and Psychopathology, 15* (2003): 529–551.

10. Emily Nussbaum, "Say Everything," *New York*, February 12, 2007, 24–29, 102–105.

11. For information on the stigmatization of mental illness, see Patrick W. Corrigan,

ed., *On the Stigma of Mental Illness: Practical Strategies for Research and Social Change* (Washington, D.C.: American Psychological Association, 2005); Stephen P. Hinshaw, "The Stigmatization of Mental Illness in Children and Parents: Developmental Issues, Family Concerns, and Research Needs," *Journal of Child Psychology and Psychiatry, 46* (2005): 714–734; Stephen P. Hinshaw, "Stigma and Mental Illness: Developmental Issues," in *Developmental Psychopathology*, 2nd ed., vol. 3: *Risk, Disorder, and Adaptation*, ed. Dante Cicchetti and Donald J. Cohen (New York: Wiley, 2006); Stephen P. Hinshaw, *The Mark of Shame: Stigma of Mental Illness and an Agenda for Change* (New York: Oxford University Press, 2007); Bruce G. Link and Jo C. Phelan, "Conceptualizing Stigma," *Annual Review of Sociology,* 27 (2001): 363–385; and Graham Thornicroft, *Shunned: Discrimination Against People with Mental Illness* (Oxford, U.K.: Oxford University Press, 2006).

12. Findings from my summer research programs for girls, as well as the five-year follow-up investigation, are found in the following articles: Stephen P. Hinshaw, "Preadolescent Girls with Attention-Deficit/Hyperactivity Disorder: I. Background Characteristics, Comorbidity, Cognitive and Social Functioning, and Parenting Practices," *Journal of Consulting and Clinical Psychology, 70* (2002): 1086–1098; Stephen P. Hinshaw, Estol T. Carte, Nilofar Sami, Jennifer J. Treuting, and Brian A. Zupan, "Preadolescent Girls with Attention-Deficit/Hyperactivity Disorder: II. Neuropsychological Performance in Relation to Subtypes and Individual Classification," *Journal of Consulting and Clinical Psychology, 70* (2002): 1099–1111; Dara R. Blachman and Stephen P. Hinshaw, "Patterns of Friendship in Girls With and Without Attention-Deficit/Hyperactivity Disorder," *Journal of Abnormal Child Psychology, 30* (2002): 625–640; Christine Zalecki and Stephen P. Hinshaw, "Overt and Relational Aggression in Girls with Attention-Deficit Hyperactivity Disorder," *Journal of Clinical Child and Adolescent Psychology,* 33 (2004): 131–143; Stephen P. Hinshaw, Elizabeth B. Owens, Nilofar Sami, and Samantha Fargeon, "Prospective Follow-up of Girls with Attention-Deficit/Hyperactivity Disorder into Adolescence: Evidence for Continuing Cross-Domain Impairment," *Journal of Consulting and Clinical Psychology,* 74 (2006): 489–499; Steve S. Lee and Stephen P. Hinshaw, "Predictors of Adolescent Functioning in Girls with Attention-Deficit/Hyperactivity Disorder: The Role of Childhood ADHD, Conduct Problems, and Peer Status," *Journal of Clinical Child and Adolescent Psychology,* 35 (2006): 356–368; Amori Mikami and Stephen P. Hinshaw, "Resilient Adolescent Adjustment Among Girls With and Without Peer Rejection and Attention-Deficit/Hyperactivity Disorder," *Journal of Abnormal Child Psychology,* 34 (2006): 823–837; and Stephen P. Hinshaw, Estol T. Carte, Catherine Fan, Jonathan S. Jassy, and Elizabeth B. Owens, "Neuropsychological Functioning of Girls with Attention-Deficit/Hyperactivity Disorder Followed Prospectively into Adolescence: Evidence for Continuing Deficits?" *Neuropsychology, 21* (2007): 263–273.

13. Narrative accounts of psychological problems are powerful means of conveying the raw material of personal experience. See, for example, Stephen P. Hinshaw, "Parental Mental Disorder and Children's Functioning: Silence and Communication, Stigma, and Resilience," *Journal of Clinical Child and Adolescent Psychology,* 33 (2004): 400–411. It is particularly important that those individuals who work in the mental health professions recognize and disclose their own (and their families') experiences with mental illness: Stephen P. Hinshaw, *Breaking the Silence: Mental Health Professionals Disclose Their Personal and Family Experiences of Mental Illness* (New York: Oxford University Press, 2008). See also Julian Rappaport, "Community Narratives: Tales of Terror and Joy," *American Journal of Community Psychology,* 28 (2000): 1–24.

14. This book benefits from an intellectual history that spans the past twenty-five years, in the form of writings about female adolescent development and the unique problems experienced by girls as they enter their teenage years. Carol Gilligan opened up the

field to consider that the developing "moral sense" of girls and women is based strongly on relationships rather than constituting a truncated form of male development. See Carol Gilligan, *In a Different Voice: Psychological Theory and Women's Development* (Cambridge, Mass.: Harvard University Press, 1982). The work of Eleanor Maccoby on girls' social preferences and networks—and how they differ from those of boys as early as the preschool years—is essential; see Eleanor E. Maccoby, "Gender and Relationships: A Developmental Account," *American Psychologist, 45* (1990): 513–520.

A report by the American Association of University Women, *Shortchanging Girls, Shortchanging America: A Call to Action* (Washington, D.C.: Author, 1991), made it quite clear that the onset of adolescence is associated with a precipitous drop in self-esteem across girls in our society. Intriguingly, this drop is far stronger for white girls and Latinas than it is for African American girls. Following this report, two key books appeared: Lyn Mikel Brown and Carol Gilligan, *Meeting at the Crossroads: Women's Psychology and Girls' Development* (Cambridge, Mass.: Harvard University Press, 1992), which expanded Gilligan's earlier work and brought in issues of adolescent development through a rich series of vignettes of girls from age seven through the late teen years, and Peggy Orenstein and the American Association of University Women, *Schoolgirls: Young Women, Self-Esteem, and the Confidence Gap* (New York: Anchor Books, 1994), which presented poignant portraits of a white middle-class middle school and a predominantly minority lower-class middle school, illustrating how and why parents and teachers unknowingly shape the plummet in girls' academic and social self-concepts at the beginning of adolescence.

A huge influence on our society's thinking about adolescent girls is the classic work of Mary Pipher, *Reviving Ophelia: Saving the Selves of Adolescent Girls* (New York: Ballantine, 1994), in which she chronicled the surge of eating disturbances and suicidal behavior in teenage girls as a function of relentless commercialization, unhealthy media influences, and other cultural forces that erode strong identity formation in our daughters, particularly as adolescence emerges. She placed the blame squarely on the shoulders of cultural messages rather than on parents per se, presaging key themes in the current book, but things have been changing rapidly since the time of Pipher's analysis in the early 1990s. Pipher also wrote the foreword for the engrossing, devastating book by Jean Kilbourne, *Deadly Persuasion: Why Women and Girls Must Fight the Addictive Power of Advertising* (New York: Free Press, 1999), a must-read for all interested in the effects of media images of girls, women, sexuality, and products in the modern era.

Although not focused exclusively on girls and although exaggerated in its claims, Alvin Rosenfeld and Nicole Wise's *The Overscheduled Child: Avoiding the Hyper-Parenting Trap* (New York: St. Martin's Press, 2001), has sensitized families to the problems inherent in overscripting children's lives, leaving no time for basic play and exploration and self-discovery. The crucial role (and destructive potential) of indirect, social, and relational aggression in girls' development was investigated by several trail-blazing scholars (especially Nicki Crick) during the 1990s (see Chapter 8) and summarized, in lucid fashion, by Rachel Simmons in *Odd Girl Out: The Hidden Culture of Aggression in Girls* (New York: Harcourt, 2002).

Another qualitative investigation was undertaken in Sharon Lamb, *The Secret Lives of Girls: What Good Girls Really Do—Sex Play, Aggression, and Their Guilt* (New York: Free Press, 2002), revealing the hidden currents of sexuality, aggression, and drive for power among "normal" girls and pointing out the hypocrisy of our culture's denial of such currents in all girls.

Finally, I highlight recent books dealing with both adolescent girls/young women and the plight of families of children and teens, including Laura Sessions Stepp, *Unhooked: How Young Women Pursue Sex, Delay Love, and Lose at Both* (New York: Riverhead, 2007), an indictment of the "hookup" culture (but with the insight that, as young women are surpassing young men in academics and careers in recent years, they may simply not want to invest the time in traditional relationships that might slow down their newfound competitive spark); Madeline Levine, *The Price of Privilege: How Parental Pressure and Material Advantage Are Creating a Generation of Disconnected and Unhappy Kids* (New York: HarperCollins, 2006), a critique of overscheduled lives and emotionally underinvolved parents in affluent suburban America; and Alexandra Robbins, *The Overacheivers: The Secret Lives of Driven Kids* (New York: Hyperion, 2006), a case study of highly competitive young women. For a searing self-examination of motherhood in the current age, see Judith Warner, *Perfect Madness: Motherhood in the Age of Anxiety* (New York: Riverhead, 2005), and for a particularly poignant examination of mother-daughter relationships in this age of increasing problems in adolescent girls, see Nancy L. Snyderman and Peg Streep, *Girl in the Mirror: Mothers and Daughters in the Years of Adolescence* (New York: Hyperion, 2002). In all, consensus is growing that girls have major opportunities in today's society, but major risks, problems, and pitfalls exist as well.

On the clinical and research front, there is voluminous research from psychobiological, psychological, developmental, family-systems, and psychiatric perspectives on the problems of female socialization and on girls' distressingly high rates of clinical problems. Yet no existing work deals fully with the recent increases in the displays of such problems and the lowering age of onset of depression, phenomena that beg for explanations at the level of environmental context and cultural messages. In other words, as discussed in Chapter 2, although there is undoubted biological and even genetic risk for many of the problems under consideration in this book, changes in genes cannot explain the rise in girls' self-reported violence or in trends toward cutting (or the tragic, recent increases in suicide rates among preteen and early teenage girls) that we have witnessed recently. Thus, in this book, I go beyond my usual investigations and perspectives by considering the confusing and objectifying cultural messages and images that are (a) accentuating biological vulnerabilities and placing more and more girls into the clinical range of major disorders and (b) increasing levels of distress for all girls.

Chapter 1: Impossible Expectations

1. Dwight L. Evans and Martin E. P. Seligman, "Introduction," and Commission on Adolescent Disorder and Depression, "Defining Depression and Bipolar Disorder," in *Treating and Preventing Adolescent Mental Health Disorders: What We Know and What We Don't Know*, ed. Dwight L. Evans, Edna B. Foa, Racquel E. Gur, Herbert Hendin, Charles P. O'Brien, Martin E. P. Seligman, and B. Timothy Walsh (New York: Oxford University Press, 2005); Constance Hammen and Karen D. Rudolph, "Childhood Mood Disorders," in *Child Psychopathology*, 2nd ed., ed. Eric J. Mash and Russell A. Barkley (New York: Guilford, 2003). For a key historical review on the concept of depression prior to adulthood, see Gabrielle A. Carlson and Dennis P. Cantwell, "Unmasking Masked Depression in Children and Adolescents," *American Journal of Psychiatry* 137 (1980): 445–449, who note the transition from the 1960s (and earlier), when depression was held not to exist in children, to the concept of "masked depression"—in which all mental disturbance in childhood was thought to be a form of depression—to the current view that depression can and does exist in young people.

Since the late 1970s, when current thinking on this topic began to solidify, it has been known that boys and girls are essentially equal in their rates of serious depression during childhood; if anything, boys may have slightly higher rates. But during early adolescence, girls quickly surge in their rates of this disorder, such that by age fifteen or sixteen, they are twice as likely to have experienced major depression—a difference that is maintained throughout adulthood (at least through the oldest years, when depression can emerge strongly in both sexes). Thus, early adolescence is a period of ultrahigh risk for depression in girls; see Susan Nolen-Hoeksema and Joan S. Girgus, "The Emergence of Gender Differences in Depression During Adolescence," *Psychological Bulletin, 115* (1994): 424–443. For an overview of traditional risk factors for teen depression, especially in girls, see Jill M. Cyranowski, Ellen Frank, Elizabeth Young, and Kathleen Shear, "Adolescent Onset of the Gender Difference in Lifetime Rates of Major Depression: A Theoretical Model," *Archives of General Psychiatry,* 57 (2000): 21–27. Synthesizing a vast literature, these authors document that depression represents a confluence of many causal factors, including genetic risk, insecure attachments to parents during the early years of life, pubertal timing, negative life events, responses to stress, reactions to loss, ruminative coping styles, and the like. Thus, the reasons for the surge in girls' depression during adolescence are complex. Still, if the environment makes impossible demands on girls during this period of life, as I contend with respect to the Triple Bind, distress and depression are likely.

Depression during adolescence is highly likely to be followed by repeated episodes of depression during the adult years. Beyond the usual patterns of impairment it yields, depression is associated with poor physical health, high rates of health care utilization, and elevated levels of work-related impairment. See for example, Danielle Keenan-Miller, Constance L. Hammen, and Patricia A. Brennan, "Health Outcomes Related to Early Adolescent Depression," *Journal of Adolescent Health, 41* (2007): 256–262.

2. For recent suicide increases in teenage girls, see Centers for Disease Control and Prevention, "Suicide Trends Among Youths and Young Adults Aged 10–24 Years—United States, 1990–2004," *Morbidity and Mortality Weekly Report, 56 (35)* (September 7, 2007): 905–908, retrieved from www.cdc.gov/MMWR/preview/mmwrhtml/mm5635a2.htm, with additional Web postings at www.cbc.ca/health/story/2007/09/06/suicide-girls.html and www.cbsnews.com/stories/2007/09/06/health/main3239837.shtml. For information on adolescent suicide, see David B. Goldston, Stepanie S. Sergeant, and Elizabeth M. Arnold, "Suicidal and Nonsuicidal Self-Harm Behaviors," in *Behavioral and Emotional Disorders in Adolescents: Nature, Assessment, and Treatment*, ed. David A. Wolfe and Eric J. Mash (New York: Guilford, 2006). Risk for adolescent suicide is accentuated, among many other factors, by abuse earlier in life; see Susanne Salzinger, Margaret Rosario, and Daisy S. Ng-Mak, "Adolescent Suicidal Behavior: Associations with Preadolescent Physical Abuse and Selected Risk and Protective Factors," *Journal of the American Academy of Child and Adolescent Psychiatry, 46* (2007): 859–866. At the time of final preparation of this book, new data were released from the Centers for Disease Control and Prevention on an unexpected rise in suicide among Americans between forty-five and fifty-four years of age, signifying that adolescent female suicide is not the only crisis these days; see Patricia Cohen, "Midlife Suicide Rises, Puzzling Researchers," *New York Times*, February 19, 2008.

3. See Amelio A. D'Onofrio, *Adolescent Self-Injury: A Comprehensive Guide for Counselors and Health Care Professionals* (New York: Springer, 2007); and Mitchell J. Prinstein, "Introduction to the Special Section on Suicide and Non-Suicidal Self-Injury: A Review of Unique Challenges and Important Directions for Self-Injury Science," *Journal of Consulting and Clinical Psychology,* 76 (2008): 1–8. There are a host of known correlates of self-harmful behaviors, including family disruption, divorce or death of a parent, insecure attachment, physical abuse, high levels of "negative affect" (including pessimism and emotional reactivity), and alexithymia (the adolescent's difficulty with understanding and expressing her own emotional state and with distinguishing feelings from bodily sensations). In all, the complex causal factors are highly likely to differ across subgroups of those who self-injure (Prinstein, "Introduction to Special Section"). See also Elizabeth Lloyd-Richardson, Nicholas Perrine, Lisa Dierker, and Mary L. Kelley, "Characteristics and Functions of Non-Suicidal Self-Injury in a Community Sample of Adolescents," *Psy-*

chological Medicine, 37 (2007): 1183–1192. For data on linkages between parental rates of hostility/criticism and both suicidal behavior and self-harm, see Michelle Wedig and Matthew K. Nock, "Parental Expressed Emotion and Adolescent Self-Injury," *Journal of the American Academy of Child and Adolescent Psychiatry,* 46 (2007): 1171–1178. It is often assumed that girls show greater levels of self-injury than boys, but the data are not entirely clear. As noted in the notes to the Introduction, whereas nearly all clinicians agree that rates of self-mutilation and self-harm are drastically higher than a generation ago, definitive data are difficult to come by. Yet consensus is strong that cutting and related behavioral patterns are more prevalent today than in past years.

4. See James D. Lock and Daniel le Grange, "Eating Disorders," in *Behavioral and Emotional Disorders in Adolescents: Nature, Assessment, and Treatment,* ed. David A. Wolfe and Eric J. Mash (New York: Guilford, 2006). How early do eating problems begin? As noted in the Introduction, the data are alarming: 42 percent of girls in first to third grades report wanting to be thinner, and 51 percent of nine- and ten-year-old girls report feeling better about themselves when dieting. Furthermore, it has been reported that the number-one wish of adolescent girls is to lose weight. For a compilation, see Margo Maine, *Body Wars: Making Peace with Women's Bodies: An Activist's Guide* (Carlsbad, Calif.: Gurze Books, 2000). Also, in a recent online report, Y. May Chao, Emily M. Pisetsky, Lisa C. Dierker, Faith-Anne Dohm, Francine Russell, Alexis M. May, and Ruth H. Striegel-Moore, "Ethnic Differences in Weight Control Practices Among U.S. Adolescents from 1995–2005," *International Journal of Eating Disorders* (DOI:10.1002/eat.20479), found that dieting and the use of diet products increased strongly in adolescent girls from the mid-1990s through 2005, especially among white girls (African American girls, with more flexible standards of beauty, did not show such an increase). Also, in 2006 it was reported by Project EAT, at the University of Minnesota, that the use of diet pills among teens nearly doubled between 2000 and 2005, from 7.5 to 14.2 percent; see Project EAT, "New Study Shows Teenage Girls' Use of Diet Pills Doubles Over 5 Year Span," *Science Daily,* November 1, 2006, retrieved from www.sciencedaily.com/releases/2006/10/061030143332.htm.

5. For official data, see Federal Bureau of Investigation, *Crime in the United States 2000* (Washington, D.C.: U.S. Government Printing Office, 2001), which revealed that girls' arrests increased by 25 percent during the 1990s whereas boys' arrests actually declined by 3 percent. These data, and other information revealing even a larger increase in violent assaults in girls during this time period, are reviewed in Meda Chesney-Lind and Joanne Belknap, "Trends in Delinquent Girls' Aggression and Violent Behavior: A Review of the Evidence," in *Aggression, Antisocial Behavior, and Violence Among Girls,* ed. Martha Putallaz and Karen L. Bierman, (New York: Guilford, 2004). See also review of Marlene M. Moretti, Candice L. Odgers, and Margaret A. Jackson, "Girls and Aggression: A Point of Departure," in *Girls and Aggression: Contributing Factors and Intervention Principles,* ed. Marlene M. Moretti, Candice L. Odgers, and Margaret A. Jackson (New York: Kluwer Academic/Plenum, 2004). For results on self-reported aggression and violence, see U.S. Department of Health and Human Services, *Youth Violence: A Report of the Surgeon General* (Rockville, Md.: Author, 2001). See also the thorough review in James Garbarino, *See Jane Hit: Why Girls Are Growing More Violent and What We Can Do About It* (New York: Penguin, 2006). Comprehensive volumes on this topic include Marlene M. Moretti, Candice L. Odgers, and Margaret A. Jackson, eds., *Girls and Aggression: Contributing Factors and Intervention Principles* (New York: Kluwer Academic/Plenum, 2004), and Martha Putallaz and Karen L. Bierman, eds., *Aggression, Antisocial Behavior, and Violence Among Girls* (New York: Guilford, 2004).

As noted in the Introduction, Chesney-Lind and Belknap provide a cautionary note. They contend that crime and delinquency statistics may now overcount girls as having assault records, when in fact such girls may be status offenders or show home-based aggression but not necessarily serious out-of-home violence. Thus, some of the rapid increase in girls' violence may be more mythical than real, but even these authors contend that increases have occurred.

Aggression and violence in girls are intriguing and troubling. When adolescent girls display physical aggression, they are far more likely than boys to have comorbid depression; see Margit Wiesner and Hyoun K. Kim, "Co-Occurring Delinquency and Depressive Symptoms of Adolescent Boys and Girls: A Dual Trajectory Modeling Approach," *Developmental Psychology, 42* (2006): 1220–1235. Similarly, Thompson and colleagues found that delinquency is more closely associated with suicide in girls than in boys during adolescence: See Martie B. Thompson, Ching-Hua Ho, and J. B. Kingree, "Prospective Associations Between Delinquency and Suicidal Behaviors in a Nationally Representative Sample," *Journal of Adolescent Health, 40* (2007): 232–237.

Finally, although not the primary focus of this book, adolescent girls have apparently caught up with boys regarding rates of substance abuse, even surpassing boys in terms of abuse of prescription drugs. See Sandra A. Brown and Ana M. Abrantes, "Substance Use Disorders," in *Behavioral and Emotional Disorders in Adolescents: Nature, Assessment, and Treatment*, ed. David A. Wolfe and Eric J. Mash (New York: Guilford, 2006); Sandra A. Brown, "Development of Alcohol/Drug Abuse and Dependence," in *Child and Adolescent Psychopathology*, ed. Theodore P. Beauchaine and Stephen P. Hinshaw (Hoboken, N.J.: Wiley, 2008).

6. Overall, across the conditions of interest, is there real evidence for either increases in prevalence or a lowering of the age of onset? And when have these trends occurred during recent history? Summarizing from the citations in notes 1 through 5 and from the notes to the Introduction, for depression there is controversy as to whether there has actually been an increase in child and adolescent depression in recent decades, but the age of onset of depression is clearly decreasing, particularly in females, a trend that has been occurring across the last thirty to forty years. For youth suicide, there was a persistent increase from the 1950s through the 1980s, leading to far higher rates than in the mid-twentieth century, followed by a decrease during the 1990s. Yet a sharp spike upward for girls occurred in 2003–4, the last period for which firm data are available. As for self-harm, there has apparently been a major increase across the past decade, with great attention now paid to self-injurious behavior in girls. Regarding eating disorders, a spike in binge eating in girls and women has been noted within the past decade, which may be related, in part, to the increase in obesity during this time period, given that obesity may promote purging to control weight. Also, the use of diet pills and other means of controlling weight have also increased greatly in adolescent girls in recent years. And for the past decade and a half, rates of violence have increased in girls at the same time that they have shown either a milder rate of increase or a gradual decline in boys, with self-reported aggression in girls at alarmingly high rates. Overall, the trend toward lower age of onset for depression has been building for several decades; increases in girls' violence have been apparent since the early 1990s. Yet spikes in girls' rates of suicide, binge eating, and, in all likelihood, self-harm are more recent. Finally, although teen pregnancy rates are not a core topic of discussion in the rest of the book, please note that they underwent an increase in 2006 after 15 years of decline. It is tempting to attribute this rise to the components of the Triple Bind, but there are doubtless several reasons for this statistic. See Gardiner Harris, "Teenage Birth Rate Rises for First Time Since '91," *New York Times,* December 6, 2007.

7. Martin E. P. Seligman and Steven F. Maier, "Failure to Escape Traumatic Shock," *Journal of Experimental Psychology, 74* (1967): 1–9; Martin E. P. Seligman, "Learned Helplessness," *Annual Review of Medicine,* 23 (1972): 407–412.

8. Soon, the learned helplessness paradigm was found in other animals—and in humans. In people, however, it is not simply exposure to noncontingent punishment but

rather the patterns of expectations and attribution (i.e., beliefs that uncontrollable, negative events are related to internal, stable, and global causes) that are linked to depression. See Lyn Y. Abramson, Martin E. P. Seligman, and John D. Teasdale, "Learned Helplessness in Humans: Critique and Reformulation," *Journal of Abnormal Psychology,* 87 (1978): 49–74.

9. For a classic citation on the original double bind theory, see Gregory Bateson, Don D. Jackson, Jay Haley, and John Weakland, "Toward a Theory of Schizophrenia," *Behavioral Science, 1* (1956): 251–264; see also D. D. Jackson and John H. Weakland, "Schizophrenic Symptoms and Family Interaction," *Archives of General Psychiatry, 1* (1959): 618–621. This provocative view held that the conflicting, mutually contradictory messages given by certain parents would undermine the developing child's sense of identity and reality, ultimately leading to the psychotic states indicative of schizophrenia. Although the double bind is no longer considered a risk factor for schizophrenia, the notion that children and adolescents can be caught in mutually contradictory messages is a powerful one.

10. Regarding the nature of mental illness, see Stephen P. Hinshaw, *The Mark of Shame: Stigma of Mental Illness and an Agenda for Change* (New York: Oxford University Press, 2007), Chapter 1; Stephen P. Hinshaw, "Developmental Psychopathology as a Scientific Discipline: Relevance to Behavioral and Emotional Disorders of Childhood and Adolescence," in *Child and Adolescent Psychopathology*, ed. Theodore P. Beauchaine and Stephen P. Hinshaw (Hoboken, N.J.: Wiley, 2008); and Jerome C. Wakefield, "Disorder as Harmful Dysfunction: A Conceptual Critique of *DSM-III-R*'s Definition of Mental Disorder," *Psychological Review,* 99 (1992): 232–247.

11. Other commentators and scholars have certainly commented on the binds in which girls increasingly find themselves, especially with respect to the need to embody traditionally feminine ideals of nurturance and caring as well as the competitive, "agentic" male objectives of competition and instrumental behavior. See, for example, Lyn Mikel Brown and Carol Gilligan, *Meeting at the Crossroads: Women's Psychology and Girls' Development* (Cambridge, Mass.: Harvard University Press, 1992); Madeline Levine, *The Price of Privilege: How Parental Pressure and Material Advantage Are Creating a Generation of Disconnected and Unhappy Kids* (New York: HarperCollins, 2006); and Nancy L. Snyderman and Peg Streep, *Girl in the Mirror: Mothers and Daughters in the Years of Adolescence* (New York: Hyperion, 2002). To my knowledge, however, the third prong of the Triple Bind (the lack of viable alternatives) has not been emphasized.

12. *America's Next Top Model* began in 2003 on WB and subsequently moved to the CW. In 2007, it was the CW's highest-rated program. It has generated spin-off shows in at least thirty-four nations, including Afghanistan, Malaysia, and Nigeria. Its heaviest winner weighed 138 pounds, at 5'11", but most winners have been far lighter. See en.wikipedia.org/wiki/America's_Next_Top_Model.

13. In 2005, 54 percent of college enrollees were women, an all-time high; see Mark Mather and Dia Adams, "The Crossover in Female-Male College Enrollment Rates," *Population Reference Bureau*, February 2007, retrieved from www.prb.org/Articles/2007/CrossoverinFemaleMaleCollegeEnrollmentRates.aspx. By 2007, 33 percent of women between the ages of twenty-five and twenty-nine had earned a bachelor's degree, compared to 25 percent of men in this age group; see Lauren B. Cooper, "Census: Women Beat out Men When It Comes to Higher Education in 2007," *Birmingham Business Journal*, January 14, 2008, retrieved from www.bizjournals.com/birmingham/stories/2009/01/14/daily6.html. Thus, 57 percent of bachelor's degrees now go to women. Also, regarding the claim that one-fourth of women now outearn husbands in two-income households, the statistics in 2005 showed that 25.5 percent of women were in this category; see Elaine L. Chao, "Remarks at the Women's Leadership Board, John F. Kennedy School

of Government," December 4, 2007, retrieved from www.dol.gov/_sec/media/speeches/20071204_JFK.htm.

14. For information on the status of women's intercollegiate sports, see the report "Who's Playing Women's Sports? Trends in Participation," June 5, 2007, retrieved from www.womenssportsfoundation.org/cgi-bin/iowa/issues/disc/article.html/?record=1201.

15. By 2001, medical schools enrolled 45 percent women and 55 percent men; see Association of American Medical Colleges, "Total Enrollment by Gender and Race/Ethnicity 1992–2001," January 16, 2002, retrieved from www.aamc.org/data/facts/archive/famg82001.htm. As of 2007, the ratio was nearly 50:50; see Chao, "Remarks." For law schools, in 2006–7, total enrollment percentages were 47 percent women and 53 percent men; see American Bar Association, "First Year and Total J.D. Enrollment by Gender," retrieved from www.abanet.org/legaled/statistics/charts/stats%20-%206.pdf.

16. See Bureau of Labor Statistics, "Women at Work: A Visual Essay," 2003, retrieved from www.bls.gov/opub/mlr/2003/10/ressum3.pdf. For earnings figures, women's annual earnings, relative to those of men, are currently between 77 percent and 80 percent, depending on job status and on statistical controls used. Indeed, in 2005, among full-time workers, women's average weekly earnings were $585, compared to men's comparable earnings of $722; see Mather and Adams, "The Crossover," retrieved from www.prb.org/Articles/2007/CrossoverinFemaleMaleCollegeEnrollmentRates.aspx. However, for highly paid professions, such as medicine, the ratio is more skewed, with women earning 63 percent of men's salaries; see Daniel H. Weinberg, "Earnings by Gender: Evidence from Census 2000," *Monthly Labor Review Online 130* (2007), retrieved from www.bls.gov/opub/mlr/2007/07/art3exc.htm.

17. Weinberg, "Earnings by Gender."

18. See "Who's Playing Women's Sports?" Furthermore, there is a vast difference in the salary structures of top men's professional sports, for which multimillion-dollar contracts are now modal for basketball and baseball, contrasted with the far lower figures for women's teams. For example, in 2007–8, the average National Basketball Association (NBA) player earned millions of dollars per year in salary, with the minimum salary for a rookie set at $427,000 annually. Contrast these figures with the Women's National Basketball Association (WNBA), where the 2007 salary minimum was $49,134 annually and the maximum was $93,000. See data on women's salaries, retrieved from www.WomensBasketballOnline.com/wnba/rosters/salary.html.

19. Lisa Belkin, "The Feminine Critique," *New York Times*, November 1, 2007.

20. Cited in ibid.

21. Cited in ibid.

22. Peter Glick, Sadie Larsen, Cathryn Johnson, and Heather Branstiter, "Evaluations of Sexy Women in Low- and High-Status Jobs," *Psychology of Women Quarterly*, 29 (2005): 389–395.

23. See Michelle Conlin, "More on the Bully Broad Syndrome," July 30, 2007, retrieved from www.businessweek.com/careers/managementiq/archives/2007/07/more_on_the_bul.html. For a formal scientific article based on this research, published in a leading psychological journal, see Victoria Brescoll and Eric Uhlmann, "Can an Angry Woman Get Ahead? Status Conferral, Gender, and Expression of Emotion in the Workplace," *Psychological Science*, 19 (2005): 268–275.

24. See Sam Dillon, "A Great Year for Ivy League Schools, but Not So Good for Applicants to Them," *New York Times*, April 4, 2007. The admissions rates at Ivy League and other prestigious colleges are at an all-time low, revealing ultrahigh pressures regarding admission.

25. Judith Warner, "The Med Scare," *New York Times*, February 21, 2008.

26. It clearly appears that more and more colleges are weighing extracurricular activities highly in admissions decisions, although university websites state that it is quality and leadership in such activities, rather than quantity of activities per se, that are paramount. As indicated in the text and in note 24 to this chapter, the nation's most selective colleges have undergone dramatic increases in their selectivity in recent years. For a sample website providing guidance to high school students regarding the importance of extracurricular activities for admission, see collegeapps.about.com/od/collegeapplications/a/activitytips.htm.

27. As I emphasize in later chapters, it is just such "demand" for activities that teens may actually seek as pleasurable in their own right—that is, the extrinsic pressure and the incentive to build one's resumé—that undermines intrinsic motivation, as researchers have continually demonstrated. For a classic investigation with younger children, see Mark R. Lepper, David Greene, and Richard E. Nisbett, "Undermining Children's Intrinsic Interest with Extrinsic Reward: A Test of the 'Overjustification' Hypothesis," *Journal of Personality and Social Psychology,* 28 (1973): 129–137.

28. A mass of recent evidence documents the extensive media culture in which today's teens live. See Amanda Lenhart and colleagues, "Teens and Technology: Youth Are Leading the Transition to a Fully Wired and Mobile Nation," Pew Internet and American Life Project, July 27, 2005, retrieved from www.pewinternet.org/pdfs/PIP_Teens_Tech_July_ 2005web.pdf. For example, between 2000 and 2005, the percent of U.S. teens using the Internet rose from 73 percent to 87 percent. Instant messaging was estimated to be performed by 64 percent (with about half of IMers reporting daily use of this technology). The amount of time with peers face-to-face has nearly been equaled by the amount of time with peers online (see Chapter 7 for details). For recent data, see also another Pew report by Amanda Lenhart and colleagues, "Teen Content Creators," December 17, 2007, retrieved from pewresearch.org/pubs/670/teen-content-creators.

29. For essays on potential benefits of the Internet for girls, see Sharon R. Mazzarella, ed., *Girl Wide Web: Girls, the Internet, and the Negotiation of Identity* (New York: Peter Lang, 2005).

30. See the Kaiser Family Foundation report by Ulla G. Foehr, "Media Multitasking Among American Youth: Prevalence, Predictors, and Pairings," March 9, 2005, retrieved from www.kff.org/entmedia/entmedia121206pkg.cfm.

31. *Studio 360*, National Public Radio, February 22, 2008, retrieved from www.studio360.org/episodes/2008/02/22.

32. See a critique of upper-middle-class parenting in Levine, *The Price of Privilege.*

33. Thomas L. Friedman, *The World Is Flat: A Brief History of the Twenty-first Century* (New York: Farrar, Straus and Giroux, 2006).

34. Ibid., 14–15.

35. Barbara Ehrenreich, *Bait and Switch: The (Futile) Pursuit of the American Dream* (New York: Metropolitan Books, 2005); the quote is from 216–217.

36. Avery Johnson, "As Drug Industry Struggles, Chemists Face Layoff Wave: Lipitor Pioneer Is Out at Doomed Pfizer Lab," *Wall Street Journal*, December 11, 2007, retrieved from www.democraticunderground.com/discuss/duboard.php?az=view_all&address=114x31296.

Chapter 2: Blue Jeans and "Blue" Genes

1. See Dwight L. Evans and Martin E. P. Seligman, "Introduction," and Commission on Adolescent Disorder and Depression, "Defining Depression and Bipolar Disorder," in *Treating and Preventing Adolescent Mental Health Disorders: What We Know and What We Don't Know,* ed. Dwight L. Evans, Edna B. Foa, Racquel E. Gur, Herbert Hendin, Charles

P. O'Brien, Martin E. P. Seligman, and B. Timothy Walsh (New York: Oxford University Press, 2005). See also Centers for Disease Control and Prevention, "Suicide Trends Among Youths and Young Adults Aged 10–24 Years—United States, 1990–2004," *Morbidity and Mortality Weekly Report, 56 (35)* (September 7, 2007): 905–908, retrieved from www.cdc.gov/MMWR/preview/mmwrhtml/mm5635a2.htm.

2. Evans and Seligman, "Introduction," and Centers for Disease Control and Prevention, "Suicide Trends." See also CBS News, "Girls' Suicide Rates Rise Dramatically: CDC Advises Prevention Programs to Focus on Gender and Age Groups Most at Risk," September 6, 2007, retrieved from www.cbsnews.com/stories/2007/09/06/health/main3239837.shtml.

3. For two individuals to have parallel family histories of depression does not necessarily mean that these individuals have precisely the same "vulnerability" genes. It would take actual genotyping to determine the exact variants of selected genes that each of them carries. But family history of mood disorders is quite influential: if a person has one biological parent with depression, the chances that he or she will become clinically depressed are quite strong—as high as 60 percent before age 30. See William R. Beardslee, Eve M. Versage, and Tracy R. G. Gladstone, "Children of Affectively Ill Parents: A Review of the Last 10 Years," *Journal of the American Academy of Child and Adolescent Psychiatry,* 37 (1998): 1134–1141. The genes likely to be involved include the serotonin transporter gene (as discussed later in this chapter). Still, it is combinations of genes and a host of other factors—such as parental irritability and unresponsiveness, the modeling of emotion dysregulation, disrupted attachments, and the like—that "carry" the effects of parental depression on the risk for mood disorders in their offspring. See Sherryl Goodman and Ian H. Gotlib, eds., *Children of Depressed Parents: Mechanisms of Risk and Implications for Treatment* (Washington, D.C.: American Psychological Association, 2002), and Stephen P. Hinshaw, "Parental Mental Disorder and Children's Functioning: Silence and Communication, Stigma, and Resilience," *Journal of Clinical Child and Adolescent Psychology,* 33 (2004): 400–411.

4. Biological tendencies may be indicated by vulnerability genes per se, by a strong family history of depression or other mood disorders, and/or by such temperamental characteristics as high levels of negative affect (fearfulness, pessimism, emotional reactivity), which appears as a temperamental trait in childhood. Such characteristics may predispose certain individuals to a ruminative style and to high levels of stress reactivity—which, when associated with negative life events and loss experiences, may predict the onset of depression.

5. Over the past decade, mental illnesses have been recognized as the most impairing illnesses in the world, with depression poised to become the single most debilitating illness worldwide, surpassing infectious diseases, cancer, heart disease, and the like. The reasons have to do with both the high prevalence of depression and its extremely deleterious effects on productivity—and even on physical health. See, for example, World Health Organization, *Mental Health: New Understanding, New Hope* (New York: Author, 2001).

6. There have been many attempts to form subcategories of the clinical entity known as depression. Some are based on the severity of the symptoms (e.g., mild, moderate, or severe depression; minor versus major depression). Others combine symptom severity with a strongly biological set of tendencies—i.e., early morning awakening, distinct diurnal variation in depressive symptoms (with the most severe of these in the morning, giving way to some relief later in the day), and other biological features—in what is termed "melancholia." This variant of depression is highly heritable, is greatly associated with suicidal tendencies, and appears to be qualitatively distinct from other forms of depression;

see Theodore P. Beauchaine, Stephen P. Hinshaw, and Lisa Gatzke-Kopp, "Genetic and Environmental Influences on Behavior," in *Child and Adolescent Psychopathology*, ed. Theodore P. Beauchaine and Stephen P. Hinshaw (Hoboken, N.J.: Wiley, 2008).

7. See, for example, Susan Nolen-Hoeksema and Joan S. Girgus, "The Emergence of Gender Differences in Depression During Adolescence," *Psychological Bulletin, 115* (1994): 424–443, and Jill M. Cyranowski, Ellen Frank, Elizabeth Young, and Kathleen Shear, "Adolescent Onset of the Gender Difference in Lifetime Rates of Major Depression: A Theoretical Model," *Archives of General Psychiatry,* 57 (2000): 21–27.

8. Can one become clinically depressed without a genetic vulnerability? Because the full set of genetic vulnerabilities to depression has not yet been ascertained, this answer is not clear, but it would appear that sufficient life stressors could push many people toward major depression, although repeated depressive episodes may not appear in the absence of underlying vulnerability. On the other hand, for disorders showing more substantial heritability (e.g., schizophrenia or bipolar disorder), it is probable that the clinical condition will not appear without both the genetic liability and a particular set of environmental stressors or challenges.

9. For mental disorders (unlike some clear-cut cases of single-gene medical disorders, such as sickle-cell anemia or phenylketonuria), there is no one gene that causes the condition. Rather, a set of small-impact genes may each increase the potential for the individual's having the disorder. These are termed "vulnerability" genes. For an erudite critique of the notion that single genes lead to single mental disorders, see Kenneth A. Kendler, " 'A Gene For . . .': The Nature of Gene Action in Psychiatric Disorders," *American Journal of Psychiatry, 162* (2005): 1243–1252.

10. For analyses of current thinking about genes, and their interplay with environments in shaping behavioral traits and mental disorders, see Michael Rutter, *Genes and Behavior: Nature-Nurture Interplay Explained* (Oxford, U.K.: Blackwell, 2006); Michael Rutter, Terrie E. Moffitt, and Avshalom Caspi, "Gene-Environment Interplay and Psychopathology: Multiple Levels but Real Effects," *Journal of Child Psychology and Psychiatry,* 47 (2006): 226–261; and Beauchaine, Hinshaw, and Gatzke-Kopp, "Genetic and Environmental Influences on Behavior."

11. The full complement of DNA in the nucleus of each of our cells includes three billion nucleotide pairs—but only a small fraction of this material constitutes genes, those portions of the genome that code for the making of proteins. (It is now known, however, that the nongenetic material is not useless: it has important functions, just now being discovered.) Genes are structurally invariant throughout life, except through mutations, but chemical changes in the body's cells, in response to environmental triggers, can aid in making a given gene "come to life" and perform its functions. Many genes come in two or more forms, called alleles; certain alleles may confer risk for disease or disorder. The utter complexity of our genes and how they differ in intriguing ways from individual to individual are discussed in Elizabeth Pennisi, "Breakthrough of the Year: Human Genetic Variation," *Science, 318* (2007): 1842–1843.

12. A "vulnerability" gene is one that, in a certain allelic form, predisposes to certain traits or characteristics of the individual, but leads to disease or disorder only if other vulnerability genes are also in place and/or certain environmental factors unleash its potential.

13. The gene in question is called the serotonin transporter promoter gene (abbreviated as 5-HTTLPR), as it is related to the workings of the molecule (the serotonin transporter) that removes excess serotonin (chemical abbreviation: 5-HT) from the synapse and escorts it back into the presynaptic neuron from which it had been released. It comes in two allelic forms: "l" (for long) and "s" (for short). Because individuals get one copy from

their mothers and one from their fathers, they can have the genotype of "l/l," "l/s," or "s/s." It is individuals with the "s/s" genotype who have the most inefficient serotonin processing, with the "s/l" subgroup intermediate between "s/s" and "l/l" individuals.

14. As discussed later in this chapter, it is the interaction between specific genes and certain environments that produces the highest risk for mental disorder.

15. Here we see an example of a different type of gene-environment interplay, known as "gene-environment correlation." The principle here is that genetically mediated traits of parents influence the child's exposure to certain environments, and traits of children (transmitted genetically from their parents) influence the child's own exposure to certain environments or settings. An example of "passive" gene-environment correlation occurs when bright parents, who are more likely than average to have bright children given the heritability of intelligence, also provide high stimulation to their offspring (e.g., more books in the home than average), accentuating the potential for the child's intellectual abilities and learning. In "active" forms of gene-environment correlation, a child's temperamental tendencies cause her to seek the kinds of settings that reinforce those initial tendencies—for example, a shy, inhibited youngster backs away from social contact, preventing development of needed social skills. In "evocative" gene-environment correlation, the child's tendencies elicit responses from adults, peers, and the general environment that serve to accentuate the child's initial tendencies. For instance, an impulsive child is likely to evoke frustration and negative reactions from her parents, and the resultant harsh parental treatment perpetuates and escalates her oppositionality or impulsivity. For reviews, see Beauchaine, Hinshaw, and Gatzke-Kopp, "Genetic and Environmental Influences on Behavior," and Robert Plomin, J. C. DeFries, and John C. Loehlin, "Genotype-Environment Interaction and Correlation in the Analysis of Human Behavior," *Psychological Bulletin,* 84 (1977): 309–322.

16. A relevant concept here is "kindling," as applied to bipolar disorder, recurrent depression, schizophrenia, seizure disorders, and other psychiatric and neurological conditions. The idea is that although it may take considerable environmental stress to elicit an initial episode in a vulnerable individual, once that episode has occurred, progressively lower amounts of stress are needed to "trigger" a subsequent episode. In some cases, episodes may begin to occur spontaneously, without the stressor. For discussion, see Susan R. B. Weiss and Robert B. Post, "Kindling: Separate vs. Shared Mechanisms in Affective Disorders and Epilepsy," *Neuropsychobiology,* 38 (1998): 167–180.

17. See Lyn Y. Abramson, Martin E. P. Seligman, and John D. Teasdale, "Learned Helplessness in Humans: Critique and Reformulation," *Journal of Abnormal Psychology,* 87 (1978): 49–74.

18. Susan Nolen-Hoeksema and Benita Jackson, "Mediators of the Gender Difference in Rumination," *Psychology of Women Quarterly,* 25 (2001): 37–47. For a popular yet scientifically grounded work on women's propensities toward rumination, and consequences for eating problems, alcohol use, and depression, see Susan Nolen-Hoeksema, *Eating, Drinking, and Overthinking: The Toxic Triangle of Food, Alcohol, and Depression—and How Women Can Break Free* (New York: Henry Holt, 2006).

19. Note that even though height is highly heritable, there is no "height gene." Like most traits and all forms of mental illness, height is polygenic, meaning that many different, small-effect genes work together to produce the phenotype (trait or behavior) of interest. And consider this crucial question: even though height has a heritability of 90 percent, why are we all taller, on average, than our great-grandparents? The answer is that even for traits or conditions with substantial heritability, the environment (in the case of height, our diet, including higher levels of fats and hormones) can raise or lower the "level" of that trait across the whole population, even across a relatively short time period. It may be that the Triple Bind (and other features of the environment) raise the potential

for all of us to become distressed and disordered, despite the moderate heritability of the conditions under discussion in this book.

20. Sickle-cell anemia results from inheriting two copies of a recessive gene, one from each parent. It is therefore 100 percent heritable. So is phenylketonuria (PKU), another recessive disorder, which causes the child not to be able to metabolize key substances in certain foods, quickly leading to mental retardation, as toxic levels build in the brain. Note, however, that the treatment for PKU involves dietary restrictions—which, when enforced rigorously, can allow the child to develop with normal intelligence. This example makes the important point that even entirely heritable conditions can be managed or controlled with the "right" environments (in this case, dietary "environments"). Heritability is not destiny.

21. For extensive data on the heritability of depression, see Patrick F. Sullivan, Michael C. Neale, and Kenneth S. Kendler, "Genetic Epidemiology of Major Depression: Review and Meta-Analysis," *American Journal of Psychiatry,* 157 (2000): 1552–1562.

22. Again, for Jeannie and Melinda, we are inferring their equal liability to depression through an identical pattern of family history of mood disorder. In the future, genetic testing is likely to be performed to understand the specific "risk alleles" that we have for a variety of conditions. A crucial study by Kenneth Kendler and colleagues, utilizing an extremely large sample of Swedish twins, established that the heritability of major depression in women was 42 percent—moderately but significantly higher than that for men (29 percent). See Kenneth S. Kendler, Margaret Gatz, Charles O. Gardner, and Nancy L. Pederson, "A Swedish National Twin Study of Lifetime Major Depression," *American Journal of Psychiatry, 163* (2006): 109–114. Thus, there are some indications of a larger genetic propensity toward depression in females than in males. Still, over half of the individual differences in depression in women are attributable to environmental rather than genetic factors.

23. Other conditions—autism, ADHD, and bipolar disorder, for example—have heritabilities substantially greater than the figure for depression. It is clear, however, that even highly heritable traits and conditions can be modulated, in certain individuals, by environments and treatment strategies.

24. Avshalom Caspi, Karen Sugden, Terrie E. Moffitt, Alan Taylor, Ian W. Craig, Honalee Harrington, Joseph McClay, Jonathan Mill, Judy Martin, Anthony Braithwaite, and Richie Poulton, "Influence of Life Stress on Depression: Moderation by a Polymorphism in the 5-HTT Gene," *Science, 301* (2003): 386–389.

25. Among many examples, see Terrie E. Moffitt, Avshalom Caspi, Honalee Harrington, and Barry J. Milne, "Males on the Life-Course-Persistent and Adolescence-Limited Antisocial Pathways: Follow-Up at Age 26 Years," *Development and Psychopathology, 14* (2002): 179–207; Sara Jaffee, Avshalom Caspi, Terrie E. Moffitt, Jay Belsky, and Phil Silva, "Why Are Children Born to Teen Mothers at Risk for Adverse Outcomes in Young Adulthood? Results from a 20-Year Longitudinal Study," *Development and Psychopathology, 13* (2001): 377–397.

26. In the Dunedin population, 17 percent had the "s/s" allele for the 5HTTLPR gene (associated with the most inefficient serotonin transmission), 51 percent were heterozygotes (i.e., they had the "s/l" allele), and 31 percent were "l/l." Although the highest risk for depression and suicidality existed in the "s/s" subgroup who had been exposed to high levels of negative life events (e.g., financial, health, housing, and relationship stressors), a similar though less pronounced effect showed up in the "s/l" group as well. It is not the case that there is some rare, obscure genotype that confers risk for depression; rather, an allele that is quite frequent is involved. Still, this risk is realized only when there are significant environmental stressors. The same pattern of results occurred for an additional life stressor: maltreatment the child had experienced during the first ten years of life (see

Caspi et al., "Influence of Life Stress on Depression"). Additionally, another vulnerability gene—this one linked to the brain chemical monoamine oxidase (MAO)—is associated with antisocial behavior in young adulthood only when the child has been exposed to maltreatment relatively early in life; see Avshalom Caspi, Joseph McClay, Terrie Moffitt, Jonathan Mill, Judy Martin, Ian W. Craig, Alan Taylor, and Richie Poulton, "Role of Genotype in the Cycle of Violence," *Science,* 297 (2002): 851–854. These findings have been replicated in different samples; see Alan Taylor and Julia Kim-Cohen, "Meta-Analysis of Gene-Environment Interactions in Developmental Psychopathology," *Development and Psychopathology, 19* (2007): 1029–1037. Neither genes nor environments alone produce high risk for important forms of mental disturbance, but their confluence does.

27. Evans and Seligman, "Introduction"; Commission on Adolescent Disorder and Depression, "Defining Depression and Bipolar Disorder," Constance Hammen and Karen D. Rudolph, "Childhood Mood Disorders," in *Child Psychopathology*, 2nd ed., ed. Eric J. Mash and Russell A. Barkley (New York: Guilford, 2003); David B. Goldston, Stephanie Sergent Daniel, and Elizabeth Mayfield Arnold, "Suicidal and Nonsuicidal Self-Harm Behaviors," in *Behavioral and Emotional Disorders in Adolescents: Nature, Assessment, and Treatment*, ed. David A. Wolfe and Eric J. Mash (New York: Guilford, 2006).

28. Statistics for these alarming trends have been presented throughout the Introduction and Chapter 1. For suicide, see, for example, Centers for Disease Control and Prevention, "Suicide Trends." For binge eating and indicators of distorted body image, see Eric Stice and Cynthia Bulik, "Eating Disorders," in *Child and Adolescent Psychopathology*, ed. Theodore Beauchaine and Stephen P. Hinshaw (Hoboken, N.J.: Wiley, 2008); G. Terence Wilson, Carolyn Block Becker, and Karen Heffernan, "Eating Disorders," in *Child Psychopathology*, 2nd ed., ed. Eric J. Mash and Russell A. Barkley (New York: Guilford Press, 2003); and James I. Hudson, Eva Hiripi, Harrison G. Pope Jr., and Ronald C. Kessler, "The Prevalence and Correlates of Eating Disorders in the National Comorbidity Survey Replication," *Biological Psychiatry, 61* (2007): 348–358. For self-harm, see Amelio A. D'Onofrio, *Adolescent Self-Injury: A Comprehensive Guide for Counselors and Health Care Professionals* (New York: Springer, 2007); Kristin L. Croyle and Jennifer Waltz, "Subclinical Self-Harm: Range of Behaviors, Extent, and Associated Characteristics," *American Journal of Orthopsychiatry,* 77 (2005): 332–342; and Elizabeth Lloyd-Richardson, Nicholas Perrine, Lisa Dierker, and Mary L. Kelley, "Characteristics and Functions of Non-Suicidal Self-Injury in a Community Sample of Adolescents," *Psychological Medicine,* 37 (2007): 1183–1192.

29. Like the example of height, for which environmental factors have increased this trait across the whole population despite its substantial heritability, antisocial behavior and violence rose throughout much of the twentieth century (despite their moderate heritability) on the basis of the environment (e.g., urbanization, poverty, access to weapons, etc.). In parallel, the swift changes in girls' rates of self-harm, suicide, binge eating, and physical aggression (and the lowering of the age of onset of depression) cannot be "genetic" effects per se, despite the moderate heritabilities of each. For compelling discussion, see Michael Rutter, Henri Giller, and Ann Hagell, *Antisocial Behavior by Young People* (Cambridge, U.K.: Cambridge University Press, 1998).

30. A particularly difficult aspect of the Triple Bind is the effortlessness with which girls are supposed to negotiate the dangerous shoals of being nurturing and competitive in the absence of viable role models or alternative identities. Attempting difficult if not impossible tasks while revealing no effort in doing so is the source of huge strain.

31. The "maturity gap"—the increasingly long time period between the ever-earlier onset of puberty and the long-delayed time of social and financial independence, making for a period of "adolescence" that stretches for fifteen years or more—was cited as a key factor in the large number of youth who commit antisocial behavior during adolescence

(even if they have not had a history of aggression in childhood); see Terrie E. Moffitt, "Adolescence-Limited and Life-Course-Persistent Antisocial Behavior: A Developmental Taxonomy," *Psychological Review, 100* (1993): 674–701. And no less an authoritative source than the *New England Journal of Medicine* is currently claiming that there is an "epidemic" of mental illness among teens; see Richard M. Friedman, "Uncovering an Epidemic: Screening for Mental Illness in Teens," *New England Journal of Medicine,* 355 (2006): 2717–2719. For a lucid review of brain development during adolescence, see Ronald E. Dahl, "Adolescent Brain Development: A Period of Vulnerabilities and Opportunities," in *Adolescent Brain Development: Vulnerabilities and Opportunities*, ed. Ronald E. Dahl and Linda P. Spear, *Annals of the New York Academy of Sciences,* vol. 1021 (New York: New York Academy of Sciences, 2004). Adolescence is a time of massive reorganization of the body and the brain, a period of risk taking, and a time of increasing socialization via peers; see David A. Wolfe and Eric J. Mash, "Behavioral and Emotional Problems in Adolescents: Overview and Issues," in *Behavioral and Emotional Disorders in Adolescents: Nature, Assessment, and Treatment*, ed. David A. Wolfe and Eric J. Mash (New York: Guilford, 2006). Also, the experience of early puberty is a stronger risk factor for behavioral and emotional problems in girls than in boys; see Grayson N. Holmbeck, Deborah Friedman, Mona Abad, and Barbara Jandasek, "Development and Psychopathology in Adolescence," in *Behavioral and Emotional Disorders in Adolescents: Nature, Assessment, and Treatment*, ed. David A. Wolfe and Eric J. Mash (New York: Guilford, 2006).

32. Sharon R. Mazzarella, ed., *Girl Wide Web: Girls, the Internet, and the Negotiation of Identity* (New York: Peter Lang, 2005).

Chapter 3: Life in the Pressure Cooker

1. See "Ellen Interviewed by *SELF* Magazine," March 7, 2008, retrieved from www.greysanatomyinsider.com/2006/03/ellen-interviewed-by-self-magazine.html.

2. See the article by Pulitzer Prize–winning reporter David Cay Johnston, "Report Says the Rich Are Getting Richer Faster, Much Faster," *New York Times*, December 15, 2007. This article highlights a Congressional Budget Office report revealing that between 2003 and 2005, the incomes of the top 1 percent of Americans rose 42.6 percent (an average of $465,000 per individual), whereas the incomes of the middle fifth of the population rose by 4.3 percent ($2,400 per individual) and those of the poorest fifth rose by 1.3 percent ($200 per individual). In fact, as of 2007, the top echelon of Americans had the greatest proportion of wealth, relative to the poorest, since the late 1920s. For expanded coverage, see David Cay Johnston, *Free Lunch: How the Wealthiest Americans Enrich Themselves at Government Expense (and Stick You with the Bill)* (New York: Portfolio, 2008). In this book he amplifies the above argument, contending that, adjusting for inflation, the average income for the lowest 90 percent of U.S. families has declined since 1980, while the wealthiest Americans have made substantial gains. See also Bob Herbert, "Good Jobs Are Where the Money Is," *New York Times*, January 18, 2008.

3. For a recent edition, see David Elkind, *The Hurried Child: Growing Up Too Fast Too Soon*, 3rd ed. (Cambridge, Mass.: Perseus, 2001).

4. Alvin Rosenfeld and Nicole Wise, *The Over-Scheduled Child: Avoiding the Hyper-Parenting Trap* (New York: St. Martin's Press, 2001); William C. Crain, *Reclaiming Childhood: Letting Children Be Children in Our Achievement-Oriented Society* (New York: Times Books, 2003). There are certainly some good observations in these accounts. For example, Rosenfeld and Wise emphasize the importance of parents' spending "unproductive" down time with their children (rather than always being on the go) and note, with dismay, the crass consumerism (and the perfectionism) present in contemporary society.

Yet many of their claims and prescriptions go well beyond the effects of extracurricular activities or overscheduling per se.

5. Joseph L. Mahoney, Angel L. Harris, and Jacquelynne S. Eccles, "Organized Activity Participation, Positive Youth Development, and the Over-Scheduling Hypothesis," *Social Policy Report, 20 (4)* (2006): 3–31. This study was performed as part of a systematic evaluation of a nationally representative sample. It received considerable media attention. As just one example, a story in the *Boston Globe* led with the following words: " 'Our kids are over-scheduled!' is a major worry and rallying cry for parents today. But is it really just a suburban legend?" See Bryant Uestadt, "Bring It On," *Boston Globe Sunday Magazine*, July 8, 2007, 26. The effects of structured after-school activity participation are especially beneficial for impoverished children; see Joseph Mahoney, Heather Lord, and Erica Carryl, "An Ecological Analysis of After-School Program Participation and the Development of Academic Performance and Motivational Attributes in Disadvantaged Children," *Child Development,* 78 (2005): 811–825.

6. See Suniya S. Luthar and Shawn J. Latendresse, "Children of the Affluent: Challenges to Well-Being," *Current Directions in Psychological Science, 14* (2005): 49–53, and Suniya S. Luthar and Bronwyn E. Becker, "Privileged but Pressured? A Study of Affluent Youth," *Child Development,* 73 (2002): 1593–1610. Achievement pressures, perfectionistic tendencies, and low levels of closeness with parents appear to underlie this unexpected tendency for affluent adolescents to show higher levels of distress and disorder than inner-city teens—in particular, their extremely high risk for depression. Such high levels of distress and disorder among affluent youth appear during the transition to middle school, as adolescence begins.

7. Suniya S. Luthar, Karen A. Shoum, and Pamela J. Brown, "Extracurricular Involvement Among Affluent Youth: A Scapegoat for 'Ubiquitous Achievement Pressures'?" *Developmental Psychology,* 42 (2006): 583–597. It was noted that girls with extremely high levels of academic extracurricular activities had markedly high rates of substance abuse, a finding on the border of statistical significance. Still, parental and family factors—especially teens' perceptions of their parents' levels of criticism and academic pressure—were far more predictive of anxiety, depression, and substance abuse than were extracurricular activity involvements.

8. Stevie Smith, *Not Waving but Drowning* (London: Andre Deutsch, 1957). The interviews conducted for this book were lengthy and "qualitative"; through them, the girls revealed a level of pressure and distress that may not emerge in structured questionnaires or time diaries (the latter were used in the report of Mahoney et al., "Organized Activity Participation").

9. Alfie Kohn, *The Homework Myth: Why Our Kids Get Too Much of a Bad Thing* (Cambridge, Mass.: Da Capo Press, 2006). See also U.S. Department of Education, America Counts, *TIMSS Overview and Key Findings Across Grade Level,* 1998, retrieved from www.ed.gov/inits/Math/tmpres2.html.

10. U.S. Department of Education, National Center for Education Statistics, *The Condition of Education 2007*, NCES 2007–064 (Washington, D.C.: U.S. Government Printing Office, 2007).

11. David P. Baker and Gerald K. Letendre, *National Differences, Global Similarities: World Culture and the Future of Schooling* (Stanford, Calif.: Stanford University Press, 2005), 120. Homework estimates are not always reliable; indeed, youths' versus parents' estimates are not always highly correlated. Also, both youth with achievement problems and youth with high achievement motivation may spend inordinate amounts of time on homework. Alfie Kohn's argument, in *The Homework Myth,* is that homework is of questionable learning value, particularly for children in elementary school. For a systematic review, revealing benefits of homework, see Harris Cooper, Jorgianne Civey Robinson, and

Erika A. Patall, "Does Homework Improve Academic Achievement? A Synthesis of Research, 1987–2003," *Review of Educational Research,* 76 (2006): 1–62. For a rejoinder, read Kohn, *The Homework Myth.*

12. The college admissions calculator is available at www.college-admission-essay.com/formula.html. Statistics on the numbers of high schoolers taking SAT prep courses or utilizing private college admissions "advisors" are hard to come by, although Kaplan reported in 2004 that 270,000 high school students had participated in its courses (see www.kaplan.com/aboutkaplan/pressreleases/archive/2004/August_26-ktp_juniors_0804.htm). Currently, an inquiry at any relatively affluent high school is bound to yield high estimates.

13. See Alan Finder, "Elite Colleges Reporting Record Lows in Admissions," *New York Times,* April 1, 2008. See also, regarding the previous year, Sam Dillon, "A Great Year for Ivy Schools, but Not So Good for Applicants to Them," *New York Times*, April 4, 2007. Among the statistics cited: Harvard's acceptance rate in 2007 was the lowest in its long history, at 9 percent; Columbia's was 8.9 percent; Stanford's, 10.3 percent. In 2008, the acceptance rate at Harvard was 7.1 percent; at Yale, 8.3 percent; and at Columbia, 8.7 percent. Reasons include a demographic bulge in college-age youth; the fact that more youth than in past decades are going directly to college from high school; and that each student, on average, is applying to more and more colleges, further lowering acceptance rates.

14. For the more recent data, see U.S. Department of Education, *The Condition of Education.* Regarding data from the 1990s, see Ina V. S. Mullis, Michael O. Martin, Albert E. Beaton, Eugenio J. Gonzalez, Dana L. Kelly, and Teresa A. Smith, *Mathematics and Science Achievement in the Final Years of Secondary School: IEA's Third International Mathematics and Science Study* (Chestnut Hill, Mass.: TIMSS International Study Center, 1998), retrieved from http://isc.bc.edu/timss1995i/MathScienceC.html.

15. See National Sleep Foundation, "Summary of Findings—Sleep in America Poll."

16. Seung-Schik Yoo, Ninad Gunar, Peter Hu, Ferenc A. Jolesz, and Matthew P. Walker, "The Human Emotional Brain Without Sleep: A Prefrontal-Amygdala Disconnect," *Current Biology,* 17 (2007): 877–878.

17. See Po Bronson, "Snooze or Lose," *New York,* October 15, 2007, 34.

18. For example, Mary Carskadon of Brown University has performed pioneering research, noting adolescents' tendencies (even beyond the social pressures to stay up later and later) to have delayed onset of sleep, as a result of shifting hormone patterns and altered circadian rhythms. She and others have lobbied for regulations against having high schools start too early in the morning, because of the high risk for driving accidents related to sleep deprivation. See Mary A. Carskadon, Christine Acebo, and Oskar G. Jenni, "Regulation of Adolescent Sleep: Implications for Behavior," in *Adolescent Brain Development: Vulnerabilities and Opportunities*, ed. Ronald E. Dahl and Linda P. Spear, *Annals of the New York Academy of Science,* vol. 1021 (New York: New York Academy of Sciences, 2004). From the abstract to this review chapter, the following quote is salient: "[M]any adolescents have too little sleep at the wrong circadian phase. This pattern is associated with increased risks for excessive sleepiness, difficulty with mood regulation, impaired academic performance, learning difficulties, school tardiness and absenteeism, and accidents and injuries."

19. Even though the official workweek has shrunk across the last century, working couples are combining to put in more than 20 percent more working hours than did families several decades ago, according to the U.S. Department of Labor; see Bureau of Labor Statistics, "Working in the 21st Century," retrieved from www.bls.gov/opub/working/page17b.htm. With regard to sleep, perhaps the single most important influence on sleep patterns in the past several hundred years has been the invention of the electric light, which has turned night into day for countless millions worldwide. Certainly, historical

patterns of child labor and child exploitation led to devastating effects on youth, involving both intellectual and physical stunting. But today's patterns are nonetheless troublesome.

20. The tendency for girls to be more empathic than boys is discussed in more detail in Chapter 5. Research shows as well that girls have a higher level of sensitivity and anxiety to social situations than do boys; see, for example, Trudi M. Walsh, Sherry H. Stewart, Elizabeth McLaughlin, and Nancy Comeau, "Gender Differences in Childhood Anxiety Sensitivity Index (CASI) Dimensions," *Anxiety Disorders, 18* (2004): 695–706.

21. It has long been known that many children have a tendency to cheat to advance their academic or social standing; cheating is associated with high achievement motivation rather than with antisocial tendencies. For a classic work, see Hugh Hartshorne and Mark A. May, *Studies in the Nature of Character* (New York: Macmillan, 1928). But rampant cheating, related to performing rather than learning, indicates wrong-minded priorities in the culture at large.

22. The classic article is Mark R. Lepper, David Greene, and Richard E. Nisbett, "Undermining Children's Intrinsic Interest with Extrinsic Reward: A Test of the 'Overjustification' Hypothesis," *Journal of Personality and Social Psychology, 28* (1973): 129–137; see also Mark R. Lepper and David Greene, "Turning Play into Work: Effects of Adult Surveillance and Extrinsic Motivation on Children's Intrinsic Motivation," *Journal of Personality and Social Psychology, 31* (1975): 479–486, plus a host of additional studies across the past three decades. The essential finding is that when children are given external rewards for performing behaviors that they already engage in and enjoy, they subsequently fail to perform the action unless they are rewarded. As the authors of these reports have commented, however, this result does not mean that rewards should never be used. For example, for children with developmental disorders, learning disabilities, or other problems—who do not engage in academic or social behaviors with intrinsic motivation—external rewards may well be necessary. The key is that an overreliance on reward for behaviors that youth naturally enjoy and seek out is counterproductive.

23. In other words, coming to expect an external reward for one's performance is likely to change self-perceptions: for example, "I must be doing this behavior only because I am being induced or enticed to do so." These altered views of oneself may then lead to the undermining of intrinsic motivation for performing the task.

24. Claudia M. Mueller and Carol S. Dweck, "Praise for Intelligence Can Undermine Children's Motivation and Performance," *Journal of Personality and Social Psychology, 75* (1998): 33–52. Such praise can shape children and adolescents to believe that "performance goals" (i.e., seeming smart; not failing) are more important than actual learning, with negative consequences when failure occurs. That is, praise for ability or intelligence makes it difficult to muster motivation to lift effort when things aren't going well, fostering a helpless approach and a tendency to give up. On the other hand, praise for effort has extremely beneficial effects on subsequent performance, particularly after failure experiences. As stated by Mueller and Dweck: "Intelligence praise led children to wish to continue looking smart, whereas effort praise led children to want to learn new things" (p. 41). In addition, praise for intelligence led to lying about one's performance with peers, fostering overconcern with "how one did" rather than with how to improve. For a thorough examination of the ways in which praise may (or may not) undermine an individual's motivation, see Jennifer Henderlong and Mark R. Lepper, "The Effects of Praise on Children's Intrinsic Motivation: A Review and Synthesis," *Psychological Bulletin, 128* (2002): 774–795.

25. For a review of the effects of two divergent beliefs about intelligence—that it is a fixed "entity" versus a malleable, changeable process—see Carol S. Dweck, "Messages That Motivate: How Praise Molds Students' Beliefs, Motivation, and Performance (in Surprising Ways)," in *Improving Academic Achievement: Impact of Psychological Factors on*

Education, ed. Joshua Arnonson (San Diego: Academic Press, 2002). For a provocative review of how people forge meaning from everyday traits and events, well beyond intelligence per se, and how such "meanings" shape motivations and actions, see Daniel C. Molden and Carol S. Dweck, "Finding 'Meaning' in Psychology: A Lay Theories Approach to Self-Regulation, Social Perception, and Social Development," *American Psychologist, 61* (2006): 192–203.

26. For example, see Jennifer S. Beer, "Implicit Self-Theories of Shyness," *Journal of Personality and Social Psychology,* 83 (2002): 1009–1024.

27. See Molden and Dweck, "Finding 'Meaning' in Psychology," for a thoughtful examination of additional domains in which "entity" versus "incremental" perspectives may have consequences for people's actions and motivations, although beauty and looks are not included in this argument.

Chapter 4: No Place to Run, No Place to Hide

1. For the ABC homepage regarding this series, see abc.go.com/primetime/greysanatomy/index?pn=index. For the web-player for this series, see dynamic.abc.go.com/streaming/landing?lid=ABCCOMGlobalMenu&lpos=FEP.

2. Sara Rimer, "For Girls, It's Be Yourself and Be Perfect, Too," *New York Times*, April 1, 2007.

3. For the ABC homepage regarding this series, see abc.go.com/primetime/uglybetty/index?pn=index. For the web-player for this series, see dynamic.abc.go.com/streaming/landing?lid=ABCCOMGlobalMenu&lpos=FEP.

4. Emily Nussbaum, "The Incredible Shrinking Model," *New York*, February 26, 2007, 44–54.

5. Cicely Von Ziegesar, *Gossip Girl* (New York: Alloy, 2002); Cicely Von Ziegesar, *The It Girl* (Boston: Little Brown, 2005); Zoey Dean, *The A-List* (New York: Alloy, 2003).

6. Dean, *A-List*, 92–93.

7. von Ziegesar, *Gossip Girl*, 45.

8. Dean, *A-List*, 225.

9. von Ziegesar, *Gossip Girl*, 39.

10. Meg Cabot, *The Princess Diaries* (New York: HarperCollins, 2000).

11. Cabot, *The Princess Diaries*, back jacket.

12. Ibid., 24.

13. Ibid., 135–136, 267.

14. Scott Westerfeld, *Uglies* (New York: Simon Pulse, 2005).

15. Scott Westerfeld, *Pretties* (New York: Simon Pulse, 2005).

16. Jerry Spinelli, *Stargirl* (New York: Knopf, 2000).

17. Ibid., 141–142.

18. Jerry Spinelli, *Love, Stargirl* (New York: Knopf, 2007).

19. For information on *Juno,* see the Internet Movie Database, *Juno*, 2007, retrieved from www.imdb.com/title/tt0467406/.

20. Logan Hill, "Pregnant with Possibilities," *New York*, December 3, 2007, 80.

21. Amanda Marcotte, "Woe to She Born with a Uterus," *Pandagon,* posted January 13, 2008, at pandagon.blogsome.com/2008/01/13/woe-is-she-born-with-a-uterus.

22. Hill, "Pregnant with Possibilities," 80.

23. See imdb.com/title/tt0427327/ and www.mylifetime.com/on-tv/movies/queen-sized.

24. Campbell Robertson, "Tweens Love Broadway, but Can't Save It Alone," *New York Times*, October 2, 2007.

25. Gregory McGuire, *Wicked: The Life and Times of the Wicked Witch of the West* (New York: HarperCollins, 1995).

Chapter 5: When Virtue Is Its Own Punishment

1. Panic disorder is a severe, concentrated form of anxiety in which a person experiences panic attacks, which are brief periods of extreme distress (e.g., heart palpitations, chest pain, dizziness, shortness of breath, sweating, trembling, fear of losing control, feeling of being disconnected from oneself) that often feel, to the individual, as though he or she is having a heart attack or otherwise dying. Because panic attacks are events that people would do almost anything to avoid in the future, they are often related to the development of agoraphobia: a fear of being outside or in situations that seem to have been linked to the attack. Not surprisingly, panic attacks are also associated with depression. See American Psychiatric Association, *Diagnostic and Statistical Manual of Mental Disorders, 4th Edition, Text Revision* (Washington, D.C.: Author, 2000); and Philip C. Kendall, Kristina A. Hedtke, and Sasha G. Aschenbrand, "Anxiety Disorders," in *Behavioral and Emotional Disorders in Adolescents: Nature, Assessment, and Treatment*, ed. David A. Wolfe and Eric J. Mash (New York: Guilford, 2006).

2. In Nicola's vivid account, one can see the propensity for those with serious anxiety and panic to catastrophize, overgeneralize, and believe that almost any event may come to trigger a severe outbreak of anxiety and panic. The inner pain is truly overwhelming.

3. See Carolyn Zahn-Waxler, "The Development of Empathy, Guilt, and Internalization of Distress," in *Anxiety, Depression, and Emotion*, ed. Richard Davidson (New York: Oxford University Press, 2000); Kate Keenan and Daniel Shaw, "Developmental and Social Influences on Young Girls' Early Problem Behavior," *Psychological Bulletin, 121* (1997): 95–113.

4. Zahn-Waxler, "The Development of Empathy."

5. See Susan Nolen-Hoeksema and Joan S. Girgus, "The Emergence of Gender Differences in Depression During Adolescence," *Psychological Bulletin, 115* (1994): 424–443; Jill M. Cyranowski, Ellen Frank, Elizabeth Young, and Kathleen Shear, "Adolescent Onset of the Gender Difference in Lifetime Rates of Major Depression: A Theoretical Model," *Archives of General Psychiatry,* 57 (2000): 21–27. Note that panic disorder is believed to have a moderate heritability (see Chapter 2 for explanation), on the order of 40 to 50 percent; see Kendall et al., "Anxiety Disorders."

6. For the classic article on vulnerability genes for depression, which are amplified by negative life events, see Avshalom Caspi, Karen Sugden, Terrie E. Moffitt, Alan Taylor, Ian W. Craig, HonaLee Harrington, Joseph McClay, Jonathan Mill, Judy Martin, Anthony Braithwaite, and Richie Poulton, "Influence of Life Stress on Depression: Moderation by a Polymorphism in the 5-HTT Gene," *Science, 301* (2003): 386–389 (also see Chapter 2). For a lucid exposition on risk factors, see Helena C. Kraemer, Alan E. Kazdin, David R. Offord, Ronald C. Kessler, Peter S. Jensen, and David J. Kupfer, "Coming to Terms with the Terms of Risk," *Archives of General Psychiatry,* 54 (1997): 337–343.

7. The puberty-related hormone surge in girls serves to "express" vulnerability genes for depression. Regarding the cognitive styles that trigger and maintain depression, especially in females, see Lyn Y. Abramson, Martin E. P. Seligman, and John D. Teasdale, "Learned Helplessness in Humans: Critique and Reformulation," *Journal of Abnormal Psychology,* 87 (1978): 49–74; and Cyranowski et al., "Adolescent Onset of the Gender Difference." For data on the heritability of depression, see Patrick F. Sullivan, Michael C. Neale, and Kenneth S. Kendler, "Genetic Epidemiology of Major Depression: Review and Meta-Analysis," *American Journal of Psychiatry,* 157 (2000): 1552–1562.

8. In fact, Keenan and Hipwell identify empathy, compliance, and emotion regulation as potential strengths that may turn into risk factors for girls; see Kate Keenan and Alison E. Hipwell, "Preadolescent Clues to Understanding Depression in Girls," *Clinical Child and Family Psychology Review,* 8 (2003): 89–105. Although usually thought of as desirable,

these traits, when excessive and when compounded by non-harmonious families or depressed parents, turn out to predict depression and self-harm. Keenan and Hipwell contend that excessive emotional empathy (i.e., taking on the feelings of others) rather than cognitive empathy (i.e., understanding the feelings of another) is particularly problematic, because overzealous emotional empathy leads to the ignoring of one's own feelings and needs.

Why does it take until adolescence for these variables to become activated as female risk factors? First, although empathy, compliance, and the ability to regulate emotions may serve girls well in childhood, adolescence requires individuation and demands "boy"-like qualities, particularly during the current era of the Triple Bind. If a girl has become overly effective in suppressing anger, individuality, and her own needs, depression may not be far behind. Second, the surge of female hormones during and after puberty may "express" vulnerability genes in girls; see Dwight L. Evans and Martin E. P. Seligman, "Introduction," and Commission on Adolescent Disorder and Depression, "Defining Depression and Bipolar Disorder," in *Treating and Preventing Adolescent Mental Health Disorders: What We Know and What We Don't Know*, ed. Dwight L. Evans, Edna B. Foa, Racquel E. Gur, Herbert Hendin, Charles P. O'Brien, Martin E. P. Seligman, and B. Timothy Walsh (New York: Oxford University Press, 2005). See also Grayson N. Holmbeck, Deborah Friedman, Mona Abad, and Barbara Jandasek, "Development and Psychopathology in Adolescence," in *Behavioral and Emotional Disorders in Adolescents: Nature, Assessment, and Treatment*, ed. David A. Wolfe and Eric J. Mash (New York: Guilford, 2006), who highlight that it is not puberty per se but rather early puberty in combination with other risk factors that predicts the onset of depression (and other conditions) in girls.

9. Mona Simpson, *Anywhere but Here* (New York: Knopf, 1986).

10. Still, it may take additional risks before such a girl becomes depressed. As indicated throughout this chapter, the risk for depression (and other forms of self-harm) grows as the number of risk factors (e.g., genetic predisposition, depressed parent, maltreatment, high rates of loss events) increases. Risk factors are known to magnify one another; their effects are compared metaphorically to a cascading waterfall or to a mutually reinforcing "symphony" of events. See W. Thomas Boyce, "Symphonic Causation and the Origins of Childhood Psychopathology," in *Developmental Psychopathology*, 2nd ed., vol. 2: *Developmental Neuroscience*, ed. Dante Cicchetti and Donald J. Cohen (Hoboken, N.J.: Wiley, 2006).

11. For a review of gender differences in psychopathology, with reference to aggression and depression, and the role of peers and social interactions in fostering risk for girls' psychopathology, see Eleanor E. Maccoby, "Aggression in the Context of Gender Development," in *Aggression, Antisocial Behavior, and Violence Among Girls*, ed. Martha Putallaz and Karen L. Bierman (New York: Guilford, 2004).

12. Harriette Cole, "Alicia Keys," *Ebony*, November 2007, 69–74, 220–222.

13. Zahn-Waxler, "The Development of Empathy." Her argument is that, in girls, emotional empathy, verbal skills, compliance, and high levels of emotion regulation may serve to predict later problems—especially in the domains of depression and distress—when other vulnerabilities and risk factors exist in a girl's life, particularly a parent's depression. "Young girls, on average, show better regulation of emotions, better ego control, greater language skills, more rapid physical maturation, internalization of standards of interpersonal conduct, social maturity, and responsible interpersonal behavior than young boys. With these initial advantages, why do so many girls later become depressed?" (p. 242). Her answer, in brief, is that an overabundance of empathy may become linked to guilt, whereby the girl comes to believe that she may have been responsible for her mother's distress. This overidentification and emotional overinvolvement hinder female self-development and predispose to later depression. This process is particularly likely to

occur with the emergence of adolescence, when girls are prone to ruminate and to become preoccupied with body image.

Girls show higher levels of empathy than boys, from young ages, because of "internal" tendencies as well as socialization practices that tune girls in to the feelings of others. Indeed, as noted in the text, girls show greater heart-rate deceleration than boys—revealing greater attention focused outwardly—when they witness the distress of another person, as early as the preschool years. At the same time, girls are socialized by families to anticipate the consequences of their negative actions more than boys are, promoting their tendencies to internalize. When a girl comes to feel that she is responsible for her mom's distress, a vicious cycle of rumination and overattribution of responsibility to herself may result. That is, her very empathy may cause her to fail to take care of her own emotions, as she struggles to solve the problems of others. Still, some empathy is clearly a good thing for development in both boys and girls, as a lack of empathy may predispose individuals to high levels of aggression or other forms of antisocial behavior; see Carolyn Zahn-Waxler and Nicole Polanichka, "All Things Interpersonal: Socialization and Female Aggression," in *Aggression, Antisocial Behavior, and Violence Among Girls*, ed. Martha Putallaz and Karen L. Bierman (New York: Guilford, 2004).

14. Zahn-Waxler, "The Development of Empathy"; Zahn-Waxler and Polanichka, "All Things Interpersonal."

15. According to Keenan and Hipwell in "Preadolescent Clues," researchers and clinicians are so conditioned to believe that empathy and emotional regulation are strengths that they may fail to attend to girls' tendencies to overregulate their emotions or be excessively empathic—which can, in the presence of additional risk factors, thwart girls' own individuation and sense of agency, placing them at risk for depression.

16. See, again, Keenan and Hipwell, "Preadolescent Clues," particularly with regard to their contentions about excessive compliance.

17. The messages of the Triple Bind are likely to influence most strongly those girls with genetic, trauma-related, familial, and school- or neighborhood-related risk factors (see note 10).

18. For early work on rumination, see Sonja Lyubormirsky and Susan Nolen-Hoeksema, "Effects of Self-Focused Rumination on Negative Thinking and Interpersonal Problem Solving," *Journal of Personality and Social Psychology*, 69 (1995): 176–190. Book-length coverage is found in Susan Nolen-Hoeksema, *Eating, Drinking, Overthinking: The Toxic Triangle of Food, Alcohol, and Depression and How Women Can Break Free* (New York: Henry Holt, 2006).

19. Lev S. Vygotsky, *Thought and Language* (Oxford, U.K.: Wiley, 1962). This is a translation, from the Russian, of Vygotsky's classic 1934 book. See also Keenan and Shaw, "Developmental Influences."

20. Eleanor E. Maccoby, *Growing Up Apart, Coming Together* (Cambridge, Mass.: Harvard University Press, 1998).

21. See review in Zahn-Waxler, "The Development of Empathy."

22. See review in Keenan and Hipwell, "Preadolescent Clues."

23. For recent research on the predictability of suicidal ideation, eating symptomatology, and depression from ruminative tendencies, see Regina Miranda and Susan Nolen-Hoeksema, "Brooding and Reflection: Rumination Predicts Suicidal Ideation at One-Year Follow-up in a Community Sample," *Behavior Research and Therapy*, 45 (2007): 3088–3095, and Susan Nolen-Hoeksema, Eric Stice, Emily Wade, and Cara Bohon, "Reciprocal Relations Between Rumination and Bulimic, Substance Abuse, and Depressive Symptoms in Female Adolescents," *Journal of Abnormal Psychology*, 116 (2007): 198–207.

24. Tara S. Peris and Robert E. Emery, "Redefining the Parent-Child Relationship Following Divorce: Examining the Risk for Boundary Dissolution," *Journal of Emotional*

Abuse, 5 (2005), 169–189; Tara Sophia Peris, "An Investigation of Emotional Parentification in Adolescence," *Dissertation Abstracts International, Section B: The Sciences and Engineering,* 66 (2006): 5101.

25. See Amelio A. D'Onofrio, *Adolescent Self-Injury: A Comprehensive Guide for Counselors and Health Care Professionals* (New York: Springer, 2007). He writes, "It [self-mutilation] is a physical manifestation of profound psychological wounding that is often inaccessible to the sufferer and, as such, represents a kind of psychological pain that is literally unspeakable" (p. xv).

26. Lisa Zacheim, "Alexithymia: The Expanding Realm of Research," *Journal of Psychosomatic Research,* 63 (2007): 345–347, introduces a special issue on this topic. See also Erin Polk and Miriam Liss, "Psychological Characteristics of Self-Injurious Behavior," *Personality and Individual Differences,* 43 (2007): 567–577.

27. Cole, "Alicia Keys."

Chapter 6: Bratz Dolls and Pussycat Dolls

1. See CW website, "Pussycat Dolls Present: The Search for the Next Doll," 2008, retrieved from www.cwtv.com/shows/pussycat-dolls/about.

2. American Psychological Association, Task Force on the Sexualization of Girls, *Report of the APA Task Force on the Sexualization of Girls* (Washington, D.C.: Author, 2007), retrieved from www.apa.org/pi/wpo/sexualization.html. This landmark review synthesizes information from a large number of primary-source articles regarding the effects of sexual imagery in television, music videos and music lyrics, magazines, films, video games, the Internet, and advertisements on the psychological development of girls and women. The task force defined "sexualization" as a person's self-valuation that emerges solely from sexual appeal or sexual behavior—to the exclusion of other characteristics—and "sexual objectification" as a person's being made into a thing for another's sexual pleasure or use. The report, cited throughout this chapter, claims that sexual imagery in the media has increased markedly in recent years and concludes that sexualization has negative effects on many aspects of female development: achievement and cognitive functioning, mental health, physical development, and the development of sexuality. Indeed, the report's summary contends that sexualization and objectification undermine a girl's confidence in and comfort with her own body, leading to emotional and self-image problems, eating disorders, low self-esteem, depressed mood, and a restricted sexual self-image. See also Jean Kilbourne, *Deadly Persuasion: Why Women and Girls Must Fight the Addictive Power of Advertising* (New York: Free Press, 1999); and Deborah L. Tolman, *Dilemmas of Desire: Teenage Girls Talk About Sexuality* (Cambridge, Mass.: Harvard University Press, 2002).

3. Brian Lowery, "Pussycat Dolls Present: The Search for the Next Doll," *Variety,* posted Sunday, March 4, 2007, retrieved from www.variety.com/review/VE1117932979.html?categoryid=32&cs=1.

4. Jacqueline Cutler, "Wanted: Singer/Dancer Who's Hot Like the Pussycat Dolls," *Media Village,* retrieved from www.zap2it.com/tv/zap-story-pcatdolls,0,6744402.story.

5. Cecily von Ziegesar, *All I Want Is Everything: A Gossip Girl Novel* (New York: Alloy, 2003), 155.

6. Janet Reitman, "Sex and Scandal at Duke," *Rolling Stone,* June 1, 2006; retrieved from www.rollingstone.com/news/story/10464110/sex_scandal_at_duke.

7. See Tolman, *Dilemmas of Desire*; see also American Psychological Association Task Force, *Report of the APA Task Force,* for details on the many negative impacts (cognitive, psychological, self-esteem-related, and health-related) given by messages of sexualization and objectification from multiple forms of media. These messages not only objectify girls and women (see details later in this chapter) but also give boys and men the explicit sense

that females are there chiefly for the direct pleasure of males, fueling a culture in which objectification, sexual harassment, and abuse are far too prevalent.

8. See American Psychological Association Task Force, *Report of the APA Task Force*.

9. See Martha K. McClintock and Gilbert Herdt, "Rethinking Puberty: The Development of Sexual Attraction," *Current Directions in Psychological Science,* 5 (1996): 178–183, who contend that sexual attraction typically begins around fourth grade, two years prior to menarche, when the adrenal glands send out an early surge of hormones. Terming this event "adrenarche," they call for reconsideration of the timing of the development of sexual attitudes and cognitions.

10. See Sarah E. Anderson, Gerard E. Dallal, and Aviva Must, "Relative Weight and Race Influence Average Age at Menarche: Results from Two Nationally Representative Surveys of US Girls Studied 25 Years Apart," *Pediatrics, 111* (2003): 844–850. The researchers found that the age of menarche for girls has declined by as much as two years across the past century. This lowering of the age at menarche has been associated with a concomitant increase in girls' body mass indexes during this time (that is, girls are getting heavier as well). For African American girls, the age of menarche is several months lower than it is for white girls, controlling for any differences in body mass. See also Margaret A. McDowell, Deborah J. Brody, and Jeffrey P. Hughes, "Has Age at Menarche Changed? Results from the National Health and Nutrition Examination Survey (NHANES) 1999–2004," *Journal of Adolescent Health, 40* (2007): 227–231, who found definitive evidence for a one-year drop in the age at menarche from before 1920 until the 1990s. Regarding obesity, see Phil McKenna, "Childhood Obesity Brings Early Puberty for Girls," New Scientist.com, who reports on recent data from Joyce Lee of the University of Michigan; retrieved from www.newscientist.com/article/dn11307-childhood-obesity-brings-early-puberty-for-girls.html. In the article, Marcia Herman-Giddens (an original discoverer of the linkage between obesity and early puberty) states, "There are huge health and social complications. . . . Imagine being eight or nine years old and having men hit on you because you have breasts. Grown women have enough trouble dealing with unwanted sexual advances—imagine being in the fourth grade."

11. For details, see American Psychological Association Task Force, *APA Task Force Report*. See also Margaret Talbot, "Little Hotties," *New Yorker*, December 4, 2006, 74.

12. See, for example, Kathleen Deveny with Raina Kelley, "Girls Gone Bad," *Newsweek*, February 12, 2007, 40–47, which evaluates the attraction of Lindsay, Paris, and Britney and probes whether today's girls are really in crisis. Sarah Rimer, "For Girls, It's Be Yourself and Be Perfect, Too," *New York Times*, April 1, 2007, points out that girls have trouble navigating the conflicting messages they've received, such as "bring home A's . . . do everything . . . get into a top college," but also "be yourself . . . have fun . . . don't work too hard." See also Emily Nussbaum, "Say Everything," *New York*, February 12, 2007, 24–29, 102–105.

13. Kathleen A. Kendall-Tackett, Linda M. Williams, and David Finkelhor, "Impact of Sexual Abuse on Children: A Review and Synthesis of Recent Empirical Studies," *Psychological Bulletin, 113* (1993): 164–180. As for the prevalence of child victimization, maltreatment, and exposure to violence, see David Finkelhor, Richard Ormrod, Heather Turner, and Sherry L. Hamby, "The Victimization of Children and Youth: A Comprehensive, National Survey," *Child Maltreatment, 10* (2005): 5–25, who found that more than half of their sample (ages two to seventeen years) had experienced a physical assault in the study year, a fourth had experienced a property offense, more than one in eight had experienced a form of child maltreatment, about one in twelve had experienced sexual victimization, and more than a third had been a witness to violence or experienced another form of indirect victimization. For work on abuse experiences and their association

with aggressive behavior and peer rejection in girls with ADHD, see Allison Briscoe-Smith and Stephen P. Hinshaw, "Linkages Between Child Abuse and Attention-Deficit/Hyperactivity Disorder in Girls: Behavioral and Social Correlates," *Child Abuse and Neglect, 30* (2006): 1239–1255.

14. See Deborah L. Tolman, Emily A. Impett, Tracy J. Allison, and Alice Michael, "Looking Good, Sounding Good: Femininity Ideology and Adolescent Girls' Mental Health," *Psychology of Women Quarterly, 30* (2006): 85–95, who found that body objectification and inauthenticity in relationships were strongly related to eighth-grade girls' depression and self-esteem scores. Body objectification and inauthenticity in relationships were also predictive of poor sexual self-efficacy and less use of protection during sex; see Emily A. Impett, Deborah Schooler, and Deborah L. Tolman, "To Be Seen and Not Heard: Femininity Ideology and Adolescent Girls' Sexual Health," *Archives of Sexual Behavior, 35* (2006): 131–144. For a review, American Psychological Association Task Force, *Report of the APA Task Force*.

15. See Alison Gopnik, Andrew N. Meltzoff, and Patricia K. Kuhl, *The Scientist in the Crib: Minds, Brains, and How Children Learn* (New York: William Morrow, 1999).

16. For more on objectification, see Barbara L. Fredrickson and Tomi-Ann Roberts, "Objectification Theory: Toward Understanding Women's Lived Experiences and Mental Health Risks," *Psychology of Women Quarterly, 21* (1997): 173–206. The distinction between pretending or faking sexuality and actual sexuality is crucial here. See also Sharon Lamb, *The Secret Lives of Girls: What Good Girls Really Do—Sex Play, Aggression, and Their Guilt* (New York: Free Press, 2002), who states that girls well before puberty often engage in sex play, which should not be a source of shame, so long as it is not exploitative or forced upon them by older youth or adults and it is not prompted and promoted by a premature "push" toward being sexual.

17. American Psychological Association Task Force, *APA Task Force Report*; Kendall-Tackett, Williams, and Finkelhor, "Impact of Sexual Abuse on Children"; David A. Wolfe, Jennine S. Rawana, and Debbie Chiodo, "Abuse and Trauma," in *Behavioral and Emotional Disorders in Adolescents: Nature, Assessment, and Treatment,* ed. David A. Wolfe and Eric J. Mash (New York: Guilford, 2006).

18. Barbara L. Fredrickson, Tomi-Ann Roberts, Stephanie M. Noll, Diane M. Quinn, and Jean M. Twenge, "The Swimsuit Becomes You: Sex Differences in Self-Objectification, Restrained Eating, and Math Performance," *Journal of Personality and Social Psychology,* 75 (1998): 269–284. One of the most pernicious consequences of self-objectification, according to Fredrickson and colleagues, is that girls and women who constantly monitor themselves regarding how they look will lack the cognitive reserves for concentrated academic performance. This work stems from their theoretical model on objectification and self-objectification, which posits that in a culture (such as ours) with a penchant for sexualizing girls and women, females internalize an observer's perspective and overly monitor themselves, producing shame and anxiety and promoting risk for depression and eating disorders as well as sexual dysfunction (see Fredrickson and Roberts, "Objectification Theory"). In a recent replication, the swimsuit condition led to reduced capacity in young women's basic attention, with clear implications for their ability to perform in the world; see Diane M. Quinn, Rachel W. Kallen, Jean M. Twenge, and Barbara L. Fredrickson, "The Disruptive Effect of Self-Objectification on Performance," *Psychology of Women Quarterly, 30* (2006): 59–64.

19. The original, highly cited investigation is Claude M. Steele and Joshua Aronson, "Stereotype Threat and the Intellectual Test Performance of African Americans," *Journal of Personality and Social Psychology, 69* (1995): 797–811. Steele and Aronson found that black participants who were in the "diagnostic" condition—that is, those who were told

that the test was a measure of verbal and reading ability—performed worse because they activated concerns about their own abilities and made excuses in advance about how they might perform. Having to indicate their race on a pre-test questionnaire also depressed performance. See also Claude M. Steele, "A Threat in the Air: How Stereotypes Shape Intellectual Identity and Performance," *American Psychologist,* 52 (1997): 613–629.

20. See Steven J. Spencer, Claude M. Steele, and Diane M. Quinn, "Stereotype Threat and Women's Math Performance," *Journal of Experimental Social Psychology,* 35 (1999): 4–28.

21. Toni Schmaer and Michael Johns, "Converging Evidence That Stereotype Threat Reduces Working Memory Capacity," *Journal of Personality and Social Psychology,* 85 (2003): 440–452.

22. See review in Neil M. Malamuth and Emily A. Impett, "Research on Sex in the Media: What Do We Know about Effects on Children and Adolescents," in *Handbook of Children and the Media*, ed. Dorothy G. Singer and Jerome L. Singer (Thousand Oaks, Calif.: Sage, 2001); see also American Psychological Association Task Force, *Report of the APA Task Force*. For the television commercial experimental study, see Paul G. Davies, Steven J. Spencer, Diane M. Quinn, and Rebecca Gerhardstein, "Consuming Images: How Television Commercials That Elicit Stereotype Threat Can Constrain Women Academically and Professionally," *Personality and Social Psychology Bulletin,* 28 (2002): 1615–1628. See also, more recently, Paul G. Davies, Steven J. Spencer, and Claude M. Steele, "Clearing the Air: Identity Safety Moderates the Effects of Stereotype Threat on Women's Leadership Aspirations," *Journal of Personality and Social Psychology,* 88 (2005): 276–287.

23. American Psychological Association Task Force, *Report of the APA Task Force*, 33.

24. Tolman, *Dilemmas of Desire*. Overall, how influential is exposure to media on child and adolescent behavioral patterns and attitudes? First, there is a massive literature on the topic of violent imagery and aggression, with considerable experimental and longitudinal evidence that exposure to violence through television, video games, and other media is clearly associated with increases in aggressive behavior. See Craig A. Anderson, Leonard Berkowitz, Edward Donnerstein, L. Rowell Huesmann, James D. Johnson, Daniel Linz, Neil M. Malamuth, and Ellen Wartella, "The Influence of Media Violence on Youth," *Psychological Science in the Public Interest,* 4 (2003): 81–110. See also L. Rowell Huesmann, "The Impact of Electronic Media Violence: Scientific Theory and Research," *Journal of Adolescent Health,* 41 (2007): S6–S13, and L. Rowell Huesmann and Laramie D. Taylor, "The Role of Media Violence in Violent Behavior," *Annual Review of Public Health,* 27 (2006): 393–415.

Second, for reviews on the effects of sexual imagery in the media on youths' sexual attitudes and behavior, see Malamuth and Impett, "Research on Sex in the Media," and Nancy Signorelli, "Television's Gender Role Images and Contribution to Stereotyping," in *Handbook of Children and the Media*, ed. Dorothy G. Singer and Jerome L. Singer (New York: Sage, 2001). There is a far smaller literature on media effects on sexual attitudes and behavior, largely because of investigators' hesitation to expose youth (as opposed to adults) to sexual images in experimental studies. Correlational studies, however, show that there is an association between the proportion of all media viewing that contains sexual content, on the one hand, and engagement in sexual behavior, on the other. As noted in the text, experimental studies, in which youth are assigned randomly to watch music videos with sexual content versus those without, reveal that such exposure is linked with the youths' subsequent approval of sexist attitudes.

Third, there is a substantial literature on the effects of pornography, largely on men's propensity toward sexual violence. Whereas boys and men who tend toward exploitation of and violence toward girls and women watch pornography more than the norm, their exposure to violent pornography serves to increase their initial tendencies. See Vanessa Vega and Neil M. Malamuth, "Predicting Sexual Aggression: The Role of Pornography in the Context of General and Specific Risk Factors," *Aggressive Behavior,* 33 (2007): 104–117, and Neil M. Malamuth, Tamara Addison, and Mary Koss, "Pornography and Sexual Aggression: Are There Reliable Effects and Can We Understand Them?" *Annual Review of Sex Research, 11* (2000): 26–91.

How can exposure to media images increase the tendencies in question? Viewers may model the behaviors that they witness, and repeated exposure may cultivate a set of beliefs about how to act in the world. Also, witnessing media images from a young age may blur distinctions between fantasy and reality, and repetitive exposure may wear away the inhibitions against violence (sexual or physical) that one has typically been socialized to hold. See Malamuth and Impett, "Research on Sex in the Media"; Anderson et al., "The Influence of Media Violence on Youth"; and Signorelli, "Television's Gender Role Images."

25. For statistics on girls' distorted body images, see James D. Lock and Daniel le Grange, "Eating Disorders," in *Behavioral and Emotional Disorders in Adolescents: Nature, Assessment, and Treatment*, ed. David A. Wolfe and Eric J. Mash (New York: Guilford, 2006), and Dwight L. Evans and Martin E. P. Seligman, "Introduction," and Commission on Adolescent Disorder and Depression, "Defining Depression and Bipolar Disorder," in *Treating and Preventing Adolescent Mental Health Disorders: What We Know and What We Don't Know*, ed. Dwight L. Evans, Edna B. Foa, Racquel E. Gur, Herbert Hendin, Charles P. O'Brien, Martin E. P. Seligman, and B. Timothy Walsh (New York: Oxford University Press, 2005). Regarding self-objectification, see Tolman et al., "Looking Good, Sounding Good"; Impett et al., "To Be Seen and Not Heard"; and the general review in American Psychological Association Task Force, *Report of the APA Task Force*.

26. See American Society for Aesthetic Plastic Surgery, "11.5 Million Cosmetic Procedures in 2006," March 9, 2007, retrieved from www.surgery.org/press/newsprint.php ?iid=465§ion.

27. See Monica Rizzo, "High School Musical's Ashley Tisdale Gets a Nose Job," December 3, 2007, retrieved from www.people.com/people/article/0,,20163982,00.html; "Did Blake Get Her Nose and Lips Done," *Life and Style*, January 28, 2008, 45; "The Only Way Heidi Will Marry Spencer," *Life and Style*, January 28, 2008, 26–29.

28. See American Association of University Women, *Hostile Hallways: Bullying, Teasing, and Sexual Harassment in School* (Washington, D.C.: Author, 2001), retrieved from www.aauw.org/research/upload/hostilehallways.pdf.

29. The American Psychological Association Task Force, *APA Task Force Report*, highlights that, increasingly, adult women are portrayed sexually as young girls—while at the same time, young girls are portrayed sexually as women.

30. For data on the linkage between sexual abuse and prostitution, see Cathy Spatz Widom and Joseph B. Kuhns, "Childhood Victimization and Subsequent Risk for Promiscuity, Prostitution, and Teenage Pregnancy: A Prospective Study," *American Journal of Public Health, 86* (1996): 1607–1612, and Lisa A. Kramer and Ellen C. Berg, "A Survival Analysis of Timing of Entry into Prostitution: The Differential Impact of Race, Educational Level, and Childhood/Adolescent Risk Factors," *Sociological Inquiry,* 73 (2003): 511–528.

31. Tim Kasser and Richard M. Ryan, "A Dark Side of the American Dream: Correlates of Financial Success as a Central Life Aspiration," *Journal of Personality and Social Psychology,* 65 (1993): 410–422; Tim Kasser, Richard M. Ryan, Melvin Zax, and Arnold J. Sameroff, "The Relations of Maternal and Social Environments to Late Adolescents' Materialistic and Prosocial Values," *Developmental Psychology,* 31 (1995): 907–914. A book-length account is found in Tim Kasser, *The High Price of Materialism* (Cambridge, Mass.:

MIT Press, 2002), in which he argues that once people have their basic needs addressed, additional materialistic pursuits add almost nothing to their sense of well-being. Furthermore, a preoccupation with wealth and possessions predicts unhappiness, low self-esteem, relationship problems, and even depression.

32. See "Bratz Beat Barbie in Q4," *Playthings*, February 6, 2007, retrieved from www.playthings.com/article/CA6413828.html.

33. I am indebted to Tim Cusack for this insight.

34. Bratz dolls website, www.bratz.com.

35. For the conflicting statements, see The National Labor Committee, "Made in China: The Sweatshop Behind the Bratz," December 21, 2006, retrieved from www.nlcnet.org/article.php?id=197 and Tina Benitez, "MGA Refutes Bratz Sweatshop Story," *Playthings,* December 26, 2006, retrieved from www.playthings.com/article/CA6402684.html.

36. Jeff Leeds, "As Pop Music Seeks New Sales, the Pussycat Dolls Head to Toyland," *New York Times,* April 17, 2006.

37. James Montgomery, "Hasbro Decides Not to Stick With Pussycat Dolls Toy Line," MTV News, posted May 25, 2006, retrieved from www.vh1.com/artists/news/1532498/05252006/the_pussycat_dolls.jhtml.

38. Peggy Orenstein, "What's Wrong with Cinderella?" *New York Times Magazine,* December 24, 2006, 34–39.

39. Peggy Orenstein and the American Association of University Women, *Schoolgirls: Young Women, Self-Esteem, and the Confidence Gap* (New York: Anchor Books, 1994).

40. Lev Grossman, "Tila Tequila," *Time,* December 16, 2006, retrieved from www.time.com/time/magazine/article/0,9171,1570728,00.html.

41. See Amanda Wagner, "Cultural Norms of Shaving Pubic Hair Considered," *Wheaton Wire,* December 5, 2007, retrieved from media.www.thewheatonwire.com/media/storage/paper1132/news/2007/12/05/Commentary/Cultural.Norms.Of.Shaving.Pubic.Hair.Considered-3132472.shtml.

42. Tom Robbins, *Even Cowgirls Get the Blues* (Boston: Houghton Mifflin, 1976).

43. Kilbourne, *Deadly Persuasion,* 26–27.

44. See *The Show Buzz,* CBS, "How to Look Good Naked: In New TV Show, 'Queer Eye' Fashion Guru Carson Kressley Shows Women How to Feel Beautiful from the Inside Out," January 4, 2007, retrieved from www.showbuzz.cbsnews.com/stories/2008/01/04/tv_realty_tv/main3676889.shtml?source=RSSattr=Entertainment_3676889.

Chapter 7: The Wired Child

1. Lauren Collins, "Friend Game," *New Yorker,* January 21, 2008, 34–41; Christopher Maag, "A Hoax Turned Fatal Draws Anger but No Charges," *New York Times,* November 28, 2007, A23.

2. Collins, "Friend Game," 36.

3. Ibid., 38.

4. Maag, "A Hoax," A23.

5. American Psychological Association, Task Force on the Sexualization of Girls, *Report of the APA Task Force on the Sexualization of Girls* (Washington, D.C.: Author, 2007), retrieved from www.apa.org/pi/wpo/sexualization.html.

6. Children with ADHD are particularly prone to be rejected by their peers; see Stephen P. Hinshaw and Sharon Melnick, "Peer Relationships in Children With Attention-Deficit Hyperactivity Disorder With and Without Comorbid Aggression," *Development and Psychopathology,* 7 (1995): 627–647, and Betsy Hoza, Sylvie Mrug, Alyson C. Gerdes, Stephen P. Hinshaw, William M. Bukowski, Joel A. Gold, Helena C. Kraemer, William E.

Pelham, Timothy Wigal, and L. Eugene Arnold, "What Aspects of Peer Relationships Are Impaired in Children with Attention-Deficit/Hyperactivity Disorder?" *Journal of Consulting and Clinical Psychology,* 73 (2005): 411–423. For depression, which also engenders difficulty in peer relationships, see Karen D. Rudolph, Constance Hammen, and Shannon E. Daley, "Mood Disorders," in *Behavioral and Emotional Disorders in Adolescents: Nature, Assessment, and Treatment,* ed. David A. Wolfe and Eric J. Mash (New York: Guilford, 2006).

7. Collins, "Friend Game," 36.

8. Kimberly J. Mitchell, David Finkelhor, and Janis Wolak, "Youth Internet Users at Risk for the Most Serious Online Sexual Solicitation," *American Journal of Preventive Medicine,* 32 (2007): 532–537; Kimberly J. Mitchell, Michele Ybarra, and David Finkelhor, "The Relative Importance of Online Victimization in Understanding Depression, Delinquency, and Substance Abuse," *Child Maltreatment, 12* (2007): 314–324.

9. Thanks to Andrea Stier for providing details about such procedures. Note that one can search a site by the target person's name. Thus, if a target had used her real name when she signed up and allowed herself to be searched by name, she could have been found this way (although this feature can be blocked). Also, a "friend" may know a target person's screen name from communicating with her in person and would also be able to search for her in that way, too.

10. See Roy F. Baumeister and Mark R. Leary, "The Need to Belong: Desire for Interpersonal Attachments as a Fundamental Human Motivation," *Psychological Bulletin, 117* (1995): 497–525, for the devastating consequences to individuals who are rejected from social groups.

11. See Janis Whitlock, Wendy Lader, and Karen Conterio, "The Internet and Self-Injury: What Psychotherapists Should Know," *Journal of Clinical Psychology,* 63 (207): 1145–1153, and Janis L. Whitlock, Jane L. Powers, and John Eckenrode, "The Virtual Cutting Edge: The Internet and Adolescent Self-Injury," *Developmental Psychology,* 32 (2006): 407–417, who note the potential of the Internet for gaining support versus learning further means of self-harm.

12. See Amanda Lenhart, Mary Madden, and Paul Hitlin, *Teens and Technology: Youth Are Leading the Transition to a Fully Wired and Mobile Nation* (Washington, D.C.: Pew Internet and American Life Project, 2005); retrieved from www.pewinternet.org/pdfs/PIP_Teens_Tech_July2005web.pdf.

13. Sharon R. Mazzarella, ed., *Girl Wide Web: Girls, the Internet, and the Negotiation of Identity* (New York: Peter Lang, 2005).

14. A large literature documents that rejection from one's peer group is a strong predictor (even controlling for one's initial problem behavior) of negative outcomes, such as school dropout, delinquency, internalizing problems (anxiety and depression), and need for mental health services in adulthood. See Jeffrey G. Parker and Steven R. Asher, "Peer Relations and Later Personal Adjustment: Are Low-Accepted Children at Risk?" *Psychological Bulletin, 102* (1987): 357–389, and Jeffrey G. Parker, Kenneth H. Rubin, Stephan A. Erath, Julie C. Wojslawowicz, and Allison A. Buskirk, "Peer Relations, Child Development, and Adjustment: A Developmental Psychopathology Perspective," in *Developmental Psychopathology,* 2nd ed., vol. 1: *Theory and Method,* ed. Dante Cicchetti and Donald J. Cohen (Hoboken, N.J.: Wiley, 2006).

15. Lenhart et al., *Teens and Technology.*

16. See data memo from Amanda Lenhart on "Cyberbullying and Online Teens." Pew Internet and American Life Project, July 27, 2007, retrieved from www.pewinternet.org/pdfs/PIP%20Cyberbullying%20Memo.pdf.

17. For i-SAFE information, see www.isafe.org/channels/sub.php?ch=op&sub_id edia_cyber_bullying.

18. Collins, "Friend Game," 40.

19. Judith Rich Harris, *The Nurture Assumption: Why Children Turn Out the Way They Do* (New York: Free Press, 1998).

20. Camille Jackson, "E-Bully," retrieved from www.tolerance.org/teach/printar.jsp?p=0&ar=653&pi tm.

21. Mazzarella, *Girl Wide Web.*

22. Emily Nussbaum, "Say Everything," *New York*, February 12, 2007, 24–29, 102–105; quote from 28.

23. Ibid., 29.

24. Ibid.

25. The quote and the following figures come from Ulla G. Foehr, "Media Multitasking Among American Youth: Prevalence, Predictions, and Pairings," Kaiser Family Foundation, pub. 7593, retrieved from www.kff.org/entmedia/upload/7593.pdf. The larger study from which this sample was obtained was from Donald F. Roberts, Ulla G. Foehr, and Victoria Rideout, *Generation M: Media in the Lives of 8–18 Year Olds*, Kaiser Family Foundation, March 2005, retrieved from www.kff.org/entmedia/upload/Generation-M-Media-in-the-Lives-of-8-18-Year-olds-Report.pdf.

26. See Foehr, "Media Multitasking." See also Walter Kirn, "The Autumn of Multitasking," *Atlantic Monthly*, November 2007, retrieved from www.theatlantic.com/doc/200711/multitasking.

27. Kirn, "The Autumn of Multitasking."

28. Karin Foerde, Barbara J. Knowlton, and Russell A. Poldrack, "Modulation of Competing Memory Systems by Distraction," *Proceedings of the National Academy of Sciences, 103 (31)* (2006): 11778–11783. This team concluded that multitasking may be optimal for certain situations—for example, listening to music while exercising, because the latter activity does not require complex processing of information. But with competing cognitive tasks, the danger is that multitasking will result in knowledge that cannot be applied flexibly in new contexts.

29. Karin Foerde, Russell A. Poldrack, and Barbara J. Knowlton, "Secondary-Task Effects on Classification Learning," *Memory and Cognition,* 35 (2007): 864–874.

30. In interpreting the effects of life situations or activities on subsequent behavior, there may well be "selection" (i.e., certain individuals or families gravitate toward such environments or activities). For example, do different neighborhoods, schools, or peer groups—or in the case at hand, does multitasking—exert causal effects on outcomes of interest, or is it just that certain youth select such settings or activities? Strong evidence exists that although youth who are aggressive tend to gravitate toward media violence, the effects of such violence on child and adolescent antisocial behavior go beyond such selection effects. See Craig A. Anderson, Leonard Berkowitz, Edward Donnerstein, L. Rowell Huesmann, James D. Johnson, Daniel Linz, Neil M. Malamuth, and Ellen Wartella, "The Influence of Media Violence on Youth," *Psychological Science in the Public Interest, 4* (2003): 81–110.

31. Patricia J. Williams, "The 600 Faces of Eve," *The Nation*, July 31/August 7, 2006, 8.

32. Tim Kasser, *The High Price of Materialism* (Cambridge, Mass.: MIT Press, 2002).

33. I am indebted to Krista Page for this observation.

Chapter 8: See Jane Hit

1. Donna Koehn, "Hype Over More Violent Girls Lacks Statistics to Back It Up," *Tampa Tribune*, December 16, 2007, retrieved from www2.tbo.com/static/special_reports_news/tbo-special-reports-news-girl-fight.

2. " 'I Can't Believe That's Me,' Says Girl in Video Attack," Cincinnati News/WLTW, Channel 5, updated October 9, 2007, retrieved from www.wlwt.com/news/14304375/detail.html; "Online Video Shows Girl Attacked at Area School," Cincinnati News/WLTW, Channel 5, updated October 9, 2007, retrieved from www.wlwt.com/news/14295313/detail .html.

3. KCTV5.com, Kansas City, Missouri, updated December 28, 2007, retrieved from www.kctv5.com/news/14934661/detail.html.

4. James Garbarino, *See Jane Hit: Why Girls Are Growing More Violent and What We Can Do About It* (New York: Penguin, 2006). For comprehensive volumes on female aggression, see Martha Putallaz and Karen L. Bierman, eds., *Aggression, Antisocial Behavior, and Violence Among Girls* (New York: Guilford, 2004), and Marlene M. Moretti, Candice L. Odgers, and Margaret A. Jackson, eds., *Girls and Aggression: Contributing Factors and Intervention Principles* (New York: Kluwer Academic/Plenum, 2004).

5. Meda Chesney-Lind and Joanne Belknap, "Trends in Delinquent Girls' Aggression and Violent Behavior: A Review of the Evidence," in *Aggression, Antisocial Behavior, and Violence Among Girls*, ed. Martha Putallaz and Karen L. Bierman (New York: Guilford, 2004).

6. Marge Piercy, *Woman on the Edge of Time* (New York: Knopf, 1976).

7. See discussion in Chesney-Lind and Belknap, "Trends." They also argue that some self-report statistics show a decrease in female violence and homicide from the 1960s through the 1990s, in contrast to the depiction from the surgeon general's report of 2001, which provided evidence of extremely high rates of self-reported aggression and violence in girls. See U.S. Department of Health and Human Services, *Youth Violence: A Report of the Surgeon General* (Rockville, Md.: Author, 2001), discussed in this chapter.

8. See discussion in Stephen P. Hinshaw, *The Mark of Shame: Stigma of Mental Illness and an Agenda for Change* (New York: Oxford University Press, 2007). For example, Los Angeles County Jail is thought to be the largest mental health facility in the world, as thousands of people with mental illness are confined there each day, receiving no treatment. In states such as California, drug possession has been increasingly criminalized, leading to swelling imprisonment rates.

9. Chesney-Lind and Belknap, 216.

10. U.S. Department of Health and Human Services, *Youth Violence*. The behaviors included here are those that could seriously injure or kill another person. This range of 16 to 32 percent for girls contrasts with the 30 to 40 percent figure for boys. In short, boys are more violent, even by self-report, but girls' rates are alarmingly high, and most female incidents never enter official delinquency statistics. Although some readers may wonder whether teens' self-reports of violent behavior may be exaggerated, the relevant research utilizes sophisticated and confidential means of asking questions of youth in current survey methods. Thus, the figures above do not appear to be distortions (see U.S. Department of Health and Human Services, *Youth Violence*, for details).

11. Rosalind Wiseman, *Queen Bees and Wannabes: Helping Your Daughter Survive Cliques, Gossip, Boyfriends, and Other Realities of Adolescence* (New York: Crown, 2002).

12. For example, see Nicki R. Crick and Jennifer K. Grotpeter, "Relational Aggression, Gender, and Social-Psychological Adjustment," *Child Development,* 66 (1995): 710–722, and Nicki R. Crick, "The Role of Overt Aggression, Relational Aggression, and Prosocial Behavior in the Prediction of Children's Future Social Adjustment," *Child Development,* 67 (1996): 2317–2327. See also Nicki R. Crick, Jamie M. Ostrov, and Nicole E. Werner, "A Longitudinal Study of Relational Aggression, Physical Aggression, and Children's Social-Psychological Adjustment," *Journal of Abnormal Child Psychology,* 34 (2006): 131–142, in which Crick and colleagues found that whereas the combination of relational

and physical aggression predicted maladjustment across a two-year longitudinal interval, relational aggression alone was an important predictor as well. For early work in this area, see Kaj Bjorkqvist, Kirsti M. Lagerspetz, and Ari Kaukiainen, "Do Girls Manipulate and Boys Fight? Developmental Trends into Direct and Indirect Aggression," *Aggressive Behavior, 18* (1992): 117–127.

13. See, for example, Crick et al., "A Longitudinal Study."

14. Girls are not the only sex to engage in relational aggression; see, for example, Melanie J. Zimmer Gembeck, Tasha C. Geiger, and Nicki R. Crick, "Relational and Physical Aggression, Prosocial Behavior, and Peer Relations: Gender Moderation and Bidirectional Associations," *Journal of Early Adolescence, 25* (2005): 421–452. However, recent data suggest that relational aggression (at least as measured by parents and youth themselves, rather than by peers, who may be the optimal source of information) does not merit inclusion in the next edition of the official diagnostic manual of mental disorders. See Kate Keenan, Claire Coyne, and Benjamin B. Lahey, "Should Relational Aggression Be Included in DSM-V?" *Journal of the American Academy of Child and Adolescent Psychiatry,* 47 (2008): 86–93.

15. The overall conceptual model is presented in Terrie E. Moffitt, "Adolescence-Limited and Life-Course-Persistent Antisocial Behavior: A Developmental Taxonomy," *Psychological Review, 100* (1991): 674–701. However, longitudinal research reveals that not all of the "early starter" boys go on to display persistent antisocial activities, and a number of youth (boys and girls) with adolescent onset of delinquent and aggressive behavior do *not* necessarily remit by the end of their teenage years: the consequences ("snares") related to drug abuse, a criminal record, becoming pregnant or getting a girl pregnant, and the like may have serious long-term consequences. See Terrie E. Moffitt, Avshalom Caspi, Honalee Harrington, and Barry J. Milne, "Males on the Life-Course-Persistent and Adolescence-Limited Antisocial Pathways: Follow-Up at Age 26 Years," *Development and Psychopathology, 14* (2002): 179–207. For an overview, see Terrie E. Moffitt, "Life-Course-Persistent Versus Adolescence-Limited Antisocial Behavior," in *Developmental Psychopathology*, 2nd ed, vol. 3: *Risk, Disorder and Adaptation*, ed. Dante Cicchetti and Donald J. Cohen (Hoboken, N.J.: Wiley, 2006).

16. See Moffitt, "Adolescence-Limited," and Moffitt, "Life-Course-Persistent."

17. See Kenneth A. Dodge, "Public Policy and the 'Discovery' of Girls' Aggressive Behavior," in *Aggression, Antisocial Behavior, and Violence Among Girls*, ed. Martha Putallaz and Karen L. Bierman (New York: Guilford, 2004). Dodge posits a general dichotomy: boys' aggression and violence are often related to early-onset manifestations of genetic, biological, and temperamental risk, whereas girls' aggression and violence are embedded in social relationships and response to trauma, with late-childhood or early-adolescent onset for the display of such behaviors.

18. Terrie E. Moffitt and Avshalom Caspi, "Childhood Predictors Differentiate Life-Course-Persistent and Adolescence-Limited Antisocial Pathways Among Males and Females," *Development and Psychopathology, 13* (2001): 355–375.

19. See, for example, Carolyn Zahn-Waxler and Nicole Polanichka, "All Things Interpersonal: Socialization and Female Aggression," in *Aggression, Antisocial Behavior, and Violence Among Girls*, ed. Martha Putallaz and Karen L. Bierman (New York: Guilford, 2004).

20. The Girls' Study Group comprises scientists who examine statistics and underlying theories of female delinquency and violence (see the group's website, http://girlsstudy group.rti.org). In a report made to the Office of Juvenile Justice and Delinquency Prevention in 2006, the group systematically reviewed the literature, indicating that the risk factors for aggression in girls are similar to those for boys, but that for girls, the factors of

early puberty, sexual assault, depression/anxiety, influence of the opposite sex, and low attachment to school are especially salient; see Margaret A. Zahn, Office of Juvenile Justice and Delinquency Prevention, "Girls' Study Group," October, 2006, retrieved from girlsstudygroup.rti.org/docs/2006%2010%20Utah.pdf.

21. See Avshalom Caspi, Donald Lynam, Terrie E. Moffitt, and Phil A. Silva, "Unraveling Girls' Delinquency: Biological, Dispositional, and Contextual Contributions to Adolescent Misbehavior," *Developmental Psychology,* 29 (1993): 19–30.

22. See Kathleen A. Pajer, "What Happens to 'Bad' Girls? A Review of the Adult Outcomes of Antisocial Adolescent Girls," *American Journal of Psychiatry,* 155 (1998): 862–870.

23. The overlap between aggressive behavior and depression, and between aggressive behavior and suicidality, is larger in girls than in boys. See Margit Wiesner and Hyoun K. Kim, "Co-Occurring Delinquency and Depressive Symptoms of Adolescent Boys and Girls: A Dual Trajectory Modeling Approach," *Developmental Psychology,* 42 (2006): 1220–1235, and Martie B. Thompson, Ching-Hua Ho, and J. B. Kingree, "Prospective Associations Between Delinquency and Suicidal Behaviors in a Nationally Representative Sample," *Journal of Adolescent Health,* 40 (2007): 232–237. The exception to the material presented in the text occurs in the rare instances of truly psychopathic behavior in girls and women, in which there is an absence of empathy, compassion, or remorse (as depicted, for example, by Charlize Theron in the movie *Monster*, for which she won the Oscar for Best Actress).

24. See Christopher J. Patrick, ed., *Handbook of the Psychopathy* (New York: Guilford, 2006).

25. ADHD is linked with impulsivity: See, for example, Russell A. Barkley, *Attention-Deficit Hyperactivity: A Handbook for Diagnosis and Treatment*, 3rd ed. (New York: Guilford, 2006).

Chapter 9: Is There a Triple Bind Solution?

1. See Sandra A. Brown and Ana M. Abrantes, "Substance Use Disorders," in *Behavioral and Emotional Disorders in Adolescents: Nature, Assessment, and Treatment*, ed. David A. Wolfe and Eric J. Mash (New York: Guilford, 2006); and Cathy Spatz Widom and Joseph B. Kuhns, "Childhood Victimization and Subsequent Risk for Promiscuity, Prostitution, and Teenage Pregnancy: A Prospective Study," *American Journal of Public Health,* 86 (1996): 1607–1612.

2. For a thorough review of risk factors related to ADHD, see Joel T. Nigg, *What Causes ADHD? Understanding What Goes Wrong and Why* (New York: Guilford Press, 2006), and Russell A. Barkley, *Attention-Deficit Hyperactivity Disorder: A Handbook for Diagnosis and Treatment*, 3rd ed. (New York: Guilford Press, 2006). Despite the substantial heritability of ADHD, contributing factors also include maternal smoking, alcohol, and drug use during pregnancy, as well as low birth weight.

3. See Wystan Hugh Auden, *The Age of Anxiety* (New York: Random House, 1947), which spawned Leonard Bernstein's Symphony No. 2 for Piano and Orchestra and Jerome Robbins' ballet, both of the same name. For data on secular trends of increasing anxiety in American children between the 1950s and 1990s, see Jean M. Twenge, "The Age of Anxiety? The Birth Cohort Change in Anxiety and Neuroticism, 1952–1993," *Journal of Personality and Social Psychology,* 79 (2000): 1007–1021.

4. For narcissism, see Christopher Lasch, *The Culture of Narcissism: American Life in an Era of Diminishing Expectations* (New York: Warner Books, 1979).

5. For thorough reviews of borderline personality disorder, see Joel Paris, "The Nature

of Borderline Personality Disorder: Multiple Dimensions, Multiple Symptoms, but One Category," *Journal of Personality Disorders, 21* (2007): 457–473, and Timothy J. Trull, Stephanie D. Stepp, and Marika Solhan, "Borderline Personality Disorder," in *Comprehensive Handbook of Personality and Psychopathology*, vol. 2: *Adult Psychopathology*, ed. Frank Andrasik (Hoboken, N.J.: Wiley, 2006). The core symptoms include extreme emotional instability, an impulsive lifestyle, highly unstable relationships, and selective problems with cognition—including, in some cases, occasional difficulties in distinguishing reality from fantasy. Indeed, it was this latter symptom that led, early on, to the "borderline" designation, as the clinical picture seemed to straddle the border between neurotic and psychotic functioning.

6. See Patricia B. Sutker and Albert N. Allain Jr., "Antisocial Personality Disorder," in *Comprehensive Handbook of Psychopathology*, 3rd ed., ed. Patricia B. Sutker and Henry E. Adams (New York: Kluwer Academic/Plenum, 2001). For a lucid account of the role of splitting and emptiness in the lives of individuals with borderline personality disorder, see Thomas Fuchs, "Fragmented Selves: Temporality and Identity in Borderline Personality Disorder," *Psychopathology, 40* (2007): 389–397. See also Les R. Greene, "Primitive Defenses, Object Relations, and Symptom Clusters in Borderline Personality Disorder," *Journal of Personality Assessment, 67* (1996): 294–304.

7. See, for example, E. David Klonsky and E. David Molino, "Identifying Clinically Distinct Groups of Self-Injurers Among Young Adults: A Latent-Class Analysis," *Journal of Clinical and Consulting Psychology, 76* (2008): 22–27. Self-injury and cutting are not always connected to borderline personality disorder, however: see M. J. Marchetto, "Repetitive Skin Cutting: Parental Bonding, Personality, and Gender," *Psychology and Psychotherapy: Theory, Research, and Practice, 79* (2006): 445–459.

8. For documentation of the linkage between physical abuse and later antisocial behavior, see Kenneth A. Dodge, John D. Coie, and Donald Lynam, "Aggression and Antisocial Behavior in Youth," in *Handbook of Child Psychology*, 6th ed., vol. 3: *Social, Emotional, and Personality Development*, ed. Nancy Eisenberg, William Damon, and Richard M. Lerner (Hoboken, N.J.: Wiley, 2006). For data linking sexual abuse to borderline personality disorder, see Jiri Modestin, Roman Furrer, and Tina Malti, "Different Traumatic Experiences Are Associated with Different Pathologies," *Psychiatric Quarterly, 76* (2005): 19–32; and Rebekah Bradley, Johanna Jenei, and Drew Westen, "Etiology of Borderline Personality Disorder: Disentangling the Contributions of Intercorrelated Antecedents," *Journal of Nervous and Mental Disease, 193* (2005): 24–31.

9. Victor E. Frankl, *Man's Search for Meaning: An Introduction to Logotherapy* (Boston: Beacon, 1962).

10. See Julia Kim-Cohen, "Resilience and Developmental Psychopathology," *Child and Adolescent Psychiatric Clinics of North America, 16* (2007): 271–283; Suniya S. Luthar, "Resilience in Development: A Synthesis of Research Across Five Decades," in *Developmental Psychopathology*, 2nd ed., vol. 3: *Risk, Disorder and Adaptation*, ed. Dante Cicchetti and Donald J. Cohen (Hoboken, N.J.: Wiley, 2006); Suniya S. Luthar, Dante Cicchetti, and Bronwyn Becker, "The Construct of Resilience: A Critical Evaluation and Guidelines for Future Work," *Child Development, 71* (2000): 543–562; Michael Rutter, "Resilience in the Face of Adversity: Protective Factors and Resistance to Psychiatric Disorder," *British Journal of Psychiatry, 147* (1985): 598–611; Norman Garmezy, "Resilience in Children's Adaptation to Negative Life Events and Stressed Environments," *Pediatric Annals, 20* (1991): 459–466.

11. See E. James Anthony, "The Syndrome of the Psychologically Invulnerable Child," in *The Child in His Family: Children at Psychiatric Risk*, ed. E. James Anthony and Cyrille Koupernik (Oxford, U.K.: Wiley, 1974).

12. To provide a brief history of the concept of resilience, I wrote the following in Stephen P. Hinshaw, *The Mark of Shame: Stigma of Mental Illness and an Agenda for Change* (New York: Oxford University Press, 2007), 172:

> Although modern research on resilience dates to the 1970s, the occurrence of positive outcomes in the midst of risk has captured the interest of scholars and writers over the ages. From the view that good outcomes in the face of stress were rare, chance-driven occurrences, the focus has shifted to identifying subgroups of high-risk individuals who show more better-than-expected outcome in predictable ways. Work in this domain has been wide-ranging, with target populations including individuals with schizophrenia, persons exposed to poverty, children who endured the Great Depression, adults reared in foster homes and institutions as children, and delinquent youth children with criminal fathers. Response to trauma has also been salient, with studies involving persons exposed to the extreme violence of Northern Ireland, children of the Holocaust followed into adulthood, and individuals exposed to natural disasters. At least three levels of variables promote resilient functioning: those within the individual (e.g., positive self-esteem, easy temperament, high intelligence, a sense of humor), factors pertaining to family and relationship processes (e.g., certain child-rearing styles, positive relations and identifications with an adult outside the home), and characteristics of broader social environments (e.g., school settings, certain types of neighborhoods).

For evidence of heritable contributions to resilience, see Julia Kim-Cohen, Terrie E. Moffitt, Avshalom Caspi, and Alan Taylor, "Genetic and Environmental Processes in Young Children's Resilience and Vulnerability to Socioeconomic Deprivation," *Child Development,* 75 (2004): 651–668.

13. Ann S. Masten, "Ordinary Magic: Resilience Processes in Development," *American Psychologist,* 56 (2001): 227–238. See also Ann S. Masten, Keith B. Burt, and J. Douglas Coatsworth, "Competence and Psychopathology in Development," in *Developmental Psychopathology*, 2nd ed., vol. 3: *Risk, Disorder and Adaptation*, ed. Dante Cicchetti and Donald J. Cohen (Hoboken, N.J.: Wiley, 2006). For an insightful commentary on the concept of resilience, see Suniya S. Luthar and Pamela J. Brown, "Maximizing Resilience Through Diverse Levels of Inquiry: Prevailing Paradigms, Possibilities, and Priorities for the Future," *Development and Psychopathology, 19* (2007): 931–955. The resilience concept has received critique (see Luthar and colleagues, "The Construct of Resilience"): Do so-called protective factors operate only in conditions of high risk, or can some individuals be resilient even without life stress or trauma? Can positive outcomes be measured in one key domain, or would truly resilient functioning require healthy adaptation across several areas of functioning? Also, because "protective factors" are often simply the opposite poles of risk factors for negative outcomes (e.g., strong versus weak family support; high versus low intelligence), perhaps no special factors exist that facilitate a process known as "resilience." Still, a focus on strength provides a needed counterpoint to the field's concern with pathology and maladaptation.

14. For discussion of competence versus resilience, and whether resilience applies only to those at high risk, see Masten et al., "Competence and Psychopathology in Development."

15. Masten, "Ordinary Magic"; Luthar, "Resilience in Development."

16. See, for example, Madeline Levine, *The Price of Privilege: How Parental Pressure and Material Advantage Are Creating a Generation of Disconnected and Unhappy Kids* (New York: HarperCollins, 2006).

17. See Masten, "Ordinary Magic"; Luthar, "Resilience in Development."

18. Drew Barrymore, "Ellen Page," *Interview*, March 2008, retrieved from www.interviewmagazine.com/#section=cover-story.

Conclusion: Coming to Terms With the Triple Bind

1. Stephen P. Hinshaw, *The Years of Silence Are Past: My Father's Life with Bipolar Disorder* (New York: Cambridge University Press, 2002).

2. See Stephen P. Hinshaw, *The Mark of Shame: Stigma of Mental Illness and an Agenda for Change* (New York: Oxford University Press, 2007), and Stephen P. Hinshaw, ed., *Breaking the Silence: Mental Health Professionals Disclose Their Personal and Family Experiences of Mental Illness* (New York: Oxford University Press, 2008).

ABOUT THE AUTHORS

STEPHEN HINSHAW, PH.D., is professor and chair of the Department of Psychology at the University of California, Berkeley. He is an internationally recognized psychologist and researcher whose work on troubled children has received ongoing attention from the press. Articles and interviews featuring him and his work have appeared in the *New York Times, Washington Post, Boston Globe, San Francisco Chronicle, Chicago Tribune,* and *USA Today.* He has appeared on *Today, NBC Nightly News, ABC World News Tonight,* and CNN.

RACHEL KRANZ is a fiction and nonfiction writer and playwright who lives in New York City. Her most recent novel is *Leaps of Faith* (Farrar, Straus, & Giroux, 2000).

ABOUT THE TYPE

This book was set in Fairfield, the first typeface from the hand of the distinguished American artist and engraver Rudolph Ruzicka (1883–1978). Ruzicka was born in Bohemia and came to America in 1894. He set up his own shop, devoted to wood engraving and printing, in New York in 1913 after a varied career working as a wood engraver, in photoengraving and banknote printing plants, and as an art director and freelance artist. He designed and illustrated many books, and was the creator of a considerable list of individual prints—wood engravings, line engravings on copper, and aquatints.